READER'S DIGEST

ON THE ROAD USA

EAST-WEST ROUTES

D0126664

Reader's Digest

The Reader's Digest Association, Inc.
Pleasantville, New York / Montreal

ON THE ROAD USA

Project Editor	Carroll C. Calkins
Project Art Editor	Gilbert L. Nielsen
Art Editor	Perri DeFino
Project Coordinator	Don Earnest
Associate Editors	Noreen B. Church, Diana Marsh (Copy Desk), Thomas A. Ranieri
Assistant Editor	D. Diefendorf
Project Research Editor	Hildegard Anderson
Research Editors	Shirley Miller, Maymay Quey Lin
Art Associate	Morris Karol
Associate Picture Editor	Richard Pasqual
Project Secretary	Jason Peterson

Contributors

Editor	Margaret Perry
Writers	Shelley Aspaklaria, Robert Brown, David Caras, Laura Dearborn, Diane Hall, Signe Hammer, Guy Henle, Archie Hobson, John Kiely, Anne Lubell, Susan Macovsky, Mona Malone, Richard Marshall, Barbara Rogan, Tim Snider, Richard Sudhalter, Robert Thurston, Carol Weeg, Joseph Wilkinson, Elaine Williams, Donald Young
Copy Editor	Harriett Bachman
Researchers	Mary Hart, Nathalie Laguerre, Mary Lyn Maiscott, Raissa Silverman, Kelly Tasker
Art Associates	Joseph Dyas, Bruce McKillip
Picture Researcher	Marian Paone
Indexer	Sydney Wolfe Cohen

Reader's Digest General Books

Editor in Chief	John A. Pope, Jr.
Managing Editor	Jane Polley
Art Director	David Trooper
Group Editors	Norman B. Mack, Susan J. Wernert, Joseph L. Gardner (International), Joel Musler (Art)
Chief of Research	Monica Borrowman
Copy Chief	Edward W. Atkinson
Picture Editor	Robert J. Woodward
Rights and Permissions	Pat Colomban
Head Librarian	Jo Manning

About the directions and other information
Mileage at the beginning of an entry is rounded to the nearest half-mile; no mileage is given for a drive of 5 minutes or less. Driving time is approximate and may vary with conditions. In a city entry, mileage and time (to the tourist bureau) appear when the city is not on the interstate. In directions the word *Route* (abbreviated Rte., as in Rte. 101) is used for all numbered noninterstate highways and roads—U.S., state, and local. At the end of an entry, the dates given are inclusive; thus Mon.–Fri. and May–Sept., mean Monday *through* Friday and May *through* September. If admission fees are not mentioned, they are not required. Symbols (below) appear when relevant.

Picnicking Camping Trailers Hiking Swimming Fishing Wheelchairs

How to use this book

First, be sure you have the right volume. This is the East–West book, with the even-numbered interstates. The odd-numbered North–South routes are in the other volume.

The map on the next two pages shows all the routes in this book and refers you to detailed maps on which numbered brackets indicate segments of each interstate.

When you turn to any two-page section in this volume, you'll see a red line along the top of each page. It represents the segment of interstate covered on those two pages. The boxed exit numbers on the line are keyed to descriptions of the points of interest. The small numbers between the exit boxes indicate the distance (to the nearest mile) between exits. The total number of miles covered by a two-page section is shown at the bottom of each page. Where interstates intersect, you'll find cross-references to the appropriate section—whether in this volume or the other one.

The book works two ways

When going east, leaf through the book from front to back. When going west, leaf through from back to front. When there are two exit numbers for one destination, the first exit given is for drivers headed east; the second, for drivers headed west.

Most entries describe such sites as parks, museums, and natural wonders. But cities are included when they are on or near an interstate. A city's highlights are mentioned; for maps and further information, contact the tourist bureau that's listed. Virtually all the attractions are 30 minutes or less from the interstate exit. And when some spectacular destination—like the Grand Canyon or Mt. Rainier—is within reasonable reach, we have included it in a box entitled "If You Have Some Extra Time."

We have made every effort to provide accurate information. Our driver-reporters visited each site; our researchers contacted each place to double-check their reports. But you may still encounter surprises. A site may change the dates it's open, adopt a new admission policy—or close altogether. Exit numbers can also change, and some interstate segments, scheduled to be completed by our publication date, may not be finished. But the detailed maps in the front of the book and the mileage between exits shown on the red line should help keep you oriented. We trust that any inconvenience will be more than compensated for by the hundreds of suggestions for restful and rewarding things to see and do within easy range of the interstates. —*The Editors*

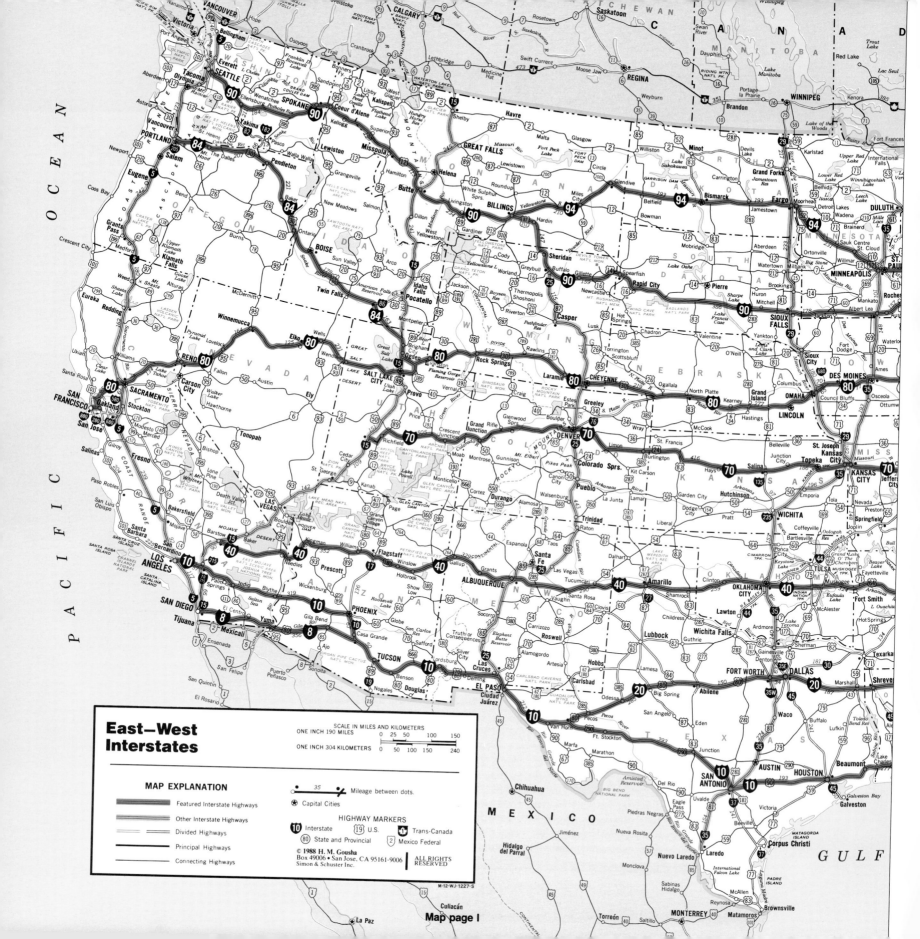

East–West Interstates

SCALE IN MILES AND KILOMETERS
ONE INCH 190 MILES
ONE INCH 304 KILOMETERS

MAP EXPLANATION

━━━ Featured Interstate Highways
━━━ Other Interstate Highways
━━━ Divided Highways
━━━ Principal Highways
━━━ Connecting Highways

•—35—✕ Mileage between dots.

✪ Capital Cities

HIGHWAY MARKERS
🛡10 Interstate   19 U.S.   🍁 Trans-Canada
80 State and Provincial   2 Mexico Federal

© 1988 H. M. Gousha
Box 49006 • San Jose, CA 95161-9006
Simon & Schuster Inc.

ALL RIGHTS
RESERVED

M-12-WJ-1227-S

Map page I

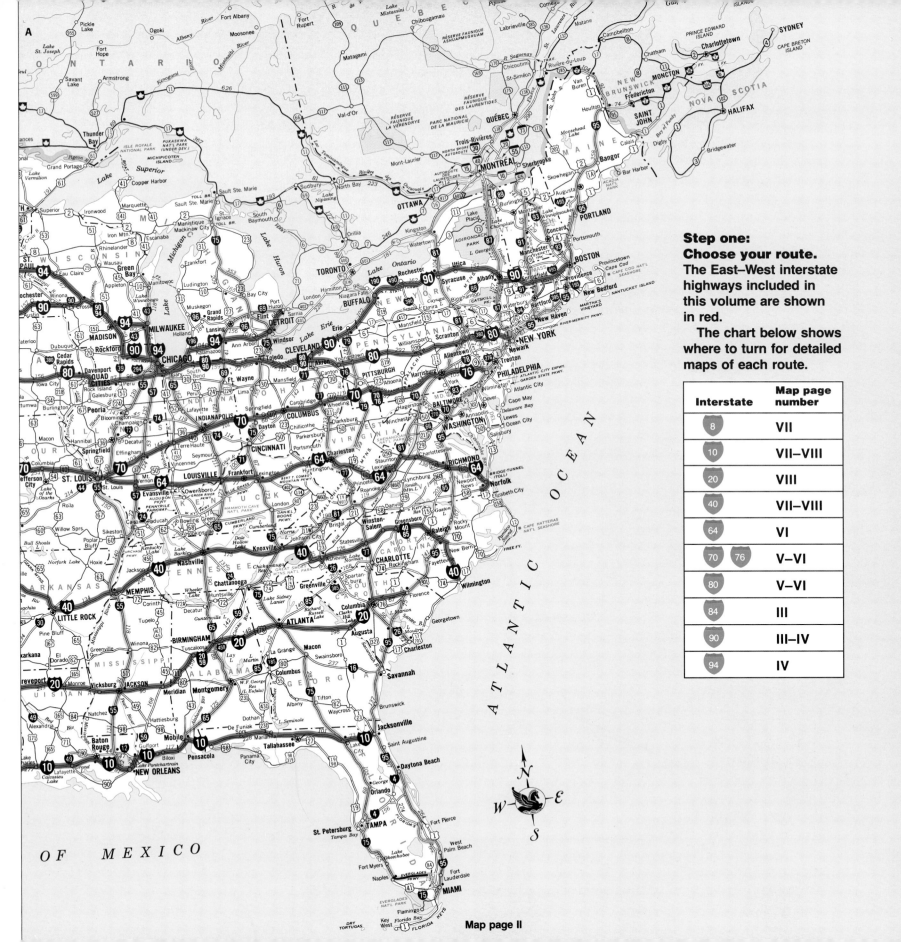

Step one:

Choose your route.

The East–West interstate highways included in this volume are shown in red.

The chart below shows where to turn for detailed maps of each route.

Interstate		Map page number
8		VII
10		VII–VIII
20		VIII
40		VII–VIII
64		VI
70	76	V–VI
80		V–VI
84		III
90		III–IV
94		IV

Map page II

Step two:

Choose a section of the route. Each interstate has been divided into segments indicated by numbered red brackets.

Each number represents a two-page section in the book. Turn to the appropriate numbered section to find the points of interest (and exit numbers) on the bracketed stretch of highway you plan to drive.

The interstates highlighted at right are included on map pages III and IV. The others are on map pages V to VIII.

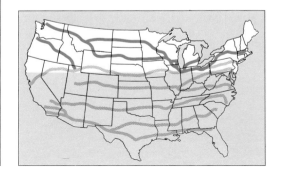

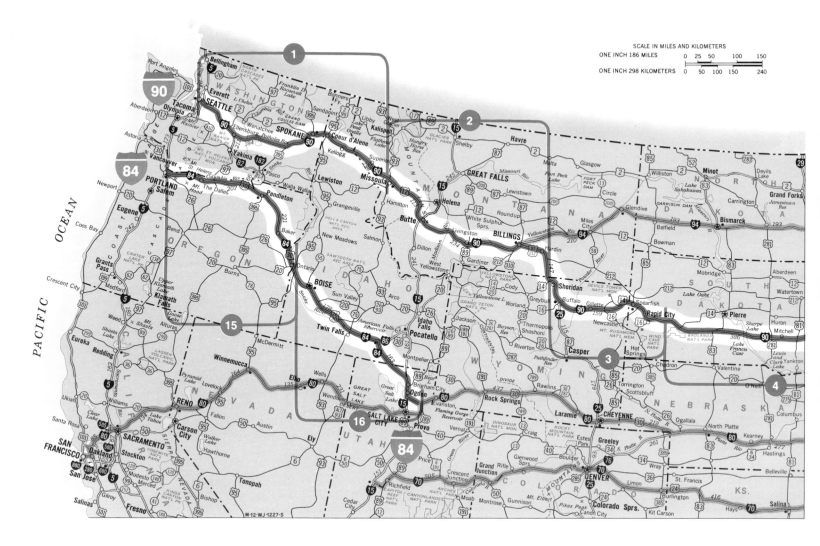

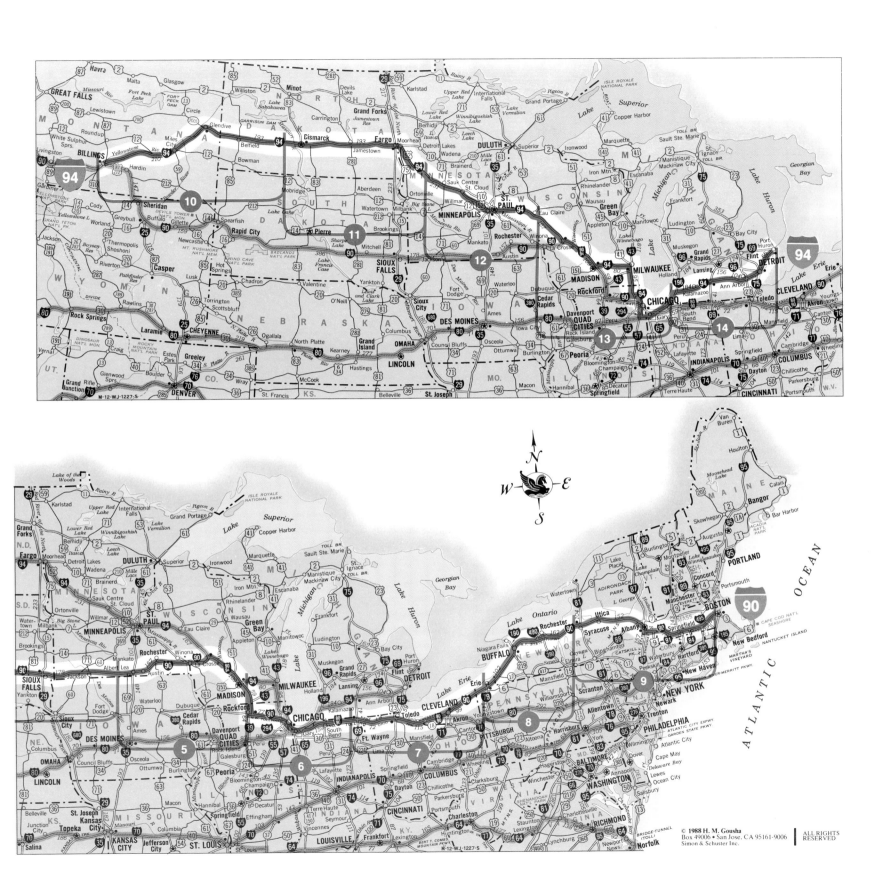

Map page IV

Step two:
Choose a section of the route.
Each interstate has been divided into segments indicated by numbered red brackets.

Each number represents a two-page section in the book. Turn to the appropriate numbered section to find the points of interest (and exit numbers) on the bracketed stretch of highway you plan to drive.

The interstates highlighted below are included on map pages V and VI. The others are on map pages III, IV, VII, and VIII.

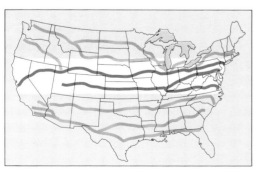

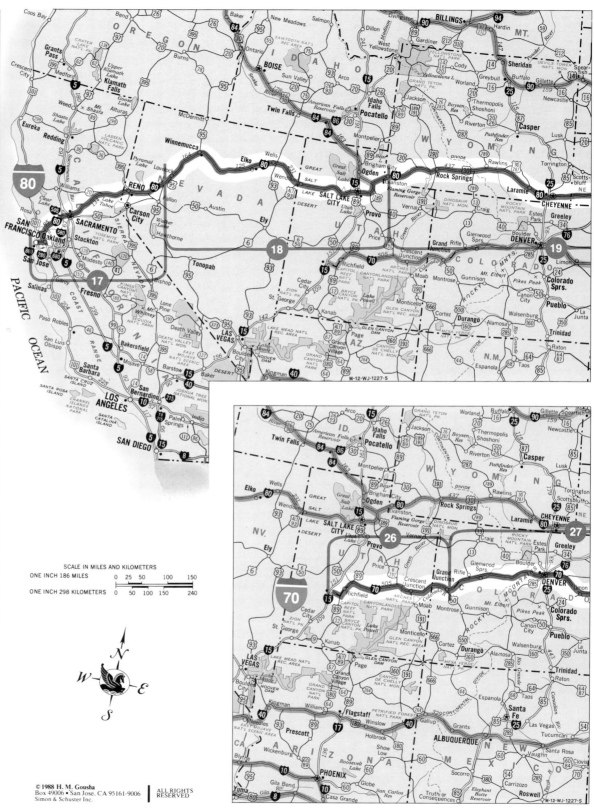

SCALE IN MILES AND KILOMETERS
ONE INCH 186 MILES   0 25 50   100   150
ONE INCH 298 KILOMETERS   0   50 100 150   240

M-12-WJ-1227-S

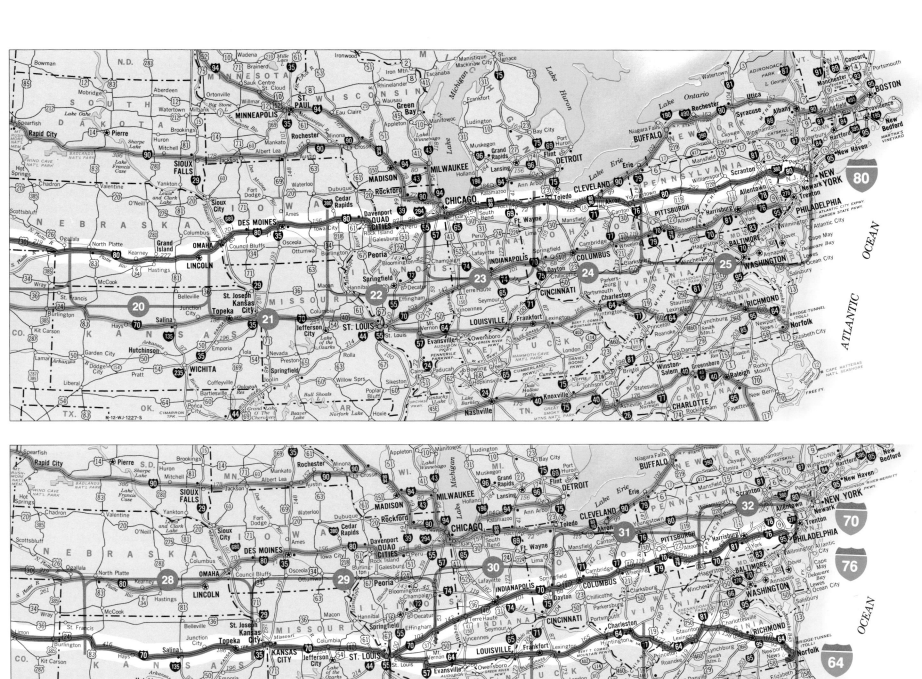

Step two:
Choose a section of the route.

Each interstate has been divided into segments indicated by numbered red brackets.

Each number represents a two-page section in the book. Turn to the appropriate numbered section to find the points of interest (and exit numbers) on the bracketed stretch of highway you plan to drive.

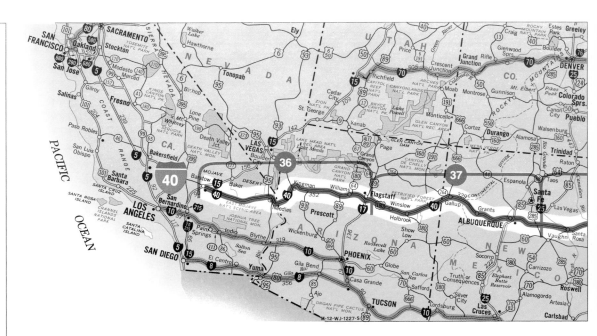

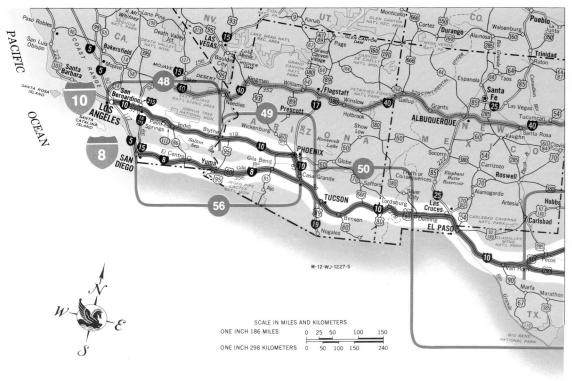

The interstates highlighted below are included on map pages VII and VIII. The others are on map pages III to VI.

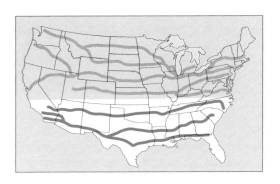

Map page VIII

4TH   Seattle, WA 98101

4th Ave. exit. Convention and Visitors Bureau, 1815 7th Ave. (206) 447-4200. Here on seven hills, almost surrounded by water, is one of America's most dramatic settings for a city. The Space Needle in Seattle Center provides stunning views of Puget Sound, Lake Washington, and (weather permitting) the distant Olympic Range, Cascade Range, and the majesty of Mt. Rainier. Downtown attractions include the waterfront, Pioneer Square, and Pike Place Market, where the display of fresh fruits and vegetables has become an art form.

31   Snoqualmie Falls Park

5 mi./10 min. North on Rte. 202; follow signs. The falls, 110 feet higher than Niagara's Horseshoe Falls, drop from a rocky cliff into a misty pool 270 feet below. The best view of the falls is from the observation platform some 300 feet above the Snoqualmie River. A trail leads from here to the cascade's base. Other pathways in the park invite more leisurely

31. *If one were to design a waterfall (with rainbow), this could be the prototype.*

walking. Carved into the rock behind the falls is one of the country's first complete underground electric generating stations. Finished in 1898, it is a civil engineering landmark and still operating. Downstream from the falls the river offers kayaking and steelhead and trout fishing. *Open year-round.*

84 / 85   Cle Elum Historical Society Museum

Exit 84: 5 min. East on town access road. Exit 85: 5 min. West on town access road. From 1901 to 1966 the switchboard operator's "Number, please?" was the human link in an otherwise impersonal system. The operators are gone, but the impressive switchboard, with its 1,200 terminals, is still here along with a collection of antique telephones, including an 1894 crank model encased in oak, a 1915 magneto model, and a dial phone circa 1920. Among the more recent models are a 1959 Princess, 1966 Trimline, and 1970 Touchtone. Graphic displays and replicas tell the story of Alexander Bell's influential invention. There's also a collection of old post office boxes along one wall. Other exhibits relate to Cle Elum's history as a coal-mining center. *Open daily late May–Sept., A.M. Mon.–Fri. Oct.–late May.*

115   Olmstead Place State Park Heritage Area

5 mi./10 min. North on Main St., left on Kittitas Hwy., left on Squaw Creek Trail Rd. Sarah and Samuel Olmstead settled in this rich valley in 1875. Today their 218-acre farm is a park celebrating our pioneer farming heritage. The family's original cabin, constructed with hand-hewn cottonwood logs, has been furnished with period pieces. A later farmhouse built by the family and the granary, the wagon shed, and the red dairy barn contain household artifacts and farm equipment mostly from the 1920's to the 1940's. The leaflet for the half-mile trail along scenic Altapes Creek explains the uses of various plants in pioneer times. The trail ends at the one-room Seaton Schoolhouse, which is more than 100 years old and was moved here from a nearby meadow. *Open year-round. Buildings open P.M. Memorial Day–Labor Day.*

136   Ginkgo Petrified Forest State Park

2 min. North on access road. About 15 million years ago upland trees were washed down into lakes and swamps here. Ancient lava flows covered the trees, and silica in the groundwater slowly turned them to stone. The petrified logs you see were exposed by erosion during the last ice age. The process is explained in an audiovisual show at the Heritage Area Interpretive Center, where exhibits also illustrate the area's natural history. The Natural Area, two miles north, features a short interpretive trail and a longer hiking trail through a prehistoric lake bed. The Wanapum Recreation Area, south of the interstate on the Columbia River, offers a swimming beach, a boat launch, and camping facilities. *Park open year-round. Interpretive center open mid-May–mid-Sept.*

176 / 179   Adam East Museum, Moses Lake

Exit 176: 3 mi./10 min. East on Broadway, right on Balsam St. Exit 179: 5 min. North on Rte. 17; continue on Pioneer Way, left on 5th St., right on Balsam St. The impressive collection of Indian artifacts, fossils, and rocks in this small museum represents the lifework of one collector. Adam East spent over 50 years scouring the Columbia River area for items detailing the history of the Sinkiuse Indians, their prehistoric ancestors, and this land they inhabited. He deeded his collection to the city of Moses Lake, and the community built this museum. Indian arrowheads and spearpoints, saddles, beads, and war bonnets; fossil bones of mammoths, camels, and elk; petrified wood, smithsonite crystals, and memorabilia from the Civil War and World Wars I and II are among the many fascinating pieces here. *Open mid-Mar.–Oct.; P.M. only Mar.–Apr., Sept.–Oct.*

179   Potholes State Park

17.5 mi./35 min. South on Rte. 17 , right on M Southeast Rd., right on O'Sullivan Dam Rd. Fear not: the potholes for which this 1,000-acre park is named are not the kind that you encounter on roads, but rather geologic de-

179. *To judge the size of these sand dunes, note the powerboat by the island at lower right.*

pressions that formed in sand dunes during the Ice Age. In spring these craters fill up with melted snow, dotting the landscape with hundreds of little lakes. Although this park is located in the middle of the Columbia Basin desert, you'll find several surprises here, including a 20-foot-high waterfall and lakes that support rainbow trout, silver salmon, large- and smallmouth bass—and occasionally a water-skier. At the nearby Columbia National Wildlife Refuge, you may spot red-tailed hawks, eagles, great horned owls, American kestrels, white pelicans, cranes, and other birds. In winter the activities here include ice fishing, snowmobiling, and cross-country skiing. *Open year-round.*

277 The John A. Finch Arboretum, Spokane

5 min. North on Rustle St., right on Sunset Hwy.; follow signs. The quiet, parklike atmosphere of this 65-acre arboretum makes it a pleasant place for a picnic or a stroll. The setting is beautiful year-round, but there are colorful highlights from spring to fall. The Corey Rhododendron Glen (which also includes azaleas) has secluded trails along Garden Springs Creek, and is most striking in April and May. In Lilac Lane more than 75 varieties of this lovely shrub add their color and fragrance in spring. The Shrub Beds bloom from spring through summer, and in fall the Maple Section is ablaze with color. All told, there are more than 2,000 trees and shrubs in this arboretum, representing some 600 species and varieties, and most are labeled. *Open year-round.*

39 Old Mission State Park

2 min. South to Dredge Rd.; follow signs. The mission, designed by a Jesuit priest and built by Coeur d'Alene Indians in the mid-1800's, is Idaho's oldest building and has served as a way station for Indians, pioneers, soldiers, miners, and construction crews. It has been restored and still has many of the original furnishings. Adjacent to the mission is the parish house, with three rooms of primitive furnishings. It also has an altar that may be older than the church. At the visitor center you can see the personal belongings of the Jesuit missionaries and Indian artifacts, including fine bead and leather work. With the aid of a trail guide, you can visualize the former way of life in this community. *Open year-round. Admission charged.*

I-90 Coeur d'Alene District Mining Museum

Museum on I-90 (Bank St.) in Wallace. This building contains visible evidence of the rich deposits of lead, zinc, and silver that brought settlers to this region. The mining museum is dedicated to the past, present, and future of mining. Paintings and photographs interpret the life and times of the Coeur d'Alene district in the 1880's. Dioramas depict the history of mining, and there are three-dimensional exhibits of actual mine shafts, and the tools and equipment needed to exploit them. Samples of rock and ore are also displayed. There's a video show on mining, and information about a tour of the Sierra Silver-Lead Mine is available here. *Open year-round except Thanksgiving Day, Christmas, and New Year's Day. Admission charged.*

62 Burke Mining Town

7 mi./10 min. Northeast on Rte. 4. At the turn of the century Burke was a boomtown wedged in a narrow canyon where the lead, zinc, and silver mines kept it alive until after World War II (one mine kept operating until 1982). The canyon is still picturesque, and there are hiking trails to explore. A few people live in town, but it takes a vivid imagination to visualize the houses, bars, hotel, main street, and railroad that were once crowded together here. Some of the brick and concrete buildings relating to the mining operations still stand, and the foundation of the hotel can be seen. On the road to Burke the past is further recalled by former mining towns and camps with such evocative names as Mace, Yellow Dog, and Gem.

96 Aerial Fire Depot Smokejumper Center

3 min. South on Rte. 10W. Those who jump out of airplanes to fight forest fires must be considered special, and this center is where they are trained and deployed. Some 400 smokejumpers are hired for the fire season nationally, and about 100 are stationed at this U.S. Forest Service facility. The 1-hour visitor tour starts with an orientation video; then the smokejumpers show the parachute loft where they repair and pack the parachutes, and the manufacturing room where much of their special equipment is made. Training sites, air cargo, various aircraft used in firefighting, and the history of smokejumping are also seen on the tour. *Open daily June–mid-Sept.*

101 Historical Museum at Fort Missoula

7 mi./15 min. South on Reserve St., right on South Ave. This open fort—typical of those designed to encourage active patrol rather than passive defense—saw very little action against the Indians but served a number of other purposes. After the Civil War the 25th Infantry Regiment, composed of black soldiers, was headquartered here. This was also headquarters for the 25th Infantry Bicycle Corps in 1896; but despite much valiant pedaling, the bikes did not replace the horses. The 32-acre site includes the main administration building, a depot, a church, a schoolhouse, a Forest Service lookout, and other historic buildings, some of which were relocated here. Several other displays have been planned. *Open Tues.–Sat. and P.M. Sun. Memorial Day–Labor Day; P.M. Tues.–Sun. Labor Day–Memorial Day.*

184 187 Grant-Kohrs Ranch National Historic Site

3 min. Exit 184: south on I-90 (business loop); follow signs. Exit 187: north on I-90 (business loop); follow signs. This is about as close as you can come to the reality of ranch life in the Old West. Although the former 25,000 acres of open range have been reduced to 266, there are still 14 original main buildings and some 10,000 artifacts that belonged to the Grant and Kohrs families. Johnny Grant established a trading post here in the 1850's, built a fine house—a two-story log building—in the 1860's, and sold the spread to Conrad Kohrs in 1866. Kohrs and his wife, Augusta, added a brick wing. The ranch became a national historic site in 1972. A guided tour of the house and a self-guiding tour of horse stalls, bunkhouses, and other outbuildings gives a close-up view of a ranch at the turn of the century. *Open year-round. Admission charged.*

208 Historic City Hall Cultural Center, Anaconda

9 mi./13 min. West on Rte. 1 (becomes Commercial St.). The emphasis here at the former city hall is on the empire of Marcus Daly, a famous copper king, and the Anaconda Minerals Company. The permanent exhibits include panels, done by a local artist, describing the process of smelting of copper from the 1880's to the 1980's. There's also a turn-of-the-century pharmacy, with medicines, cosmetics, and advertising posters. On a rotating basis the museum offers information on Indians, trappers, homesteaders, miners, and other residents whose weapons, clothing, tools, furnishings, and photographs are on display. The Arts Center also mounts changing exhibits. *Open Tues.–Sat. and P.M. Sun. July–Sept. Admission free but donations encouraged.*

124 126 Copper King Mansion, Butte

5 min. Exit 124: east on I-115, left on Montana St., left on Granite St. Exit 126: north on Montana St., left on Granite St. This luxurious 32-room mansion is an outstanding example of Victorian architecture. It was built in the 1880's by William Andrews Clark, a U.S. senator and a multimillionaire entrepreneur with interests in real estate, banking, and oil as well as copper. So vast was his wealth that the quarter of a million dollars he paid for the house represented about half a day's earnings. The opulently furnished home has frescoed ceilings, Tiffany glass windows, and hand-carved woodwork. On the guided tour you'll also see period art and glassware, dolls, toys, and women's fashions. *Open year-round. Admission charged.*

256 274 Lewis and Clark Caverns State Park

Exit 256: 11 mi./25 min. Southeast on Rte. 2. Exit 274: 20 mi./35 min. Southwest on Rte. 287/2. These limestone caverns in the foothills of the Tobacco Root Mountains resulted from millions of years of rock uplifting and faulting and eons of water seepage. As the limestone dissolved, large underground rooms were created, along with an assortment of drip formations—stalactites and stalagmites, delicate stone draperies, tiny helictites, pencil-thin soda straws, and strange shapes that remind you of such objects as an elephant's trunk, Santa Claus, a Chinese pagoda, and Freddie the Frog. A self-guiding nature trail winds through the marvelous mountainous countryside. *Open daily May–Sept. Admission charged for tour.*

306 Museum of the Rockies, Bozeman

3 mi./10 min. South on N. 7th Ave., left on Main St., right on Willson St., right on Kagy Blvd. The amazing variety of material displayed in this museum, which is part of Montana State University, creates a graphic record of the northern Rockies: dinosaur fossils (including a huge *Triceratops* skull, nests of eggs, and baby dinosaur skeletons), beadwork and leatherwork of the Sioux, Flathead, and Blackfoot Indian tribes, and artifacts representing 19th-century Montana history.

510. *Markers show where Colonel Custer and the last of his 7th Cavalry fell in battle.*

Paintings and bronzes by Western artists are exhibited along with photographs of historic figures, including Sitting Bull, Chief Rain-in-the-Face, and Buffalo Bill Cody. A planetarium and a 100-year-old homestead are the latest additions to the museum. *Open daily except Thanksgiving Day, Christmas, and New Year's Day. Admission charged.*   ♿

333   Livingston Depot Center Museum

5 min. North on Rte. 89 (business). Built in 1902, with a curving colonnade along the tracks, terrazzo walls, mosaic trim, and terracotta tiles, this impressive Italian Renaissance–style railroad station served as the gateway to Yellowstone National Park and as a major rail center until 1979. An exhibit titled "Yellowstone Days" traces the region's early history, with bronzes and paintings by such chroniclers of the West as Charles M. Russell and Frederic Remington. An assortment of memorabilia that once belonged to Buffalo Bill Cody is also shown. *Open daily May–mid-Oct. Admission charged.*   ⛲♿

377   Prairie Dog Town State Monument

2 min. South from exit; follow signs. Black-tailed prairie dogs, members of the ground squirrel family, live in "neighborhoods": a series of burrows, called towns, that they defend against intruders, including other prairie dogs in the same town. Several sharp barks, a signal of danger, send the creatures scampering underground through the conical burrow entrances. Predators include golden eagles and badgers. Signboards describe the animals' complex social system and the arrangement of their "rooms." *Open year-round.*

446   Oscar's Dreamland Amusement Park, Billings

5 min. West on S. Frontage Rd., left on Shiloh Rd. Farm machinery is Oscar Cooke's special passion. At the Yesteryear Museum his intriguing collection of 300 antique restored tractors, 40 steam engines, 100 threshing machines, and untold numbers of combines and freight wagons is housed in three enormous buildings that cover some 2 acres. Other unexpected treasures include some 19th-century hearses, a 1917 Liberty truck, road-building machines, an early airplane, and a 110-h.p. 1906 Best steam truck that pulled six 10-ton ore wagons at a time.

At the amusement park you can ride a restored railroad, and for a glimpse of pioneer life, stroll along a restored Main Street with fully appointed homes and stores and a jail. *Open daily May–Labor Day.*   ⛲

450   Peter Yegen, Jr., Yellowstone County Museum, Billings

4 mi./10 min. North on 27th St. to airport; loop through terminal to museum. An 1893 log cabin houses a major portion of this museum, where the collections range from prehistoric times to the days of the homesteaders. The cabin's living room, dominated by a huge stone fireplace and furnished in 19th-century style, evokes life in pioneer-era Montana. Collections in four additional rooms comprise Indian clothing and artifacts, military uniforms, peace pipes, dueling pistols and six-shooters, wagons, and branding irons. Dioramas interpret the age of dinosaurs and cave people and depict the legend of Sacrifice Cliff (Indian braves riding off the top to their death). *Open Mon.–Fri. and P.M. Sun. except holidays.*

510   Custer Battlefield National Monument

2 min. East on Rte. 212. On the slopes of a ridge above the Little Bighorn River, markers show where Lt. Col. George Armstrong Custer and 51 of his men fell in battle against the Sioux and Cheyenne nations in 1876. To the south and east are the vast plains of sagebrush and prairie grass of southeastern Montana, where the rest of Custer's 210 troops died. At the visitor center, dioramas of the battlefield and biographical portraits of the protagonists—Custer, Maj. Marcus Reno, Capt. Frederick Benteen, and chiefs Sitting Bull, Gall, and Two Moon—explain the reasons for the conflict and its outcome. One of Custer's buckskin suits, his Colt revolver, Chief Sitting Bull's beaded bag, and other belongings are displayed. Guided tours of the battlefield are available in the summer. *Open year-round. Admission charged.*   🚶♿

If You Have Some Extra Time:

Yellowstone National Park

333   *53 mi./75 min.* Just 5 miles from the north entrance in Gardiner, Montana, is Mammoth Hot Springs, a travertine fantasy of flat terraces and rounded forms shaped by the flow of mineral-laden water—a fitting introduction to the marvels of America's first national park. In some 3,500 square miles of wilderness, you'll find vast forests, grassy meadows, streams, and lakes. The Grand Canyon of the rushing Yellowstone River has a waterfall almost twice as high as Niagara's Horseshoe Falls. A forest of petrified trees, an obsidian cliff, and 1,000 miles of hiking trails add to the park's majesty.

The most famous of the dramatic geysers is Old Faithful, which earned its name by erupting at regular intervals. In recent years the average has been 70 to 73 minutes. You have seen the pictures, but nothing can prepare you for the event itself. Near the appointed time—posted for each eruption—there can be wisps of steam and spurts of water to announce the impending phenomenon. Then, with a roar, comes the heart-stopping surge of boiling water shooting up as high as 180 feet.

On the 142-mile Grand Loop Road, you may see moose, elk, deer, bison, and bighorn sheep. Be careful with animals; this is their territory, and we are intruders. *How to get there: south on Rte. 89 to Gardiner (only entrance open year-round). Admission charged.*

23 Trail End Historic Center, Sheridan

4 min. West on 5th St., left on Clarendon Ave. This luxurious home was built in about 1910 by John Kendricks, who became governor of Wyoming in 1914 and was elected to the U.S. Senate two years later. The house, which then cost $165,000 to build and furnish, is in the Flemish style (new to these parts at the time), with curved gables, a red tile roof, and walls and chimneys of pale brick.

The furnishings and woodwork are superb, from the piano-finish mahogany, the huge Kurdistan rug, and the French brocade wall panels in the coffered drawing room to the library's quarter-sawn oak paneling with antique English finish. On the third floor a ballroom with a musicians' loft, a dance floor of Maryland maple, and a beamed ceiling seems ready for festivities. *Open daily Memorial Day–Labor Day; limited hours Labor Day–Memorial Day.* 🌲♿

23 33 Bradford Brinton Memorial

Exit 23: 6 mi./10 min. South on Rte. 87, right on Rte. 335; follow signs. Exit 33: 13.5 mi./17 min. West on Rte. 342, right on Rte. 87, left on Rte. 335; follow signs. This part of Wyoming is prime cattle country; and the Quarter Circle A Ranch, built in 1892 and bought by Bradford Brinton as a summer home in 1923, is an authentic reminder of a way of life enjoyed by the more prosperous landowners in northern Wyoming. The ranch-style house retains its fine original furnishings and Brinton's outstanding collection of western art (Indian crafts, as well as paintings and bronzes by Charles Russell, Frederic Remington, Frank Johnson, and Edward Borein). The grounds are nicely maintained, and there are lovely views of the Bighorn Mountains' front range. *Open daily mid-May–Labor Day.*

44 Fort Phil Kearny National Historic Site

5 min. Northwest on Rte. 193; follow signs. Constructed in 1866 in violation of a treaty with the Sioux nation, Ft. Kearny was held under continual siege by Chief Red Cloud and his warriors until it was abandoned in 1868 (it was later destroyed by fire). Today the visitor center displays an outline of the fort and the barracks, along with reproductions of army weapons and bows and arrows. Panels in an adjacent cabin tell the dramatic story of the Wyoming Indian wars and the Bozeman Trail, and describe reservation and frontier life. *Open daily June–mid-Oct.* 🌲♿

153–185. *The irresistible force of an ancient volcano is documented in stone.*

56 58 Jim Gatchell Memorial Museum, Buffalo

5 min. Exit 56: west on Rte. 16; follow signs. Exit 58: proceed as above. Pioneer druggist Jim Gatchell, in dealing with the Indians of the Sioux and Cheyenne tribes, amassed a large collection of their artifacts. The treasures include guns and shell casings believed to have been used during the massacre of Custer's troops at the Little Bighorn and the switchboard of the Occidental Hotel, an inn immortalized by Owen Wister in his best-selling 1902 novel, *The Virginian. Open daily June–Labor Day.*

132 The Wyodak Mine

3 min. South from exit, right on Rte. 51. When the coal supplies here are exhausted some 30 years from now, the land will be returned to range, since there is continuous reclamation in progress. In the meantime, Wyodak mines 3 million tons of coal per year and puts nearly two-thirds of it on a conveyor belt that runs under the highway to America's largest air-cooled condensing power plant, just across the road. Visitors see both old and new mining equipment, including 120-ton-capacity coal-haulers. Free bus tours of this and other area mines are available at most local motels. For reservations for the power plant tour, call (307) 686-1248. *Mine and power plant open Mon.–Fri. June–Aug.*

153 185 Devils Tower National Monument

Exit 153: 29 mi./35 min. Northeast on Rte. 14, left on Rte. 24, left on Rte. 110. Exit 185: 28 mi./35 min. Northwest on Rte. 14, right on Rte. 24, left on Rte. 110. The neck of a 60-million-year-old volcano towers imperiously more than 860 feet above its base. It's a magnificent monolith with an aura of mystery and menace. The Indians, believing that the claws of a celestial bear had fluted its walls, called the tower Bear Lodge. These days you're likely to see rock climbers inching their way to the summit, a teardrop-shaped plateau where hawks soar and chipmunks scamper through the sagebrush and buffalo grass. A trail skirts the tower's base. *Open year-round. Admission charged.* 🌲⛺🚐🚶

12 D. C. Booth Historic Fish Hatchery, Spearfish

4 min. West on Jackson Blvd., left on Canyon St. Before D. C. Booth founded the fish hatchery here in 1899, there were no trout in the streams of the Black Hills. The original hatchery building now houses the National Fish Culture Hall of Fame and an informative museum that commemorates Booth's work and the early years of the National Fish Hatcheries. Among the memorabilia, you'll see photographs of the early railroad fish cars and old equipment that Booth and others used in their fish-culture activities. Rainbow trout abound in the hatchery ponds. Visitors will enjoy feeding the fish, and anglers will want to try their luck at adjacent Spearfish Creek, a high-quality trout stream. *Museum open daily late May–late Sept.; grounds open year-round. Admission charged.*

30   Bear Butte State Park

9 mi./14 min. East on Rte. 34, left on Rte. 79. The peak of 4,426-foot-high Bear Butte looms above the plain like an outrider, and Indians still make pilgrimages to it as a sacred mountain. It's a place of great beauty and mystery, and when clouds swirl about its peak it looks so somber and brooding that one can easily understand its importance in Indian culture. Geologically, it is called a laccolith—a place where molten rock has raised the land's surface without breaking through, similiar to a volcano that did not erupt. Buffalo graze on the mountain's slopes, and at its foot lies Bear Butte Lake, where there is camping and picnicking. A visitor center records the butte's history. *Open year-round.*

30   Broken Boot Gold Mine, Deadwood

13 mi./18 min. West on Rte. 14A. This mine, which received its name when a miner's old boot was unearthed in a pile of debris, was opened in 1878, and by the time it closed in 1904 it had produced gold worth $1.5 million in turn-of-the-century dollars. The tour (the only underground mine tour in the Black Hills region still open to the public) takes you down the "main drift," a tunnel that runs into the hill horizontally for nearly 300 yards and into the house-size "stopes," the chambers from which the ore was removed. With the aid of searchlights, you can still see pockets of gold ore in the walls. *Open daily May–Sept. Admission charged.*

46   Black Hills Petrified Forest

4 min. East from exit; follow signs. A guided tour takes you along the crest of Piedmont Butte, where numerous petrified trunks of cypress and primitive palm trees lie where they fell, or where the earth millions of years ago moved them. Some actually still stand upright, and many are half buried in a matrix of sandstone. The museum displays samples of petrified wood and provides a detailed account of Black Hills geology as well as the process of petrifaction, the gradual conversion of organic matter into stone, or a stonelike substance. *Open daily mid-May–mid-Sept. Admission charged.*

57   Sioux Indian and Pioneer Museums, Rapid City

4 min. South on I-190 (becomes West Blvd.). Two fine museums occupy the same stone building in Halley Park. The Sioux Indian Museum displays the arts and crafts of the Sioux and other North American Indians: quillwork, beadwork, carvings, paintings on hide, featherwork, musical instruments, and costumes. The Pioneer Museum, which complements the Indian Museum, chronicles the history of the Black Hills region from the time of the first fur traders, with historic photographs, tools, and other memorabilia of trappers and prospectors, as well as some fine antiques and clothing. *Both museums open Mon.–Sat. and P.M. Sun. June–Sept; Tues.–Sat. and P.M. Sun. Oct.–May except Thanksgiving Day, Christmas, and New Year's Day. Pioneer Museum closed Jan.*

57   Mount Rushmore National Memorial, Keystone

21 mi./30 min. South on I-190, east on Quincy St., right on Mt. Rushmore Rd. (Rte. 16), left on Rte. 16A. The surprise here is how natural the granite faces of Washington, Jefferson, Lincoln, and Theodore Roosevelt appear as they gaze out from their mountain fortress. They seem to belong here—as they belong to the history of our country. Far below at the visitor center, there's a viewing terrace and information on how the carving was done. The sculptor, Gutzon Borglum, began his blasting and drilling in 1927 and didn't finish his monumental labor until 1941, just short of his 74th birthday. His studio, down a steep hill from the visitor center, contains a large model of the memorial, photographs of the work at various stages, and a display of sculptor's tools. *Open year-round.*

57. *Our 1st, 3rd, 26th, and 16th chief executives are memorialized here for the ages.*

131. *This fantasyland is even more astounding seen in its setting of surrounding prairie.*

110 Wall Drug Store

2 min. Exit north; follow signs. This famous drugstore-café-shopping complex began as a humble small-town drugstore in 1931 and took off when Ted and Dorothy Hustead began to lure travelers with signs promising free ice water. These days the dramatically expanded store is still owned by the Hustead family and patronized by up to 20,000 people per day in summer. Besides the famous ice water, drugstore, and café, visitors will find shops that sell western goods, a traveler's chapel, "clothed wild animals," and the jackalope, a stuffed jackrabbit with antelopelike horns. One of the signs advertising the store says it's "like a museum—see it free." *Open daily mid-Mar.–Nov.; Mon.–Sat. Dec.–mid-Mar. except holidays.*

131 Badlands National Park

9 mi./15 min. South on Rte. 240. Some of this country's strangest and most spectacular landscapes can be seen in this part of South Dakota, where the earth has been laid bare by eons of rain and wind, and the ancient strata of mud, rock, and ash have been carved into jagged ruins, mesas, and pinnacles. In late summer golden prairie grass tops the mesas, and lone plants cling to life in the cracked mud of valley floors. There are many overlooks along the Scenic Loop Road, and the short Door Trail (accessible to the handicapped) leads to miniature ravines and spikes embedded with nodules of pink rock. The Cliff Shelf Nature Trail passes gnarled junipers where magpies nest and a pool where cattails grow. The Cedar Pass Visitor Center gives an account of the geological and natural history of the park. *Open year-round. Admission charged.*

152 Badlands Petrified Gardens

1 min. South on access road. Sixty million years ago an inland sea covered western South Dakota. Logs sank into the muddy seabed and eventually became petrified. Now an extensive collection of these stone tree remnants can be seen in the gardens here, their ancient bark, roots, and wormholes clearly visible. The museum has an excellent collection of minerals and fossils, including rare specimens of petrified wood. *Open daily May–late Oct. Admission charged.*

192 Pioneer Auto Museum and Antique Town, Murdo

1 min. North from exit; follow signs. About three dozen buildings, spread over more than 10 acres, house a variety of nostalgic displays, including exhibits of minerals, gems, and toys. A fine collection of more than 200 antique automobiles features an early camper (the Motor Palace Camp Car) and a 1909 Auburn, used on the roadless prairie to locate land for homesteaders. You can also see a train depot and telegraph office, a church, a blacksmith's shop, a bank, and a barbershop. *Open daily except Thanksgiving Day, Christmas, New Year's Day, and Easter. Admission charged.*

260 Old West Museum

1 min. East on I-90 (business loop). Here you will find an overwhelming variety of curiosities, antiques, and Old West Americana. Vintage radios, pocket knives, sausage stuffers, antique cars, clocks, Indian artifacts, musical instruments, 200 dolls, and 120 tractor seats are included, as well as an ivory-handled 1876 Colt Peacemaker pistol with cattle brands on the barrel and a pair of buffalo-head spurs. The Old Time Main Street has a number of shops and offices, including a general store with a hard-to-come-by package of Pfeiffer's Florentine Hair Promoter. Another building houses an 80-foot-long model steam train and a governess buggy attached to a stuffed zebra. *Open daily Apr.–Oct. Admission charged.*

332 Mitchell Corn Palace

2.5 mi./6 min. North on Rte. 37, left on Rte. 38, right on Sanborn St., left on E. 1st Ave., left on N. Main St. The Moorish-style exterior of the spectacular Corn Palace is decorated from top to bottom with murals made from multicolored corncobs, sorghum, wheat, rye, and native grasses. The designs change yearly, and new ones are completed before the Corn Palace Week celebration in late September. Permanent corn murals decorate the auditorium, where entertainment is presented. *Open daily Memorial Day–Labor Day, Mon.–Fri. Labor Day–Memorial Day except Thanksgiving Day, Christmas, and New Year's Day.*

I-29 Sherman Park, Sioux Falls

4.5 mi./8 min. South on I-29 to Exit 79, east on 12th St., right on Kiwanis Ave. The park, with meadows, ballfields, tennis courts, a skating rink, a children's playground, and shady picnic grounds, lies on the banks of the Big Sioux River. At the northern end is the U.S.S. *South Dakota* Battleship Memorial, a full-size concrete plan of the warship, and a museum of memorabilia. The Great Plains Zoo in the park has some 300 animals, ranging from the elegantly aloof snow leopard to the appealing Sicilian donkey. The Delbridge Museum of Natural History shows mounted animals in lifelike dioramas. *Open daily except Christmas. Admission charged.*

12 Blue Mounds State Park

5 mi./8 min. North on Rte. 75. This is a place of great beauty, named for the large purple outcrops of Sioux quartzite in cliffs that rise suddenly from the fertile plain, as if to exalt and preserve the wild prairie that crowns them. To the north are two lakes with picnic and swimming areas, and a tract of fenced prairie where bison graze. Trails cross the prairie and follow the edge of the cliffs, where oak trees and wild roses grow, and prickly pear sprouts in cracks in the lichened quartzite. *Open year-round. Admission charged.*

332. *The Corn Palace: an uncommon tribute to common crops that are cultivated here.*

42 Nobles County Pioneer Village, Worthington

4 min. Southeast on Rte. 266, left on Rte. 35 (Oxford St.), left on Rowe Ave.; follow signs. This museum-village complex presents a remarkably complete panorama of the region's history, and of the tools and institutions that shaped it. The Agricultural Building includes tools and equipment, from wire fencing to tractors, that turned the prairie into farmland, and the Transportation Building contains a wide selection of antique buggies, sleighs, and other vehicles. A restored train depot has a display of period railroad cars. Other establishments—the blacksmith's shop, firehouse, town hall, newspaper office, lawyer's office, saloon, hospital—are here too, as well as a photo shop, with its big scrapbooks of old-fashioned postcards. A farmhouse, built in Worthington around 1880, is furnished with careful fidelity to the period, and so are the two-room parsonage and the old Lutheran church nearby. *Open Mon.–Sat. and P.M. Sun. May–Sept. Admission charged.*

64 Kilen Woods State Park

12 mi./15 min. North on Rte. 86, right on Rte. 24. The park lies on the west bank of the Des Moines River in a landscape that comprises prairie, wooded ravines, and steep hillsides. From the sturdy observation tower there's a pleasant view of the river and the uplands. Trails crisscross prairie, oak savanna, woods, and floodplain, and a nature center provides a detailed account of the native birds, animals, trees, flowers, and grasses that make the park a wildlife oasis within the surrounding farmland. *Open year-round. Admission charged.*

102 Pioneer Museum, Fairmont

5 min. South on Rte. 15, right on Blue Earth Ave. The museum is the headquarters of the Martin County Historical Society, which since 1929 has been gathering pioneer and other memorabilia of early life in the area. Exhibits include the furnished interior of an 1890 home, ladies' old-fashioned gowns, a one-room schoolhouse, military relics, and tools and equipment used in local trades, professions, industries, and home life. *Open P.M. Tues.–Fri. and Mon. evenings May–Sept. Admission free but donations encouraged.*

12. *The fragile beauty of prickly-pear flowers is a refreshing surprise in hot, dry places.*

119 James B. Wakefield House Museum, Blue Earth

5 min. South on Rte. 169, right on E. 6th St. The museum occupies a two-story brick home built in 1868 by James B. Wakefield, who founded Blue Earth City and also served as a lieutenant governor of Minnesota. His office is preserved on the ground floor, along with memorabilia about Wakefield and his friend Henry Constans, who founded the Constans Hotel (at the corner of 5th and Main streets). On the second floor are such relics of local history as a kettle that belonged to the first white settler, a rolling pin made in 1867 from a tree that stood near the courthouse, and an 1865 christening dress. *Open P.M. Mon.–Sat. Admission free but donations encouraged.*

158 Freeborn County Museum and Historical Village, Albert Lea

3 min. South on Bridge Ave.; follow signs. Twelve historic buildings are preserved here in southern Minnesota, along with a variety of exhibits that tell the story of Freeborn County's early days. The main exhibition hall displays pioneer articles ranging from trunks and baby clothes to a Swedish harp. There's also a well-equipped kitchen, a comfortable parlor, an elegant millinery shop, Indian artifacts, antique bottles, a mammoth tusk from a local gravel pit, and much more. The Red Barn houses a fully equipped train depot, a barbershop, a bank, a photo studio, a jail, a firehouse, tractors, steam engines, agricultural equipment, and automobiles. Elsewhere in the historical village is the first log house built in Freeborn County (1853), a rural schoolhouse, a hardware store, a cobbler's shop, an 1870's church, and a general store that stocks everything from hatpins to horse collars. *Open P.M. Tues.–Sun. June–Aug.; P.M. Sun. May and Sept.–Oct. Admission charged.* ♿

I-35 Helmer Myre State Park

5 min. South on I-35 to Exit 11, east on Rte. 46, right on Rte. 38. The sweet smell of tallgrass prairie and the shining expanse of Albert Lea Lake (2,600 acres) are the most immediate attractions in the park. The terrain reflects its glacial past and varies from prairie to oak savanna, marsh, forest, and esker (rock and sand deposits left by glacial streams). The park is well known for its waterfowl and shorebirds, and it has more than 450 kinds of wildflowers. There are several trails, and canoes are rented. An interpretive center on Big Island has an outstanding collection of Indian artifacts. The nearby town of Albert Lea also has many excellent parks. *Open year-round. Admission charged.*

175 Mower County Historical Center, Austin

5 min. East on West Oakland Ave., right on Rte. 105 (12th St.). This complex of museums and historic buildings presents highlights of regional history and aspects of daily life in southern Minnesota since the first settlers arrived. The Indian Museum has an excellent collection of artifacts, and there is an 1862 log cabin and an 1870 rural school. The Pioneer, Rural Life, and Hormel museums illustrate the area's early settlement and later prosperity: here are surveyor's instruments, farm tools, a loon-feather cape, and George Hormel's first (1890's) meat-packing establishment. The Rahilly Museum displays a 1910 eight-seater omnibus, the Railroad Museum shows a Baldwin locomotive, and the Communications Museum specializes in telephone equipment. The Headquarters Building (1856) contains old-time county miscellany, including a general store and the county's recruiting station from the Civil War. In the Fireman's Museum a 1926 chain-driven pumper and fire-fighting badges and patches from all over the world are displayed. *Open P.M. daily, June–Aug.*

252 Julius C. Wilkie Steamboat Center, Winona

9 mi./14 min. North on Rte. 43, left on Homer Rd. (becomes Mankato Ave.), left on Sarnia St., right on Main St. This full-size replica of a paddle wheeler rests in a dry dock in Levee Park beside the Mississippi River. It features a steamboat museum with model paddleboats, photographs, steamboat prints by Currier and Ives, relics of the original *Wilkie*, bills of lading, and other mementos of the steamboat era. Perhaps the most interesting items are the manuscripts, books, and other memorabilia of Robert Fulton, father of the commercial paddleboat and a canal engineer who built early models of submarines and torpedoes. The rest of the *Wilkie,* from the pilothouse to the lavish Grand Salon, gives a vivid impression of what the old riverboats were like in their heyday. While here, try the walking tour of Winona's many turn-of-the-century structures. *Open daily May–Oct. Admission charged.*

3A Hixon House, La Crosse

4.5 mi./11 min. South on Rte. 53 (becomes Rose St., then Copeland Ave.), left on Vine St., left on 7th St. Banker, philanthropist, and lumber mogul Gideon Hixon built this home in 1859 and furnished it according to 19th-century standards of comfort and opulence. The woodwork is exceptional, from the hand-carved teak desk and bookcases in Hixon's study to the sliding birch doors in the parlor. Throughout the house elegant imported items capture one's attention: Wedgwood pottery from his personal collection, a screen of Chinese silk in the master bedroom, and a "Turkish nook" with an olivewood harem screen. The dining room has a handsome coffered ceiling and is furnished with Chippendale and Hepplewhite chairs. The place settings have hand-painted Limoges china. *Open P.M. daily June–Labor Day. Admission charged.*

41 The Little Red Schoolhouse, Tomah

3 min. North on Rte. 131 (Superior Ave.). In use from 1864 to 1965, this small, classic one-room schoolhouse, reminiscent of simpler times, now stands in Tomah's Gillette Park. You can see photographs of the students dating back to the early 1900's, schoolbooks from 1910 and the 1920's, a small collection of minerals, and map stencils for the children's geography lessons. *Open P.M. daily Memorial Day–Labor Day.*

87. *The sandstone, obviously vulnerable to erosion, is so porous that trees can grow.*

87   The Dells

2 min. East on Rte. 13/23. The Dells of the Wisconsin River are narrow chasms or ravines that have been carved out of sandstone cliffs (formed millions of years ago) by the relentless erosive action of water against rock after the Ice Age meltdown. The walls of the cliffs are corrugated and in places capped by overhangs and pedestals of rock. These picturesque formations can be seen if you take one of the commercial boat tours from the docks in downtown Wisconsin Dells. Boats operate from mid-April to mid-October. Two other outstanding attractions in this area are

The Stand Rock Indian Ceremonial *(5 mi./7 min. from Exit 87; east on Rte. 13/23, left on Rte. 12/16, right on Rte. A, left on Stand Rock Rd.)* offers a program of traditional North American Indian dances performed by Native Americans in a magnificent natural amphitheater. *Performance every evening mid-June– Labor Day. Admission charged.* ⛩ ♿

The Winnebago Indian Museum *(6.5 mi./10 min. from Exit 87; east on Rte. 13/23, across bridge, left on River Rd.)* displays an excellent collection of Indian clothing, ornaments, and weapons along with other artifacts. *Open daily Apr.–Dec. Admission charged.* ⛩ ♿

92 106   Mid-Continent Railway Museum, North Freedom

Exit 92: 13.5 mi./18 min. South on Rte. 12, right on Rte. 136, left on Rte. PF. Exit 106: 21 mi./28 min. West on Rte. 33, continue on Rte. 136, left on Rte. PF. A restored 1894 depot is the starting point for rides through the peaceful Baraboo River valley in an authentic steam train. Railroad equipment—including a snowplow, a boxcar, and a baggage car—is displayed in the Coach Shed, along with the 1884 D & R No. 9, one of the oldest steam locomotives used regularly in North America, and the 1925 Montana Western gas-electric car No. 3l, which preceded the diesel engine. Refreshments are served in an old Marquette & Huron line mountain car. A children's playground is adjacent to the picnic area. *Open daily mid-May–Labor Day; weekends only, Labor Day–mid-Oct. Admission charged.* ⛩ ♿

135. *A Norwegian who died for his adopted land is honored on the grounds of the capitol.*

92 106   Circus World Museum, Baraboo

Exit 92: 10 mi./15 min. South on Rte. 12; follow signs. Exit 106: 14 mi./20 min. West on Rte. 33; follow signs. The Ringling Brothers circus had its winter quarters in Baraboo until 1918. The complex of 30 buildings now serves as both an active showplace and a home for circus memorabilia. In season performances are presented daily under the big top, and an extensive museum of circus history includes automated miniatures, air calliopes, and displays commemorating various circus stars. The world's largest collection of circus wagons contains fine examples of gilding and carving. The menagerie, with its tigers, camels, hippos, and other animals, draws fascinated viewers. *Open daily early May– mid-Sept. Admission charged.*

135   Madison, WI 53703

Convention & Visitors Bureau, 121 W. Doty St. (608) 255-0701. The capitol, set on an isthmus between two lakes in the downtown area of this attractive city, is reputed to be the largest state capitol building in the United States and is open for tours. Architecture on a smaller scale is also important: Frank Lloyd Wright's Unitarian Meeting House (1949–51) is open to the public, and several other buildings designed by Wright, a Wisconsin native, can be viewed from the street. The State Historical Museum features Indian and French voyageur exhibits, while the University of Wisconsin's Elvehjem Museum of Art displays works of all periods. On the university campus you can visit an arboretum, Indian effigy mounds, and Babcock Hall, where you can get college-educated ice cream.

147   Lake Kegonsa State Park

3.5 mi./6 min. South on Rte. N, right on Koshkonong Rd.; follow signs. This park, near Madison, has more than 300 acres of woodland, prairie, and marsh, as well as an extensive shoreline on 3,209-acre Lake Kegonsa ("lake of many fish" in Winnebago, and the lake reportedly lives up to it). The White Oak nature trail loops through woods past a group of Indian mounds. Inviting mown paths wind through quiet prairie. *Open year-round. Admission charged.* ⛩ ⛺ 🚐 🚶 🏊 🎣 ♿

171A Milton House Museum

5 mi./7 min. North on Rte. 26. This onetime stagecoach inn and Underground Railroad station, built in 1844, was the first structure in the U.S.A. to be made from poured grout. Today the building is a lively museum of local history where one can still see the tunnel in which its builder, Joseph Goodrich, sheltered fugitive slaves. The interior of the inn, furnished with loving attention to detail, displays rope beds, period clothing, and the original guest book. On the grounds there's a buggy shed, an 1844 blacksmith's shop, and the 1837 log cabin Goodrich lived in before Milton House was built. A country store sells gifts and souvenirs. *Open daily June–Labor Day; weekends, May and Labor Day–mid-Oct. Admission charged.*

175 The Tallman Restorations, Janesville

3 mi./7 min. West on Rte. 11, right on S. Franklin St.; follow signs. Here you'll find a striking Italianate mansion considered to be one of the largest and most important mid-19th-century house museums in the Midwest. When it was built in 1855–57, this three-story residence contained many then-uncommon luxuries, including a marble sink with running water in each bedroom. The exterior is enhanced by cast-iron arches over the windows and a small cupola on the roof. The parlor where William and Emeline Tallman entertained Abraham Lincoln one weekend in

175. *The house is noted for the elegance of the proportions and decorative details.*

1859 is especially noteworthy, although the future President of the U.S. found it too formal and withdrew to the more casual family parlor. Nearby, an elegant horse barn now houses a visitor center. One of the region's earliest mansions is located on the grounds—an 1842 Greek revival house containing portraits of local citizens as well as decorative art brought to this area by pioneer families in the 19th century. *Open Tues.–Sun. June–Aug.; weekends only May and Sept.–mid-Oct. except holidays. Admission charged.*

ROUTE 20B Rockford, IL 61104

Rte. 20 (business) exit: Convention & Visitors Bureau, 220 E. State St. (800) 521-0849; (800) 423-5361 outside IL. For a pleasant introduction to Illinois's second largest city, take one of the narrated tours on a riverboat or on an old-fashioned trolley. A highlight of the trolley ride is Sinissippi Gardens Greenhouse and Lagoon, with its elegant sunken gardens, aviary, and floral clock.

A number of historic homes attest to Rockford's 19th-century heritage: the 20-room Tinker Swiss Cottage, the dwelling made of oak logs by early settler Stephen Mack, the brick home of Swedish settler John Erlander, and the Greek revival Graham Genestra House. Museum lovers will enjoy Midway Village in the Rockford Museum Center with its turn-of-the-century blacksmith's shop, jail, bank, and other town fixtures and displays. Exhibits on science topics and the state of Illinois's wildlife are housed in the Victorian mansion of the Burpee Museum of Natural History; an excellent art collection in the Rockford Art Museum invites attention; and the renowned Time Museum has some 2,500 clocks dating from ancient times to the space age.

M-H Illinois Railway Museum, Union

Marengo-Hampshire exit: 10 mi./13 min. West on Rte. 20, right on Union Rd.; follow signs. The golden age of railroading returns in all its glory at this "museum in motion." Here you'll see one of only two surviving Norfolk & Western Mallet locomotives—113 feet long and weighing 458 tons when loaded with coal and

M-H. *Enviable luxury, as enjoyed by those who could afford a private car.*

water. Also on exhibit is the oldest still operating diesel locomotive in the country, an 1859 horse-drawn streetcar, and the stainless steel *Silver Pilot.* The rolling stock includes a luxurious 1910 Pullman observation car, massive snow-sweepers with cane-bristled brushes, and a rare interurban sleeping car. Rides are available on several trains. *Open Mon.–Sat. Memorial Day–Labor Day; Sun. mid-Apr.–Oct. Admisson charged.*

ROUTE 31 Fox River Trolley Museum, South Elgin

7 mi./12 min. South on Rte. 31. The authentic clang, clang, clang of the trolley is heard here as vintage cars make their 3-mile round-trip through scenic vistas of water and trees on the Fox River Line, built in 1896. The museum's impressive collection includes the oldest working interurban trolley in America, the only surviving streetcar post office, an 1887 caboose, a 1920's elevated train from Chicago, and one of America's last streetcars—a model with rubber wheels built in 1951. *Open Sun. and holidays mid-May–Oct. and P.M. Sat. July–Labor Day. Fare charged for rides.*

OH Chicago, IL 60611

E. Ohio St. exit: Tourism Council, 163 E. Pearson St. (312) 280-5740. This great cosmopolitan metropolis, beautifully situated on the southwestern shore of Lake Michigan, boasts a number of world-class attractions. The Art Institute is known for a wide-ranging permanent collection and creative special exhibitions. The Terra Museum, opened in 1987, has a superlative collection of American art; the John G. Shedd Aquarium, the world's largest such indoor facility, with more than 200 tanks, displays some 1,000 wonders of the deep. For an intimate sense of the city, take the El (the elevated railroad) around the Loop; and for a breathtaking overview of the city and lake, try the observation area on the 103rd floor of the Sears Tower, at this writing the tallest building in the world.

1   Wolf Lake Park, Hammond

2 mi./5 min. East on Indianapolis Blvd. (Rte. 12/20), right on Calumet Ave. (Rte. 41). Despite the unpromising surroundings of highways, high-tension lines, and gas storage tanks, this 452-acre park is an obvious success, boasting a large lake, an 18-hole miniature golf course, and other recreational facilities. Canoes, paddleboats, and sailboards are rented. The annual Augustfest, held during the first week of the month, brings some 300,000 people here for entertainment, food, and carnival attractions. A fishing pier and a boat ramp entice the angler to try for walleye, northern pike, or bass. *Open daily mid-June– mid-Sept. Admission charged.*

31   Wilbur H. Cummings Museum of Electronics, Valparaiso

15 mi./25 min. South on Rte. 49, right on Rte. 130. Electronic technology changes so quickly that yesterday's marvel soon becomes today's antique. This museum has electronic devices from the period of Edison and Marconi to the present, knowing that its latest state-of-the-art exhibits will soon be obsolescent. Among the highlights are a 1950's Seeburg jukebox that plays 78-r.p.m. records, Admiral Byrd's transmitter from a South Pole expedition, one of the first pinball machines, and radios by Atwater-Kent, Crosley, Philco, and other noted manufacturers. First-generation computers and VCR's, studio TV equipment, and other outmoded wonders are displayed and ex-

plained. The museum is at Valparaiso Technical Institute; apply for free admission at the administration building. *Open year-round.*

31   Indiana Dunes National Lakeshore

8.5 mi./13 min. North on Rte. 49, right on Rte. 12. These 1,800 acres of woodland trails and 3 miles of beach dominated by towering lakefront dunes evince an almost lyrical delicacy in an obviously industrial environment. A number of plants are relics of the colder climates that existed here at the end of the Ice Age, leaving a remarkable diversity of vegetation: arctic bearberry flourishes alongside prickly-pear cacti, and northern jack pines share dune slopes with southern dogwoods. Although the dunes are large (Mt. Tom rises more than 190 feet) and are anchored against the wind by marram grass, sand cherry, cottonwoods, and other native plants, they are susceptible to erosion. A 2-mile trail leads through red oaks and sugar maples to the restored Bailly Homestead and the Chellberg Farm. *Open year-round.*

77   Fort Joseph Museum, Niles

8.5 mi./15 min. North on Rte. 33 and Rte. 31/33. This Michigan fort, built by the French in 1691, commanded a key trade route between their holdings in Canada and Louisiana. In the French and Indian War it was held by the British, then briefly by Spain.

The documents, pictures, books, implements, and furniture in the 100,000-item museum, located in a Victorian carriage house, bring the story to vivid life. Here, too, is a large collection of Sioux and other Indian artifacts, including pictographs of chiefs Sitting Bull and Rain-in-the-Face. *Open Tues.–Sun. Admission free but donations encouraged.*

77   Studebaker National Museum, South Bend

3 mi./9 min. South on Rte. 33, left on Jefferson Blvd. In the 1850's South Bend was known as the Wheel City, because of the scores of wagonmakers living and working here. Part of that tradition was created by the Studebaker Company, which in time went from building cov-

ered wagons to producing some of the 20th century's most imaginative automobiles. You will see examples of these at Century Center (Jefferson Boulevard and St. Joseph Street). Among the highlights are Studebaker's first automobile (a 1902 electric model), the Dictator Series of the 1930's, and the bullet-nosed models of the 1950's. Dodge, Oliver, and Flanders are also well represented. And not just cars: the 1923 Indestructo cabin trunk, for example, kindles nostalgic memories of those bygone days when a trip abroad was the event of a lifetime. At the nearby Archives Center (South Street and Lafayette Boulevard), you can see more than 60 historic horse-drawn and motorized vehicles, including four presidents' carriages. *Open daily June–Aug.; Tues.–Sun. Sept.–May. Admission charged.*

77   Potato Creek State Park

24 mi./30 min. South on Rte. 33 and Rte. 31 (business) through South Bend, right on Rte. 4. Fishermen come to Worster Lake for the bass, bluegill, brown trout, crappie, and channel catfish. The 300-acre reservoir was created in 1977, when Potato Creek was dammed, and in parts of the lake the ghostly trunks of the drowned trees can still be seen. The landscape, with woodland and scrubby pasture, shows how former farmland reverts to its natural state. You can enjoy several trails, including a 3-mile bicycle trail that goes through many scenic parts. *Open year-round. Admission charged.*

121   Pigeon River State Fish and Wildlife Area

9 mi./12 min. South on Rte. 9, left on Rte. 120; follow signs. The woods, ponds, streams, and marshland in this wildlife area, which covers some 11,500 acres, are home to deer, pheasants, and waterfowl as well as pike, bluegill, perch, and of course trout. The Curtis Creek Trout-Rearing Station, which is located in the wildlife area, successfully grows some 60,000 rainbow and brown trout per year. Although not native to Indiana, fingerlings are brought here from state hatcheries, raised in six 86-foot-long raceways, and released in various streams and lakes. *Open year-round.*

156 Pokagon State Park

4 min. South on I-69 to Exit 154, west on Rte. 727. This park, named for a Potawatomi chief, has year-round appeal. In winter, thrill seekers head for the 1,780-foot refrigerated toboggan slide, where they can streak down and over hills at 45 miles per hour. The slide is open from Thanksgiving to March, and toboggans, rented by the hour, can hold up to four passengers. Other attractions in this vast area include trails for hikers and cross-country skiers (rentals available), ice fishing, ice skating, and sledding. In summer, visitors fish, boat, and swim in Lake James. *Open year-round. Admission charged.*

156. *Literally breathtaking is this toboggan run down one steep hill and up another.*

2 3 Harrison Lake State Park

Exit 2: 20 mi./30 min. North on Rte. 15, right on Rte. 20, right on Rte. 27; follow signs. Exit 3: 20 mi./30 min. North on Rte. 108, left on Rte. 20, left on Rte. 66, right on Rte. M. The soggy black soil that once earned this region the nickname the Great Black Swamp is some of Ohio's most fertile farmland. Even amid vast fields of corn, oats, and soybeans, this 350-acre park sparkles with greenery. Harrison Lake—framed by shaded picnic areas and lush meadows—provides water activities in every season and yields bluegill, crappie, and largemouth bass. In spring, vesper sparrows, brown thrashers, and yellowthroats are some of the songbirds seen here. *Open year-round.*

4 Fort Meigs State Memorial

3.5 mi./6 min. South on Rte. 20 and Rte. 25, right on Rte. 65; follow signs. Set on a bluff above the rapids of the Maumee River, Ft. Meigs played a key role in the War of 1812. It was built in February 1813, and in May survived a siege and bombardment by the British; in July they were repulsed again, paving the way for their defeat in the Battle of Lake Erie. The present fort is a reconstruction; three of the seven blockhouses contain exhibits about the war and fort design. Within the stockade are the remains of earthworks that sheltered the troops from incoming cannon fire. *Open Wed.–Sat. and P.M. Sun. and holidays late May–early Sept.; Sat. and P.M. Sun. early Sept.–late Oct. Admission charged.*

6 East Harbor State Park

15 mi./23 min. North on Rte. 53, right on Rte. 2, left on Rte. 269; follow signs. The park is Ohio's largest on Lake Erie, and one of its most popular. It lies on a limestone peninsula and embraces three sheltered harbors. One of these, Middle Harbor, is a wildlife refuge, and a trail along its southeastern shore leads to an observation blind for watching waterfowl and shorebirds. For most people, though, boating, swimming, and fishing are the park's major attractions. Winter activities include ice fishing, ice skating, sledding, and snowmobiling. *Open year-round.*

7 Firelands Museum, Norwalk

7 mi./10 min. South (marked East) on Rte. 250, right on W. Main St. (Rte. 61), left on Case Ave. The museum is named for lands in Ohio given to residents of Connecticut whose property was torched by the British during the Revolutionary War. It includes such assorted items as early maps of the district, surveyor's equipment, exceptional collections of antique firearms (including a Chinese hand-cannon dating from 1000 B.C.), prehistoric Indian artifacts, old toys and household implements, and memorabilia of the Civil War. Other items of interest range from antique clothing to a diorama of the Milan ship canal and a mammoth bass viol. The museum occupies a federal-style town house dating from 1835 and contains period furnishings. *Open Mon.–Sat. and P.M. Sun. July–Aug.; P.M. Tues.–Sun. May–June and Sept.–Oct.; P.M. Sat.–Sun. Apr. and Nov. Admission charged.*

7 ROUTE 2 Great Lakes Historical Society Museum, Vermilion

Exit 7: 25 mi./32 min. North on Rte. 250, right on Rte. 2, left on Rte. 60. Exit Rte. 2: 17 mi./25 min. West on Rte. 2, right on Rte. 60. This fascinating lakeside museum offers a colorful account of shipping on the Great Lakes. Excellent photographs of storms and wrecks serve as vivid reminders of how dangerous these waters can be, and there are models of the many kinds of ships and boats that ply the lakes. Displays of maritime equipment include compass binnacles and steering wheels, radar units, an engine room console, and a complete steam engine. A comprehensive exhibit of safety and rescue equipment includes steam whistles and foghorns, shore beacons, and the lamp from a lighthouse on northern Lake Huron, gleaming like a precious chandelier of white and ruby crystal. If you are heading west, do not take Exit 144 for I-90 and the Ohio Turnpike; instead, continue west on Rte. 2. *Open daily Apr.–Dec.; weekends only Jan.–Mar. Admission charged.*

E9TH Cleveland, OH 44114

E. 9th St. exit: Convention & Visitors Bureau, 1301 E. 6th St. (216) 621-4110. The observation deck in the Terminal Tower gives the best bird's-eye introduction to the city. You can get a more intimate look on a trolley tour; and to see where some of America's great fortunes were founded, take a boat trip down the Cuyahoga River near the steel mills. You can also shop at the boutiques of the Flats entertainment district, stroll through one of Cleveland's many parks, and visit the city's renowned zoo. The cultural attractions include the Cleveland Museum of Art, the Western Reserve Historical Society, and the Cleveland Museum of Natural History, where dinosaurs, fossils, and many artifacts are displayed. The Health Education Museum depicts the workings of the human body. Not to be missed is the downtown Arcade, where shops and restaurants are housed in a marvelous five-level skylit cast-iron fantasy.

193   Holden Arboretum, Kirtland

7 mi./15 min. South on Rte. 306, left on Kirtland-Chardon Rd., left on Sperry Rd. The 3,000-acre arboretum is a park for all seasons, but is most impressive in May and June, when azaleas, crab apples, and other flowering trees and shrubs are in their full glory. There are 20 miles of hiking trails, from which many of the special plantings can be seen. Under construction is a sensory trail for the visually handicapped that will feature the aromas and textures of plants. *Open Tues.–Sun. Admission charged.*

200   Fairport Harbor Marine Museum and Light Tower

8 mi./15 min. North on Rte. 44, right on Rte. 2, north on Rte. 535, bear left on High St. at fork. The Fairport Harbor Light, during the hundred years of its service, was both a landmark

200. *Abandoned lighthouse and* Frontenac *pilothouse are part of the marine museum.*

to the settlers en route to the West and an important beacon to ships plying Lake Erie. There has been a light here since 1825, and though today's lighthouse tower, built of Berea sandstone in 1871, is no longer functional, it and the handsome red brick museum next door confirm the area's maritime heritage. *Open Sat.–Sun. Memorial Day–Labor Day. Admission charged.*

218   Geneva State Park

5 mi./8 min. North on Rte. 534. Sounds of the waves and fresh breezes blowing off Lake Erie provide a welcome respite from highway noise and fumes. The major attraction is a large marina (with completion scheduled for the spring of 1989). Beside the marina is a recreation area with a swimming beach with protected bathing and a picnic area studded with silver maple trees. There are also 91 campsites within walking distance of the lake. Nature trails through woodlands, meadows, and swampland invite further pleasant pursuits. *Open year-round.*

218   Erieview Amusement Park

6 mi./10 min. North on Rte. 534, right on Rte. 531 (Lake Rd.). The 700-foot beach, the miniature railway, and the rides for children are the relaxing side of the park. For excitement there's the Wild Water Works water slide. This maze of water chutes winding down over wooden supports resembles a work of conceptual art and is recommended only for the stout of heart. *Open weekends Mother's Day–mid-June; daily mid-June–Labor Day. Admission for rides only.*

5 / I-79   Presque Isle State Park, Erie

Exit 5: 8 mi./12 min. North on Rte. 832. I-79 exit: 8 mi./12 min. North on I-79, left on W. 12th St., right on Rte. 832. Excellent exhibits at the nature center will enhance one's appreciation of this unique park. The 7-mile-long sandy peninsula serves not only as a recreational area but also as a place to view all stages of a 600-year ecological development, from fragile sandspit to a

mature forest of hemlocks, oaks, and sugar maples. To the north is the expanse of Lake Erie, to the south Presque Isle Bay, where Commodore Perry's fleet was constructed for the War of 1812. Park amenities include fishing, a marina, sandy beaches with lifeguards, picnic areas, and miles of trails. In winter, ice fishing and cross-country skiing are popular. *Park open year-round. Beach open Memorial Day–Labor Day.*

I-79. *Dedicated fishermen, ever hopeful, continue their quest until the end of day.*

I-79   Erie, PA 16501

Chamber of Commerce, 1006 State St. (814) 454-7191. For all its success as a modern industrial center, echoes of the War of 1812 still reverberate here. In September 1813, Commodore Oliver Hazard Perry won a stunning victory over the British on Lake Erie. Six of the nine ships in Perry's fleet were built in Erie, and one of them, the reconstructed flagship *Niagara*, is proudly berthed here. The strategy and details of the historic battle are depicted in the Erie Historical Museum, a Romanesque revival mansion with handsome period rooms and beautifully restored Tiffany windows. A planetarium is housed in a building adjoining the museum. The past is further recalled at the Old Custom House, built in 1839, now an art museum. The Cashiers House, built the same year, features some fine antique furnishings. In the Dickson Tavern, Erie's oldest surviving building, you can savor the 19th-century equivalent of a cocktail bar.

59 Chadwick Bay Wine Co.

5 min. South on Rte. 60. Small vineyards have prospered on the southern shores of Lake Erie ever since Deacon Elizah Fay first planted vines here in 1824. Chadwick Bay Wine Co. is a family business that produces up to 90,000 bottles per year of various kinds, including dry Chambourcins, medium dry Chablis and Burgundy, and the sweet Cracker Ridge white and rosé. When you visit the modern but surprisingly modest-size winery building itself, you will see the whole wine-making process from the fermentation of the grapes to bottling. At the complimentary tasting counter you are invited to sample the various wines and jellies made from wine. Live entertainment is offered Saturday and Sunday afternoons. *Open daily Mon.–Sat. and P.M. Sun.*

51 Albright-Knox Art Gallery, Buffalo

6 mi./10 min. West on Rte. 33, right on Rte. 198; follow signs. Although this museum has a rather forbidding neoclassical facade reminiscent of a Greek temple, its collections represent all major periods. Especially strong are the holdings of modern American and European art, which include such major painters as Willem de Kooning, Robert Rauschenberg, Jean Dubuffet, Jackson Pollock, and many others. Henry Moore, George Segal, and other modern sculptors are given the space needed to show their impressive works. You'll also find a sampling of distinguished art from the pre–Christian Era through the Renaissance, the 18th and 19th centuries, French impressionists, and such 20th-century master artists as Braque, Matisse, Picasso, and Mondrian. *Open Tues.–Sun. except Thanksgiving Day, Christmas, and New Year's Day. Admisssion free but donations encouraged.* ♿

51 Buffalo Zoological Gardens

5 mi./13 min. West on Rte. 33, right on Rte. 198; follow signs. There are few creatures more appealing than a baby bison, as you may discover here, and few as odd-looking as the capybara, the world's largest rodent. Here, too, you'll find a functioning prairie-dog town and other favorite animals such as lions, zebras, polar bears, elephants, gorillas, and snakes—including an anaconda. The zoo is now working on its plan to further develop natural habitats for its residents. Children might want to ride on a camel or an elephant. *Open daily except Thanksgiving Day and Christmas. Admission charged.* ⛱♿

50. *Dramatic promontories enhance the view from this overlook on the American side.*

50 Niagara Falls

20 mi./30 min. North on I-290, north on I-190 to Exit N21, west on Robert Moses Pkwy.; follow signs. Pictures and descriptions—no matter how dramatic—cannot do true justice to this magnificent creation of nature, consisting of the 130-foot American Falls in New York and the 167-foot Horseshoe Falls in Canada. Only when you see and hear billions of gallons of water plummeting down to the misty maelstroms below can the awesome power of this spectacle be fully appreciated. The falls can be seen from the top, from the observation tower, or from a boat trip on the *Maid of the Mist*, which goes right up to the base of the falls, where in the foam, spray, and constant roar you are as much a part of this unforgettable phenomenon as you could ever wish to be. *Open year-round. Admission charged Apr.–Oct.* ⛱🚶♿

48A Akron Falls Park

12 mi./20 min. South on Rte. 77, right on Rte. 5, right on Rte. 93; follow signs. A modest but pleasant spot to rest or picnic, this 250-acre county park has tennis courts, baseball diamonds, a skating rink, and picnic areas in addition to the waterfall. A wooded path leads down from one of the parking areas through a gorge adorned with firs and dogwood to an observation platform, where one can enjoy the cool mist from the 50-foot falls. Swallows nest in the mossy recesses of the gorge's walls, which have been hollowed out by the cascading water. *Open year-round.* ⛱🚶🐟♿

47 Victorian Doll Museum and Chili Doll Hospital, North Chili

12 mi./20 min. East on I-490 to Exit 4, north on Rte. 259, right on Rte. 33. Linda Greenfield created this remarkable doll museum from her own childhood collection, and she has been restoring dolls in her "hospital" for some 20 years. The museum has about 1,200 dolls, dating from the 1840's to the present, and they are made of everything from china, wood, and wax to papier-mâché and felt. There are entire circuses, a Noah's Ark, Kewpie dolls, 25 years' worth of Ken and Barbie, and flappers with cigarette holders. Dolls can be left for Linda's expert ministrations at the hospital, but the workroom itself is not open to the public. A doll collector's gift shop offers a variety of dolls and accessories for purchase. *Open Tues.–Sun. except holidays and Jan. Admission charged.*

47. *A delightful assembly of dolls and related accoutrements from the Victorian era.*

47 Rochester, NY 14604

45 *10 mi./15 min. Convention & Visitors Bureau, 126 Andrews St. (716) 546-3070.* Set in the beautiful Genesee Valley, New York State's third largest city has attractions ranging from photography to lilacs. The International Museum of Photography, in the 50-room mansion built by George Eastman, houses the world's largest collection of photo exhibits. Eastman was founder of the Eastman Kodak Company, which offers guided tours of its facilities in summer. The Strong Museum has superb collections of Victorian furniture, miniatures, and dolls. The Rochester Museum and Science Center features natural science exhibits, Iroquois artifacts, and planetarium shows; and major art collections are displayed at the Memorial Art Gallery. If you want to stretch your legs, take a stroll on the University of Rochester campus or through adjacent Genesee Valley Park. In the third week of May you can enjoy the ethereal fragrance of 400 varieties of lilacs in Highland Park.

44 Granger Homestead and Carriage Museum, Canandaigua

43 *Exit 44: 7 mi./10 min. South on Rte. 332 (becomes Main St.). Exit 43: 9 mi./ 12 min. South on Rte. 21, right on Main St.* This dignified federal-style mansion was the home of Gideon Granger, a gentleman farmer, lawyer, and postmaster-general under Presidents Jefferson and Madison. Finished in 1816, the house was intended to be, in Granger's own words, "unrivaled in the nation." It features elegant woodwork, many original furnishings, a 1,400-book library, and rococo gasolier lighting fixtures. The Carriage Museum has wagons, coaches, fire-fighting vehicles, and wonderfully curvaceous sleighs. *Open daily June–Aug.; Tues.–Sat. May and Oct.; Mon.–Sat. Sept. Admission charged.*

44 Sonnenberg Gardens and Mansion, Canandaigua

43 *Exit 44: 8 mi./12 min. South on Rte. 332 (becomes Main St.), left on Rte. 21 (Gibson St.), left on Charlotte St. Exit 43: 7 mi./15 min. South on Rte. 21, right on Charlotte St.* These extraordinary gardens have

44–43. *Sonnenberg's rich mélange of styles gives the mansion a unique appeal.*

been acclaimed by the Smithsonian Institution as "one of the most magnificent late Victorian gardens ever created in America." The Japanese Garden contains a bronze Buddha and an exquisite teahouse. The Italian Garden, with its fleur-de-lis design, is laid out in the grand manner. Streams, waterfalls, and geysers accent the paths of the Rock Garden. Visitors can also tour 10 rooms of the Victorian mansion that was the summer home of F. F. Thompson and his wife Mary Clark Thompson, the gardens' developer. *Open daily mid-May–mid-Oct. Admission charged.*

42 Seneca Lake State Park

6 mi./15 min. South on Rte. 14 to Geneva, left on Rte. 5/20; follow signs. Seneca Lake is the deepest and one of the longest of the Finger Lakes, so named because in Iroquois legend they were said to be the fingerprints of the Great Spirit. Bones and artifacts from a tribe that predates the Iroquois were found during the development of this state park, which offers a 200-slip marina, a picnic area, playgrounds, and a bathhouse with hot showers. Warm, shallow water and sandy beaches invite swimmers and sunbathers, and the adventurous angler will appreciate the lake's excellent fishing and cash-prize events. *Park open year-round; marina open daily May–Oct. Admission charged daily in summer; weekends only mid-May–Memorial Day, Labor Day–Columbus Day.*

41 Women's Rights National Historical Park, Seneca Falls

6 mi./15 min. South on Rte. 414, left on Rte. 5/20. The first Women's Rights Convention, held in Seneca Falls in 1848, was planned by Elizabeth Cady Stanton and several friends, all of whom were dissatisfied with society's treatment of women. Mrs. Stanton, Mary Ann McClintock, and others drafted the Declaration of Sentiments, which stated that "all men and women are created equal" and called for more rights for women. This declaration was signed by 68 women and 32 men at the convention. The park, actually a historic district encompassing several blocks of Seneca Falls, has a visitor center that offers exhibits and audiovisuals, guided tours of the Stanton home, and walking tours to pertinent structures in Seneca Falls, such as the Seneca Falls Historical Society and the Wesleyan Chapel, where the first convention was held. The National Women's Hall of Fame here pays tribute to more than three dozen notable women whose accomplishments affected the mores, customs, and welfare of a nation and the aspirations of many individuals. *Open daily Apr.–Nov.; Mon.–Fri. Dec.–Mar. Admission free but donations encouraged.*

40 Emerson Park

10 mi./25 min. South on Rte. 34 to Auburn, left on Rte. 20, right on Rte. 38, continue on Rte. 38A. Don't be put off by the ordinary-looking kiddie rides visible from the road. There's more: the Edwardian splendor of a green-roofed 1912 garden pavilion among lawns and flower beds that carpet the hillsides to the very edge of Lake Owasco; the Merry-Go-Round Theater, which offers summer stock productions; and the longhouses and lofty tepees of a 12th-century Owasco Indian village. The village is a living illustration of the pride and elegance of prehistoric Indian life, with its advanced techniques in farming and the making of tools, clay pots, and domestic artifacts. The nearby agriculture museum has exhibits related to farming in the region from the 19th century through the 1930's. *Open daily mid-May–mid-Sept. Admission charged for some activities.*

39 Beaver Lake Nature Center, Baldwinsville

10 mi./15 min. Northwest on Rte. 690, west on Rte. 370, right on E. Mud Lake Rd. The 200-acre lake and the surrounding wetlands, meadows, and woods of this preserve are as unspoiled and tranquil as a remote wilderness. It is a major staging area for thousands of migrating Canada geese, a truly awe-inspiring sight in spring and fall. Eight different trails wind through a mixed environment of woodland, bog, and marsh. In spring a wonderful array of wildflowers appears, and blossoming trilliums carpet the forest floor. Guided canoe trips attract visitors in the summer, and skiing and snowmobiling are enjoyed in the winter. *Open year-round.*

34 Verona Beach State Park

7 mi./12 min. North on Rte. 13. Constructed in 1944, this 1,700-acre park has fortunately not been overdeveloped. It is an idyllic retreat shaded by oaks and locusts, with a mile-long beach sloping gently to the inviting clear waters of Lake Oneida. Other attractions in the area include boating, fishing, and observing the wildlife. Deer, an occasional eagle, and in the fall, flocks of migrating waterfowl may be seen. *Park open year-round; camping mid-Apr.–mid-Nov.*

32 Erie Canal Village

10 mi./20 min. North on Rte. 233, left on Rte. 69/49, left on Rte. 46/49. The prosperity created by the Erie Canal in the 19th century is explained in the Canal Museum and is evident in this reconstructed village of the 1840's. Among the buildings are Bennett's Tavern, a handsome three-story gabled house, a onetime stagecoach stop that now serves refreshments; a nicely furnished farmhouse where antique quilts are displayed; an 1839 church-meetinghouse; a livery stable and a blacksmith's shop; and the 1840 Crosby House, where spinning and weaving are demonstrated. A replica of a horse-drawn packet boat takes passengers along a stretch of the canal, and a half-scale replica of a coal-fired steam locomotive pulls a passenger train along the bank. A carriage museum displays a wide range of horse-drawn vehicles. *Open daily May–Sept. Admission charged.*

31 Munson-Williams-Proctor Institute, Utica

5 min. South on Genesee St. The institute's two contrasting sections—a museum of modern art and a 19th-century mansion—are joined by a sculpture grove. The museum features such 20th-century artists as Picasso, Kandinsky, Mondrian, Pollock, and Calder.

Fountain Elms, the mansion built in the 1850's by Alfred Munson, is the very essence of the Italianate style. Listed in *The National Register of Historic Places*, the house is elegantly decorated with fine furnishings. Everything from furniture to teaspoons was the best available in the mid-19th century. A room on the second floor contains collections of dolls, toys, china, silver, and glassware. The most prized display is a collection of 289 watches and table clocks, mostly from 18th- and 19th-century Europe. *Open Tues.–Sat. and P.M. Sun. except holidays.*

27 Schoharie Crossing State Historic Site, Fort Hunter

9 mi./15 min. North on Rte. 30, left on Rte. 5S to T intersection; follow signs. Because of the turbulence of Schoharie Creek, the builders of the Erie Canal elected to cross that waterway by aqueduct in 1841. Today the 7 remaining arches of the original 14, looking more like the ruins of a Roman aqueduct than relics of a great 19th-century engineering feat, bear further witness to the river's violence. A path of about a mile leads to what's left of the giant locks that lifted barges up to the aqueduct. Charts, photographs, and documents regarding the building of the canal, the locks, and the aqueduct can be seen at the visitor center. *Open Wed.–Sun. May–Oct.*

If You Have Some Extra Time: Cooperstown

30 / 29

Exit 30: 25 mi./45 min. Exit 29: 30 mi./50 min. Here you'll find a remarkable repository of Americana, with diverse collections devoted to village life, rural life, folk art, and the sport that is our national pastime.

Village Crossroads on the outskirts of Cooperstown features original structures from the region that date from 1795 to 1850: a tavern, a country store, a lawyer's office, a printshop, a doctor's office, a druggist's shop, a schoolhouse, a barn, a church, and a pioneer home.

The adjacent Farmers' Museum is housed in a handsome barn where one can see displays of the tools and equipment used in rural upstate New York from the early to the mid-19th century.

The nearby Fenimore House, built as a private residence in 1932, now houses an outstanding collection of landscape paintings and folk art.

In Cooperstown proper, the great American sport is honored at the National Baseball Hall of Fame and Museum—founded in 1939 to celebrate baseball's centennial. The three-story building contains several theme rooms, including a Great Moments Room featuring record-breaking events and a World Series Room where memorabilia from the October Classic are on display. You can gaze upon equipment used by such stars as Babe Ruth, Lou Gehrig, Joe DiMaggio, and Mickey Mantle. A computer data base provides information on most players and teams, and there's a fabulous collection of baseball cards. The National Baseball Library behind the museum shows films of memorable games. Nearby is Doubleday Field, the onetime cow pasture where the sport was born. *How to get there: Exit 30, south on Rte. 28; Exit 29, west on Rte. 55, southwest on Rte. 80.*

37   NY | MA   8   36   **91** See N–S book, sec. 43.   33   57   See N–S book, sec. 46. **95**   **93** See N–S book, sec. 44.

1   2   4   9   22   End I-90

4   Albany, NY 12207

Convention and Visitors Bureau, 52 S. Pearl St. (518) 434-1217; (800) 622-8464 outside NY. Settled in the early 1600's, chartered in 1686, and declared the capital city of New York State in 1797, Albany has a rich and varied history. The Dutch presence is recalled at the Van Rensselaer home and the Ten Broeck Mansion. The Schuyler Mansion was built for a general in the Revolution, and the New York State Museum provides insights into local history. Empire State Plaza is a monumental modern-day architectural extravaganza.

1   Hancock Shaker Village

9.5 mi./15 min. North on Rte. 41. Founded in 1790 on a broad meadow overlooking the Berkshire Hills, this Shaker community had some 250 inhabitants at its prime in the mid-19th century. In 1960 the last three members left, and the village fell into disrepair. Several of the 18 remaining buildings are staffed with knowledgeable craftspeople. The elegantly simple and spacious Brick Dwelling contains spindle-back chairs, fitted cabinets, polished tables, and other examples of classic Shaker furniture. The imposing circular fieldstone barn—not a typical Shaker design—stabled the cattle and served as a granary and a threshing floor. *Open daily Memorial Day–Oct. Admission charged.* 🍽 ♿

2   Chesterwood, Stockbridge

7 mi./15 min. Southwest on Rte. 102, left on Rte. 183, right on Mohawk Lake Rd.; follow signs. A splendid early 20th-century house, a large-windowed studio, and a barn–sculpture gallery compose this summer retreat of sculptor Daniel Chester French, who is best known for his statues of Abraham Lincoln at the Lincoln Memorial in Washington, D. C., and the Minute Man in Concord, Massachusetts. During the summer months, French's work is displayed on the lawns and in the gardens. The setting is an idyllic unity of woods, meadows, and the surrounding Berkshire Hills. *Open daily May–Oct. Admission charged.* 🍽 🚶

9. *A pair of oxen, bearing their heavy handcrafted yoke, make a well-rehearsed left turn.*

4   Storrowton Village, West Springfield

6 mi./10 min. South on Riverdale St. (Rte. 5), right on Memorial Ave. (Rte. 147). A collection of buildings from Massachusetts and New Hampshire, dating back to the mid-18th century and staffed with "townspeople" in costumes, has been assembled around a pretty village green. An imposing meetinghouse and the sprawling 1799 Atkinson Tavern dominate the town. Notable among the restored buildings is the Phillips House (1767), distinctive for its gambrel roof and graduated clapboarding. *Open P.M. Tues.–Sun. mid-June–Labor Day. Admission charged.*

9   Old Sturbridge Village

3 min. Southwest on Rte. 20; follow signs. Life in rural 19th-century New England has been attractively re-created on 200 acres of rolling countryside dotted with woods and ponds. Among the more than 40 buildings brought from nearby farms and towns are several houses, a tiny iron-shuttered bank, a sawmill, a gristmill, and a cidermill, a schoolhouse, a printshop, a pottery shop, and a blacksmith's shop. The typical family farm comprises the house, outbuildings, cattle, and other animals. Costumed staff members demonstrate early crafts, plow the fields, and run the community's store. *Open daily Apr.–Nov.; Tues.–Sun. Dec.–Mar. except Christmas and New Year's Day. Admission charged.* 🍽 ♿

22   Boston, MA 02199

Convention & Visitors Bureau, Prudential Plaza. (617) 536-4100. Few places are so rewarding to explore on foot as this historic city. In only a few hours one can savor the spacious tree-studded Common, the cobbled streets and elegant homes on Beacon Hill, the maze of narrow streets in the North End, and the bustling restored Quincy Market with its shops, cafés, and boutiques. You can wander at will through the city, or you can take the Freedom Trail, a self-guiding walking tour, starting at a booth in the Common.

Among the many highlights beyond the center of the city are the Museum of Fine Arts, the charmingly idiosyncratic Isabella Stewart Gardner Museum, the Arnold Arboretum, the Franklin Park Zoo, and across the Charles River, Harvard Yard and the busy streets of Cambridge.

I-90 Pictograph Caves State Historic Site, Billings

9 mi./15 min. West on I-90 to Exit 452, east on Hardin Rd., right on Coburn Rd.; follow signs. Archeologists have found more than 30,000 artifacts—projectiles, weapons, bones—buried in these caves, which may have been inhabited by hunter tribes as early as 10,000 years ago. Pictograph Cave, largest of three, is named for the primitive colored pictures—only those in red are now visible—that adorn its smooth sandstone walls. Images include tepees, animals, weapons, and shield-bearing warriors. This cave may have been the burial place of at least one group of inhabitants. Ghost Cave, the second largest, yielded bison bones and skeletons of three people. Middle Cave's steep floor made it unsuitable for occupancy. The trail to the caves leads up steep hills, and several paths branch off to overlooks and interpretive signs. *Open daily mid-Apr.– mid-Oct., weather permitting.*

I-90 Peter Yegen, Jr., Yellowstone County Museum, Billings

10 mi./15 min. West on I-90 to Exit 450, north on 27th St. to airport; loop through terminal to museum. An 1893 log cabin houses a major portion of this museum, where the collections range from prehistoric times to the days of the homesteaders. The cabin's living room, dominated by a huge stone fireplace and furnished in 19th-century style, with a high-backed rocker, Tiffany lamps, and a grandfather clock, evokes life in Montana's pioneer era. Large collections in four additional rooms comprise Indian clothing and artifacts, fossils, military uniforms, slot machines, peace pipes, dueling pistols, paintings, and branding irons. You'll also see a roundup wagon used on the Crow Indian Reservation from 1893 to 1946 and, outside, a 1031 Class L-7 locomotive, the last Northern Pacific steam switch engine that operated in Billings. Dioramas interpret the age of dinosaurs and cave people and depict the legends of Sacrifice Cliff (braves on blindfolded horses galloping off the top to their deaths as a plea to the gods to end a smallpox epidemic) and the Yellowstone River Ferry (a judge saving his wife from drowning). *Open Mon.–Fri. and P.M. Sun. except holidays.*

I-90 Oscar's Dreamland Amusement Park, Billings

13 mi./25 min. West on I-90 to Exit 446, west on S. Frontage Rd., left on Shiloh Rd. Oscar Cooke's obvious passion is farm machinery. At the Yesteryear Museum his intriguing collection of 300 restored antique tractors, 40 steam engines, 100 threshing machines, and untold numbers of combines and freight wagons is housed in three enormous buildings that cover approximately 2 acres. Other unexpected treasures include a 1917 Liberty truck, 19th-century hearses, road-building machines, an early airplane, and a 110-h.p. 1906 Best steam truck that pulled six 10-ton ore wagons at a time. At the amusement park you can ride a restored railroad, a merry-go-round, or a Ferris wheel, and for a glimpse of pioneer life, stroll along a restored Main Street with fully appointed homes and stores and a jailhouse with padded cells. *Open daily May– Labor Day.*

I-90. *This family of visitors helps to reveal the vast dimensions of Pictograph Cave.*

93 95 West and East Rosebud Recreation Areas, Forsyth

Exit 93 (West Area): 1 min. North on Rte. 12; follow signs. Exit 95 (East Area): 3 min. North on Main St., right on 15th Ave. Both of these recreation areas are on the Yellowstone River. At East Rosebud there is a campground, but a weir makes the river dangerous for swimming. West Rosebud has a picnic area and a small playground. Both sites offer fishing and views of the bluffs on the northern banks of the river. *Open year-round.*

135 Range Riders Museum and Memorial Hall, Miles City

3 min. Northeast on I-94 (business loop); follow signs. This exceptional collection of Old West memorabilia commemorates the life, times, and friendships of the cowboy era and recounts the history of the region after trappers, soldiers, and settlers arrived. There are major displays of fossils and Indian artifacts, guns, knives, swords, daggers and bayonets, stuffed birds and animals, horseshoes, bits and hobbles, saddles, spurs, buggies, and coaches. Period buildings—a trading post, a hotel, a jail, a smithy, a barbershop, a dress shop, and a livery stable—re-create the 1880's Main Street of Milestown, as this city was formerly called. The Pioneer Memorial Hall shows a large collection of photographs of pioneers of many nationalities who helped settle the northern Plains. *Open daily Mar.– Nov. Admission charged.*

215 Frontier Gateway Museum, Glendive

1 min. Exit north, right on Belle Prairie Rd. This museum is a repository of the region's history and a grab bag of engaging curiosities. There are fossils and mineral specimens, cowbells, Indian bows and arrows, saddlebags and war bonnets, and replicas of 16th- and 17th-century European suits of armor. Downstairs a re-created street scene—complete with a drugstore, a general store, a dress shop, printing equipment, early radios, and a taxidermy display—portrays a vanished way of life. Outdoor exhibits include another general store, a firehouse with a 1938 fire engine, a log cabin furnished as its owner left it during World War II, and the 1910 Golden Valley schoolhouse, with schoolbooks from 1898 to 1957. *Open Mon.–Sat. and P.M. Sun. June–Aug.; P.M. daily late May and early Sept. Admission free but donations encouraged.*

215   Makoshika State Park, Glendive

3 mi./6 min. South on Merrill Ave., left on Barry St., right on Taylor Ave., left on Snyder St. The park, in eastern Montana, preserves a spectacular tract of badlands—*makoshika* is the Sioux word for "bad lands"—and high prairie. From mesa tops there are views of weathered buttes, hogback ridges, and polychrome valleys ornamented with capped pillars, fluted walls and spires, and landslides shaped like the feet of gigantic elephants. Junipers and pines dot this arid badlands area and soften the sky-wide prairie with dark green stands. Hawks, turkey vultures, mule deer, and cottontails are abundant, and in spring the prairie and desert wildflowers bring delight. Several of the park's unimproved roads are hazardous and should not be traveled in wet weather. A detailed guide can be obtained at the park entrance for a small charge. *Open year-round.*

6   Chateau de Mores State Historic Site

5 min. South on access road; follow signs. Here the Marquis de Mores, one of the strangest figures ever to ride the western Plains, tried to make his home and fortune. Born in Paris, he went to the Dakota country in 1883 to raise beef and to build a castle in the wilderness. Within three years his venture failed; he and his wife, Medora, left Dakota forever, and in 1936 the château was given to the state. Most of its original furnishings are intact: buffalo-skin robes vie with copies of *La Vie Parisienne* and Medora's French watercolors to create the *mise-en-scène* of these cosmopolitan pioneers, and the Trophy Room preserves both Medora's black riding habit and an array of bear traps. The visitor center displays some fascinating memorabilia of the marquis and his adventures. *Open daily mid-May–mid-Sept. Admission charged.*

6–7. *Caps of resistant material on top helped shape these fantastic sculptural forms.*

6   7   Theodore Roosevelt National Park, South Unit

5 min. Exit 6: east on exit road to Medora; follow signs. Exit 7: west on exit road to Medora; follow signs. Some of North America's most memorable landscapes lie within the boundaries of this magnificent park. In places the banded colors of eroded valleys and tableland stretch for miles; elsewhere meadows of sagebrush, pale and silvery, yield to riverbanks where cottonwoods shine golden or bright green, depending on the season. You can see bison, which lend their archaic presence to the ancient hills, and golden eagles. In the visitor center the park's geology and natural history are illustrated, and there are mementos of Teddy Roosevelt, who ranched here before he became our nation's 26th president. Roosevelt was a leading advocate of the national parks system. *Open year-round. Admission charged.*

12   Patterson Lake Recreation Area

4 min. South on Rte. 10; follow signs. Man-made Patterson Lake is part of a major Missouri River valley flood-control project in western North Dakota. The park has 26 miles of low-banked shoreline with swaying reed beds, about 1,190 acres of water, and 1,200 acres of land with nature trails. Visitors will find both primitive and modern camping areas, children's playgrounds, and horseshoe pits. *Open year-round. Admission charged.*

13   Joachim Regional Museum, Dickinson

1 min. South on 3rd Ave. W., left on 12th St. The emphasis in this museum is on the history of the various ethnic groups that settled this part of western North Dakota, mostly immigrants from Hungary, Germany, Czechoslovakia, Norway, and Russia. The exhibits change annually, but they usually include colorful folk costumes, diaries, newspaper clippings, letters, books, photographs, tools, clothing, and household articles brought here by the settlers. There is a comprehensive display of Indian clothing and ornaments, as well as an authentically decorated Plains Indian tepee. The museum is named for its benefactor, Milton Joachim, a local businessman. *Open daily Memorial Day–Labor Day.*

28 Sweet Briar Lake Recreation Area

1 min. North on Rte. 48. This attractive setting is enhanced by a hillock-strewn terrain, an irregular lakeshore fringed in some places with dense reed beds, willows, cottonwoods, and prairie flowers that grow freely. In a nearby arboretum, avenues of trees that prosper locally can be seen as if in a grove. They include black and green ash, box elder, black walnuts, and butternuts. You'll also find plots of such native grasses as wild rye, big bluestem, and switch grass. On the low hills to the west and south of the park, off Exit 27, is a surreal fiberglass model of a Holstein cow— said to be the largest cow statue in the world. *Open year-round.*

33 Fort Abraham Lincoln State Park

5 mi./8 min. South on Rte. 1806. This park lies at the scenic confluence of the Heart and Missouri rivers. Ft. Abraham Lincoln was established at this strategic spot in 1872 in order to protect settlers and workers building the Northern Pacific Railroad. The fort later was the departure point for Colonel Custer's campaign against the Plains Indians; it was abandoned in 1891. Also on the grounds is the site of the Slant Indian village—formerly the home of the Mandan Indians—where you'll see four reconstructed earth lodges and the Arc of the Lone Man, a ritual site commemorating the hero who saved the Mandan nation from a great flood. *Open year-round. Admission charged.*

36 Camp Hancock State Historic Site, Bismarck

3 mi./11 min. South on State St., right on Divide Ave., left on Washington St., left on Main Ave. Here you'll see the oldest building in Bismarck, and one of the oldest in North Dakota: the supply depot of a camp built in 1872 to protect the crews then building the Northern Pacific Railroad. The structure now serves as a museum where the region's history, geology, and wildlife are described with photos, documents, and memorabilia. Colonel Custer is said to have obtained supplies from this camp at various times in the 1870's. *Open P.M. Wed.–Sun. mid-May–mid-Sept.*

36 Cross Ranch Nature Preserve

42 mi./45 min. North on Rte. 83, left on Rte. 200A. This 6,200-acre park preserves the natural and cultural history of North Dakota in all its beauty and diversity. Here you'll see a native prairie and floodplain forest that have remained virtually unchanged for the past 100 years; more than 100 archeological sites, some dating back to 6,000 B.C.; and a variety of wildlife, including mule deer and eastern and western songbirds. *Open year-round.*

37 Sertoma Riverside Park, Bismarck

7 mi./15 min. South on Centennial Rd. (becomes Bismarck Expy.), right on Washington St., left on Arbor Ave.; follow signs. Situated on the banks of the Missouri River, this 98-acre park has trails leading through a wooded area. Tennis courts and playgrounds are available, and the Dakota Zoo, the chief attraction, has some 500 animals, 125 different species, including Patagonian cavies, pygmy goats, wallabies, and African porcupines. *Park open year-round; zoo open daily early May–Sept. Admission charged for zoo.*

38 Menoken Indian Village State Historic Site

4 min. East on Frontage Rd.; follow signs. This 3-acre site, discovered in 1936, marks the spot where Indians believed to have been ancestors of the Mandans lived about 1,000 years ago. Their village was protected on one side by the steep banks of a meander in Apple Creek and on the other sides by a fortified ditch. You can still see the 20-foot-wide ditch and the depressions where some 10 to 16 earth lodges once stood. *Open year-round.*

59 Frontier Village, Jamestown

4 min. North on Rte. 281, right on 17th St. SW. Located on hills overlooking Jamestown, this reconstructed prairie town preserves the spirit and style of the Old West. The buildings, moved to the village from nearby areas, include Jamestown's first rail depot, a one-room schoolhouse, a country church, a sheriff's office, a barbershop with white enamel

33. *During the annual Frontier Army Days, Custer's 7th Cavalry is actively remembered.*

36. *Tender twigs are a staple in the diet of beavers such as this one at Cross Ranch Preserve.*

chairs, a firehouse with hose carts and hand-pumpers, and a 60-ton concrete replica of an American bison, the species that once dominated the area's plains. *Open daily Memorial Day–Labor Day.* 🍽

59 Jamestown Dam Lakeside Marina

8.5 mi./15 min. North on Rte. 281, right on 3rd St. NE, left on 5th Ave. (Rte. 20). The dam on the James River has filled a deep valley here, and the shores of the lake are indented with cliffs and small coves. A sheltering island opposite the marina provides a charming spot for a peaceful picnic. Nearby, the Martin Joos Memorial Grove offers picnickers another choice, among stands of ashes and Russian olives. *Grove open year-round; marina open May–mid-Sept.* 🍽🏕🚐🚶🏊🎣

67 Clausen Springs Recreation Complex

20.5 mi./25 min. South on Rte. 1, left on access road; follow signs. Named for three Norwegian brothers who were the first settlers in the area, this 550-acre park site dates back to the early 19th century, when French fur traders and Indians of the Pembina colony camped here while hunting beavers and buffaloes.

Indians encamped here to protest the white man's violation of their treaty rights. During the Prohibition years people came from many miles around for Saturday night dances on a floor set up in the woods. Horned owls come to nest here during February and March. *Open year-round.* 🍽🏕🚐🚶🏊🎣

85 Bonanzaville, U.S.A., West Fargo

2 min. East on Rte. 10. Bonanzaville is a regional museum complex of almost 50 buildings, each offering a carefully researched and well-tended display from the past—an aircraft museum, a collection of dolls, a fire station, an early bathroom offering "Hot Baths 25¢ With Soap and Towel," and a barn with live animals. Dwellings include a reproduction of a sod house, log cabins, and period homes, one of them owned by D. H. Houston, who devised an early type of roll film. The Red River and Northern Plains Regional Museum contains collections of toys, model ships and cars, and a comprehensive exhibit on Indians in this area. *Museum and buildings open Mon.–Fri. and P.M. Sat.–Sun. late May–late Oct.; museum open Tues.–Fri. late Oct.–late May except Thanksgiving Day, Christmas, and New Year's Day. Admission charged.*

1 Plains Art Museum, Moorhead

5 min. North on Rte. 75, left on Main Ave. A Sioux baby bonnet trimmed with dentalia shells, a dance bustle made of feathers and tin, and Ojibwa dance caps of porcupine quills and deer hair are among many excellent examples of Indian art in this museum. The permanent collection also includes works by American impressionist Mary Cassatt as well as painters Jerry Ott and Luis Jimenez. There are changing exhibits, and many items sold here were made by area artists and craftsmen. *Open Tues.–Sat. and P.M. Sun. except Thanksgiving Day, Christmas, and New Year's Day. Admission free but donations encouraged.*

6 / 15 Buffalo River State Park

Exit 6: 11 mi./13 min. North on Rte. 11, right on Rte. 10. Exit 15: 13 mi./15 min. East on Rte. 10, left on Rte. 9, right on Rte. 10. This 1,240-acre park, divided by the Buffalo River, contains one of Minnesota's largest virgin prairies. Along the trails crossing the prairie are more than 250 kinds of grasses and wildflowers; some 200 species of birds and 40 species of mammals are also in residence. Prairie chickens, upland sandpipers, bobolinks, marbled godwits, northern grasshopper mice, and rare Dakota skipper butterflies may all be seen here. You might also come across bison skulls and bones from prehistoric times. *Open year-round. Admission charged.* 🍽🏕🚐🚶🏊

61 De Lagoon Park, Fergus Falls

5 min. North on Rte. 59. There are more than 1,000 lakes in Otter Tail County, which includes the town of Fergus Falls, and this park lies on the shores of one of them. The lakes were created during the Wisconsin glacier age, which ended about 10,000 years ago. Surrounded by grasslands, De Lagoon Park is a waterfowl protection area, spacious and peaceful, containing children's playgrounds and a softball complex. Nearby Pebble Lake, which is another city park, offers a golf course and trapshooting. *Open daily mid-May–Oct.* 🍽🏕🚐🏊🎣

77 | Tipsinah Mounds Park

6 mi./10 min. South on Rte. 10, right on Rte. 79. Located near the southern end of Pomme de Terre Lake, where the Chippewa Indians once made their summer camp, this park takes its name from an Indian word for a turniplike plant. The lake and an adjoining river provided food for them and formed a natural barrier to the prairie fires that were apt to sweep across the Plains from the west. Evidence of human habitation on a peninsula jutting into the lake is indicated by bone and stone tools dated to 9400 B.C.. Just east of the entrance road, traces of some 40 Indian mounds dating from A.D. 1000 to 1600 can be seen. *Open daily May–Oct.*

103 | Kensington Runestone Museum, Alexandria

2 mi./8 min. North on Rte. 29. The centerpiece here is a slab of gray stone with a runic inscription describing an expedition made to this area by 8 Goths and 22 Norwegians in 1362. The stone was found, so the story goes, under the roots of an aspen tree by a Minnesota farmer named Olaf Ohman in 1898. Whether it genuinely records the exploits of a Viking expedition to these parts or is a 19th-century forgery has long been the subject of vigorous debate. The museum, with its adjunct, the Fort Alexandria Agricultural Museum, also displays collections of agricultural machinery, pioneer memorabilia, and several Indian artifacts. *Open daily mid-May–Sept.; Mon.–Fri. Oct.–mid-May. Admission charged.*

103 | Lake Carlos State Park

13 mi./21 min. North on Rte. 29. Glacially formed Lake Carlos is deep and clear, and its U-shaped northern shore is surrounded by the varied terrain of this beautiful 1,261-acre park. Hikers will encounter a number of different western Minnesota landscapes: marshlands, lakeshore, steep wooded hills, meadowland, and prairie as well as smaller lakes hidden in the hills. Even on a short hike the landscape can change dramatically in a matter of minutes. Those who stay near the lake may see a heron among the reeds or hear the mournful cry of a loon, the state bird of Minnesota. Anglers are attracted by the abundance of bass, crappie, walleye, and northern pike in Lake Carlos. *Open year-round. Admission charged.*

127 | Sinclair Lewis Boyhood Home, Sauk Centre

5 min. North on Rte. 71, left on Sinclair Lewis Ave. The first American to win the Nobel Prize for literature spent most of his childhood in this modest but comfortable house, just a step away from the Main Street that he would immortalize in his most famous novel, the story of a small Midwestern town. The office where his father practiced medicine is preserved, along with the RCA radio that was Lewis's gift to him in 1920, the year *Main Street* was published. Other family possessions and memorabilia include Lewis's golf clubs, childhood photographs, and the blue and white washbowl and pitcher that belonged to his first wife, Grace. Behind the home is the gray carriage house where Lewis began writing, at age 15, for the local newspaper. *Open daily Memorial Day–Labor Day. Admission charged.*

167B | Stearns County Historical Center, St. Cloud

5 mi./8 min. North on Rte. 15, right on 2nd St., right on 33rd Ave.; follow signs. One of Minnesota's largest history museums has a distinctly regional yet imaginative focus. The Stearns County granite industry, for example, is documented with a realistic full-size model of a section of a granite quarry. And as the county is one of America's largest producers of dairy products, an entire gallery is devoted to family dairy farming from 1853 to the 1980's. Dioramas with flowing water and mounted specimens illustrate local natural history. You can also see a miniature replica of a circus and memorabilia of St. Cloud's ill-fated Pan Motor Company. *Open Mon.–Sat. and P.M. Sun. Memorial Day–Labor Day; Tues.–Sat. and P.M. Sun. Labor Day–Memorial Day except holidays. Admission charged.*

207 | Oliver H. Kelley Farm, Elk River

14 mi./17 min. North on Rte. 101, east on Rte. 10; follow signs. In 1867 Oliver Kelley, an energetic Minnesota farmer, writer, and agriculture leader, founded the Order of the Pa-

I-35W. *Set like a glowing jewel in the St. Paul skyline is the Winter Carnival Ice Palace.*

trons of Husbandry, a fraternal organization for farmers, whose local chapters were called Granges. Eventually the Grange had almost a million members as well as some 25,000 local branches. Kelley's farm is now a national landmark, a living-history farm where one can see the land being managed as it was in the 1860's. The plowing is done by horse and oxen; the sheep and hogs belong to strains from Kelley's day, and so do the crops—for example, King Philip corn, black Norway oats, and purple rose potatoes. In the Farmstead the domestic arts of the period are demonstrated, and in the visitor center there is a fascinating display on Kelley's life and the work of the Grange. *Open Tues.–Sun. May–Oct. Admission charged.* ⛺

I-35W | Minneapolis–St. Paul, MN 55402

Convention & Visitors Association, 15 S. 5th St. (612) 348-4313; (800) 445-7412 outside MN. In summer the parks and waterways clearly dominate the activity here near the headwaters of the Mississippi River. Less obvious are the ways Minnesotans know how to cope with the cold. In the dead of winter the enclosed skyways can make you forget you are this far north. Nicollet Mall is a focal point in Minneapolis; its famed Guthrie Theater and Walker Art Center beckon. There's an excellent zoo, and the Grain Exchange offers a look at the operation of a grain market. Across the river in St. Paul you can visit the state capitol, the Science Museum of Minnesota, the opulent Victorian mansion of Territorial Governor Alexander Ramsey, and also, if you choose to forsake the comfort of the skyways in late January, the Winter Carnival.

1 | The Octagon House, Hudson

4 min. North on Rte. 35 (2nd St.), right on Myrtle St. This curious, elegant building, made of stucco and clapboard with a glassed-in cupola, is one of the few examples outside New York State of the eccentric eight-sided homes that were briefly in vogue during the mid-19th century. Built in 1855, it contains period furnishings, and the kitchen is fully equipped with turn-of-the-century utensils.

1. *In addition to charm, octagonal houses were said to have beneficial attributes.*

On the upstairs floors, also furnished with loving attention to detail, there are displays of antique clothing and dolls. The old carriage house museum contains a lavish dollhouse and a re-created blacksmith's shop. Other interesting memorabilia can be seen in the garden house. *Open Tues.–Sat. and P.M. Sun. May–Oct. except July 4. Admission charged.*

24 | Crystal Cave

8 mi./12 min. South on Rte. B, left on Rte. 29; follow signs. Flowstone, stalactites, and stalagmites adorn the 30 chambers of this 13,000-year-old cave. Some of the flowstone is pure white and resembles frosting on a cake; some, colored by iron oxide, looks like strips of bacon; other formations, up to 12,000 years old, resemble waterfalls frozen in time or miniature badlands. At the deepest level of the cave, chambers have been carved by whirlpools of a glacial river. Harmless bats—eastern pipistrelles and little browns—roost in the caves and hibernate in them from late October to early April. *Open daily Memorial Day–Labor Day, weekends only Apr.–May and Sept.–Oct. Admission charged.*

41 | Empire in Pine Lumber Museum, Downsville

10 mi./16 min. South on Rte. 25, left on Rte. C. In the late 1800's Downsville had one of the largest sawmills in the world. Today a fine lumber museum recalls many aspects of that era. A re-created logging camp displays "shotgun bunks" with mannequins tucked under the covers, a cook's shanty, a blacksmith's shop, a large carved bed once owned by a local lumber baron, and an unusual baking cabinet. You'll also see giant saw blades and other tools of the trade. The grounds include an old jailhouse, a lumber company payroll office, and a post office, complete with leather-hinged wooden letter boxes. *Open Mon.–Sat. and P.M. Sun. May–Oct.* ⛺

65 | Paul Bunyan Logging Camp, Eau Claire

4 mi./11 min. North on Rte. 37, left on Clairemont Ave., right on Menomonie St., left on Carson Park Dr. A statue of Paul Bunyan, mythical folk hero of the North Woods, stands at the entrance to this authentic logging camp, dwarfing his blue ox, Babe. The camp—with a cook's shanty, a bunkhouse, a barn, a blacksmith's shop, and an interpretive center—was built in 1934 and is a re-creation of the lumber camps that brought prosperity to this area in the late 1800's. Among the machinery displayed is a horse-powered derrick and a rutter shoe. *Camp open daily May–Labor Day; P.M. Tues.–Sun. rest of Sept.; interpretive center open year-round. Admission free but donations encouraged.* ⛺ ♿

65 | Chippewa Valley Museum, Eau Claire

4 mi./11 min. North on Rte. 37, left on Clairemont Ave., right on Menomonie St., left on Carson Park Dr. Adjoining the Paul Bunyan Logging Camp in Carson Park, this museum has an extensive collection that includes period furnishings, Indian artifacts, antique cars, and exhibits on farming and pioneer life in the region. Located outside the museum are the 1857 Lars Anderson cabin and a one-room schoolhouse built in 1880. *Open Tues.–Sun. June–Aug.; P.M. Tues.–Sun. Sept.–May. Admission charged.* ⛺ ♿

143   The Little Red Schoolhouse, Tomah

I-90

Exit 143: 4 mi./6 min. South on Rte. 12 (Superior Ave.) to Gillette Park. I-90 exit: 6 mi./8 min. West on I-90 to Exit 41, north on Rte. 131 (Superior Ave.) to Gillette Park. In use from 1864 to 1965, this small, classic one-room schoolhouse now stands in a Tomah city park, a reminder of the past. You can see photographs of the students dating back to the early 1900's, schoolbooks from 1910 and the 1920's, a small collection of minerals, and map stencils for the children's geography lessons. *Open P.M. daily Memorial Day–Labor Day.*

87   The Dells

2 min. East on Rte. 13/23. The Dells of the Wisconsin River are narrow chasms or ravines that have been carved out of sandstone cliffs (formed millions of years ago) by the relentless erosive action of water against rock after the Ice Age meltdown. The walls of the cliffs are corrugated and in places capped by overhangs and pedestals of rock. These picturesque formations can be seen if you take one of the commercial boat tours from the docks in downtown Wisconsin Dells. Boats operate from mid-April to mid-October. Two other outstanding attractions in this area are

The Stand Rock Indian Ceremonial *(5 mi./7 min. from Exit 87; east on Rte. 13/23, left on Rte. 12/16, right on Rte. A, left on Stand Rock Rd.)* offers a program of traditional Indian dances in a magnificent natural amphitheater. *Performance every evening mid-June–Labor Day. Admission charged.*

The Winnebago Indian Museum *(6.5 mi./10 min. from Exit 87; east on Rte. 13/23, across bridge, left on River Rd.)* displays a fine collection of Indian clothing, weapons, ornaments, and other artifacts. *Open daily Apr.–Dec. Admission charged.*

92   Circus World Museum, Baraboo

106

Exit 92: 10 mi./15 min. South on Rte. 12 to Baraboo; follow signs. Exit 106: 14 mi./20 min. West on Rte. 33; follow signs. The Ringling Brothers circus had its winter

92–106. Circus wagons provided a worthy challenge to the wood-carver's skill.

quarters in Baraboo until 1918. The complex of 30 buildings now serves as both an active showplace and a home for circus memorabilia. A circus parade and live performances under the big top are presented daily, and a museum of circus history includes automated miniatures, air calliopes, a merry-go-round, a trolley ride, and displays commemorating various circus stars. The world's largest collection of circus wagons contains fine examples of gilding and carving. The P. T. Barnum sideshow and the menagerie, with its tigers, camels, hippos, and other performing animals, draw fascinated viewers. *Open daily early May–mid-Sept. Admission charged.*

135   Madison, WI 53703

Convention & Visitors Bureau, 121 W. Doty St. (608) 255-0701. The capitol in the downtown area of this attractive city, set on an isthmus between two lakes, is reputed to be the largest state capitol in the United States and is open for tours. Architecture on a smaller scale is also important here. Frank Lloyd Wright's Unitarian Meeting House (1949–51) is open to the public, and other buildings designed by Wright, a Wisconsin native, can be viewed from the street. The State Historical Museum features Indian and French voyageur exhibits. On the University of Wisconsin campus you can visit an arboretum, Indian effigy mounds, and Babcock Hall, where you'll find college-educated ice cream.

I-90   Lake Kegonsa State Park

6 mi./15 min. South on I-90 to Exit 147; continue on Rte. N, right on Koshkonong Rd.; follow signs. This attractive park, near Madison, has more than 300 acres of woodland, prairie, and marsh, as well as an extensive shoreline on 3,209-acre Lake Kegonsa. The White Oak nature trail loops through woods past Indian mounds. Inviting mown paths wind through quiet prairie. *Open year-round. Admission charged.*

310B   Milwaukee, WI 53202

Convention & Visitors Bureau, 756 N. Milwaukee St. (414) 273-7222; (800) 231-0903 outside WI. There's still beer in Milwaukee, and three breweries offer tours, but the city has much more to offer. The arts are well represented by the vast Milwaukee Art Museum; Villa Terrace, an Italian Renaissance-style home with displays of antique furniture and decorative arts; and the extensive collection of the Charles Allis Art Museum, housed in a resplendent Tudor-style mansion.

No less interesting is the Milwaukee Public Museum, with its environmental dioramas, dinosaur skeletons, and Indian artifacts, among other displays. Mitchell Park boasts a noted horticultural conservatory; and the zoo, a few miles west of downtown, is one of the best such institutions in the country.

326   Cliffside County Park

9 mi./15 min. East on 7 Mile Rd., right on Michna Rd.; follow signs. The park has two distinct areas: one includes the campground, a

WI | IL

7   18   2   48   See N–S book, sec. 21 for I-55; sec. 25 for I-57.   IL | IN   See N–S book, sec. 26.   See E–W book, sec. 23 for I-80; sec. 6 for I-90.   IN | MI   40   25

90   50   65   90

333   ROUTE 41   ROUTE 173   OH   22B   16   94

See E–W book, sec. 6.   90   55   57   80   80   90

baseball diamond, and tennis courts; and the other, lying behind the children's playground, is an area of woods, rough meadowland, and cliff-top paths. At the first fork in the trail, bear left to cross a meadow (bright with asters and goldenrod in the fall) leading to the cliffs, or walk through the woods. The loop to the lake is a walk of 30 to 45 minutes; there are good views, but the cliff overlooking the lake is steep and crumbly, with no beach access. *Open daily mid-Apr.–mid-Oct.* 🛆 ⛺ 🚐 🚶

333   Racine Zoological Gardens

11 mi./15 min. East on Rte. 20, left on Rte. 32 to Goold St.; follow signs. Situated on the shores of Lake Michigan, this 28-acre zoo has an interesting variety of animals. Wolves and birds of prey make their home in a wooded area near a lake. Nearby, rhesus monkeys and Barbary sheep dwell on a rocky island in a smaller lake, and penguins, otters, pelicans, and other waterbirds have their own watery domains as well. Camels, elephants, kangaroos, deer, and a beautiful white tiger with blue eyes are among the other inhabitants in this zoo. *Open year-round.* 🛆

ROUTE 41 / ROUTE 173   Illinois Beach State Park (Southern Unit), Zion

Rte. 41 exit: 11 mi./15 min. South on Rte. 41, left on Wadsworth Rd. Rte. 173 exit: 8 mi./10 min. East on Rte. 173 (Rosecrans Rd.), right on Rte. 41; proceed as above. One of the most popular state parks in the country, this extensive recreation facility on Lake Michigan is divided into northern and southern units. But first-time visitors are encouraged to head for the southern unit. The long beach there is covered with fine sugarlike sand and acres of dunes. Beachcombers love to collect the large smooth rocks shaped and polished by the elements. Nature trails wind through a rapidly changing landscape of wetlands, prairie, open oak forest, and dunes. *Open year-round.* 🛆 ⛺ 🚐 🚶 🏊 🎣

OH   Chicago, IL 60611

E. Ohio St. exit: Tourism Council, 163 E. Pearson St. (312) 280-5740. This cosmopolitan metropolis, beautifully situated on the southwestern shore of Lake Michigan, boasts a number of world-class attractions. The Art Institute is known for a wide-ranging permanent collection and creative special exhibitions. The Terra Museum, opened in 1987, has a superlative collection of American art; the John G. Shedd Aquarium, the world's largest such indoor facility, with more than 200 tanks, displays some 1,000 wonders of the deep. For an intimate sense of the city, take the El (the elevated railroad) around the Loop; and for a breathtaking overview there's the observation area on the 103rd floor of the Sears Tower, at this writing the world's tallest building.

22B   Indiana Dunes National Lakeshore

5 min. East on Rte. 20, left on Mineral Springs Rd. These 1,800 acres of woodland trails and 3 miles of beach dominated by towering lakefront dunes evince an almost lyrical delicacy in an obviously industrial environment. A number of plants are relics of colder climates that existed here at the end of the Ice Age and left a remarkable diversity of vegetation. Arctic bearberries, alongside prickly-pear cacti and northern jack pines, share dune slopes with southern dogwoods. Though the dunes are large (Mt. Tom rises more than 190 feet) and are anchored against the wind by marram grass, sand cherries, cottonwoods, and other native plants, they are susceptible to erosion. A 2-mile trail leads through red oaks and sugar maples to the restored Bailly Homestead and Chellberg Farm. *Open year-round.*

🛆 🚶 🏊 ♿

16   Warren Dunes State Park

5 min. South on Red Arrow Hwy. Awesome sand dunes more then 200 feet high provide majestic views of Lake Michigan and attract hang gliders from far away. The dunes overlook several miles of white sand beach, and behind them lie hundreds of acres of unspoiled woods intersected by trails and a winding stream. The park, delightful in all seasons, is adorned with drifts of blooming wildflowers in spring and colorful foliage in fall; sledding, tobogganing, and cross-country skiing are popular winter activities. The park has almost 200 campsites and a number of pleasant picnic areas. *Open year-round. Admission charged.* 🛆 ⛺ 🚐 🚶 🏊 ♿

310B. *Domes in Mitchell Park house environmental plantings. Cannas grow in the foreground.*

78. *Chance Vought Corsair and Curtiss Warhawk, distinguished veterans of World War II.*

39 Deer Forest

3 mi./6 min. North on Friday Rd.; follow signs. Deer, goats, llamas, donkeys, elk, swans, and peacocks are at home in this 30-acre wooded playland; some animals can be fed and petted, and there are ponies and a camel to ride. There's also a train to take visitors through the park, and a number of kiddie rides. In Story Book Lane, live animals represent favorite characters in children's stories. *Open daily Memorial Day–Labor Day. Admission charged.* 🪧

76B Kalamazoo Nature Center
76C

9.5 mi./15 min. North on S. Westnedge Ave.; continue on Park St. (Rte. 131 business), right on N. Westnedge Ave. Start a visit here at the Interpretive Center, with its circular ramp descending through the glass-roofed Sun-Rain Room, a humid jungle environment, to the Growing Place, filled with cacti, orchids, and houseplants. Live animals are displayed in the ecology laboratory. The grounds include 600 acres with trails, an herb garden, an arboretum, a trout stream, and a farm with animals you can pet. Displays about agriculture and farm life and craft demonstra-

tions are offered at the nearby De Lano Homestead, a restored 1858 Greek revival farmhouse. *Open Mon.–Sat. and P.M. Sun. except Thanksgiving Day, Christmas, and New Year's Day. Admission charged.* 🚶

78 Kalamazoo Aviation History Museum

3 min. South on Portage Rd., left on Milham Rd. This museum is devoted to World War II American planes. All are beautifully restored, and most are in flying condition. Among the highlights are an F7F Grumman Tigercat, a Curtiss P-40 Warhawk with a painted shark's mouth on its nose, and an F6F Grumman Hellcat, an unsurpassed dogfighter. Also on display are the Pratt & Whitney Wasp Major R-4360, the largest mass-produced piston engine, and memorabilia. *Open Mon.–Sat. and P.M. Sun. except holidays. Admission charged.*

100 Binder Park Zoo

4 min. South on Beadle Lake Rd.; follow signs. Set in the woodland of Binder Park, the zoo provides naturalistic environments for many of its animals. A boardwalk through a pinewoods overlooks the exhibit areas, where Formosan sika deer reside; bison, peacocks,

and prairie dogs can also be seen; and llamas, Sicilian donkeys, ponies, and a yak can be fed and petted at the petting zoo. Water birds inhabit a lovely pond, and around its edge are enclosures for eagles, emus, wallabies, and white-handed gibbons. *Open daily late Apr.–late Oct. Admission charged.* 🪧 🚶 ♿

110 Honolulu House, Marshall

5 min. South on Rte. 27; follow signs. This curious home, modeled on the executive mansion in Honolulu, was built in 1860 by Judge Abner Pratt, a former U.S. consul in the Sandwich (Hawaiian) Islands, who strove to create the exotic atmosphere of the Pacific islands here in Michigan. The two-story house has a broad veranda and an observation tower reached from the central hall by a spiral staircase; the rooms have 15-foot ceilings, and the murals—wreaths of tropical plants intermixed with cattails, lilies, and classical cupids—have been restored to their appearance in 1885, when a new owner remodeled the house and had the original murals embellished. The furnishings, fine pieces from the mid- to the late 19th century, include the judge's empire sofa in the formal dining room and a handsome huntboard intricately carved with figures of fish and game. *Open P.M. daily late May–Oct. Admission charged.*

142 Michigan Space Center

7 mi./9 min. South on Rte. 127 to M50 exit, west on McDevitt Rd., left on Hague Rd., right on Emmons Rd., left on Browns Lake Rd. Rockets and rocket engines flank the gold geodesic dome of this museum of objects related to the exploration of space. Included are a Mercury Redstone, the rocket that launched a U.S. astronaut into space in 1961, and a J2 engine of the kind that was used in the Apollo moon program. The museum contains the Apollo 9 command module, collections of various satellites, space suits, lunar rocks, and a moon rover used to explore the lunar surface. *Open Mon.–Sat. and P.M. Sun. Apr.–Aug; Tues.–Sat. and P.M. Sun. Sept.–Mar. except Thanksgiving Day, Christmas, New Year's Day, and Easter. Admission charged.* 🪧 ♿

150   Waterloo Area Farm Museum

7 mi./10 min. North on Mt. Hope Rd., right on Waterloo-Munith Rd. The museum commemorates the life of a family of German settlers who came to this southern Michigan area as farmers in 1844. Their original one-room log cabin has been reconstructed, and the brick farmhouse they built later is furnished with period pieces. The barn has an assortment of tools that such a family would have used. The outbuildings include an icehouse, a bakehouse, a blacksmith's shop, a milk cellar, and a windmill with clapboard siding to reduce the noise. *Open P.M. Tues.–Sun. June–Aug.; P.M. Sat.–Sun. in Sept. Admission charged.*

180   Nichols Arboretum, Ann Arbor

7 mi./13 min. North on Rte. 23, left on Geddes Rd.; continue on Fuller Rd., left on E. Medical Center Dr.; follow signs. The arboretum, which is run by the University of Michigan, is situated in an attractive mixture of hills, woods, ravines, and parklike meadows beside the Huron River. It combines the native growth with cultivated plantings of lilac, ash, maple, euonymus, and other decorative and useful shrubs and trees; there are numerous walks for pleasant strolling and quiet corners for secluded reverie. *Open year-round.*

206   Henry Ford Museum and Greenfield Village, Dearborn

2.5 mi./6 min. West on Oakwood Blvd. The scope, variety, and quality of one of the nation's largest museum complexes are extraordinary. The museums occupy 103 acres, and the exhibits represent most of the aspects of America's cultural and technological history. Here you will see George Washington's campaign chest and the rocking chair Abraham Lincoln was sitting in when he was assassinated; steam and internal combustion engines as big as houses; the revolutionary 1938 Massey-Harris Model 20 combine harvester; and an astonishing array of printing presses, telephones, radios, and radiotelegraphy equipment. The domestic and decorative arts are also thoroughly represented here.

Greenfield Village is a world of its own, with wide, tree-lined streets and buildings of historical interest brought here from their original sites—the Wright brothers' cycle shop, Henry Ford's birthplace, and Thomas Edison's laboratory. The village also exhibits a gristmill, a working farm of the 1880's, and a community area with most of the amenities a small 19th-century town might have had. *Museum open daily except Thanksgiving Day and Christmas; village interiors open daily except early Jan.–mid-Mar. Admission charged for museum and village.*

216   Detroit, MI 48226

Convention and Visitors Bureau, 2 E. Jefferson Ave. (313) 567-1170. Although best known for its automobiles, Detroit still keeps an antique electric trolley system in service, along with an ultramodern elevated people mover, which provides an interesting perspective of the city. To tour the auto plants always requires advance planning. But the industry is powerfully represented in Diego Rivera's great frescoes in the Detroit Institute of Arts, which in addition has exceptionally well-rounded collections from every major period.

The city also offers such varied attractions as the bustling open-air Eastern Market, with its vast displays of flowers and vegetables, two zoos, a freshwater aquarium, a children's museum, a family amusement park, and a tour of a Motown recording studio.

236   Metro Beach Metropark

4 min. East on Metropolitan Pkwy. A marshy peninsula jutting into Lake St. Clair is the site of an attractive recreation area with a wide range of facilities: marinas, boat and sailboard launching ramps, a sandy beach, a swimming pool, tennis courts, a golf course, and a dance pavilion. Lessons in sailboarding are available, and visitors can help to paddle a 34-foot, 20-passenger voyageur canoe. A nature trail circles the unspoiled marsh. In winter there are 5 miles of cross-country ski trails and skating and ice-hockey rinks. *Open year-round. Admisson charged.*

I-69B   Museum of Arts and History, Port Huron

5 min. East on I-69 (business), continue on Oak St., left on Military St., left on Wall St. Housed in a stately former public library, this museum has a large variety of collections relating to southeastern Michigan and the Great Lakes. Among the attractions are the archeological remains of an ancient fishing village, exhibits on historic forts, the bones of a 10,000-year-old mammoth, and artifacts related to Great Lakes navigation. Art exhibitions supplement the regional history displays. *Open P.M. Wed.–Sun. except holidays.*

216. *Behind the misty rainbow, Renaissance Center symbolizes the new vigor of Detroit.*

I-5   Portland, OR 97204

Convention and Visitors Association, 26 SW Salmon St. (503) 222-2223. The favored flowers in the City of Roses are at their best in Washington Park from mid-May to late November. Here, too, is a superb Japanese garden, a forestry center, a museum of science and industry, and inviting picnic areas. The zoo is famous for its Asian elephants. Other attractions include a unique block-wide landscaped water fountain, a magnificent mansion, museums of Oregon's history and art, and a museum of advertising.

I-5. *Snowcapped Mt. Hood, 50 miles away, seems to be right in Portland's backyard.*

28   Multnomah Falls

35

Exit 28: 3 mi./7 min. East on Rte. 30. Exit 35: 3 mi./7 min. West on Rte. 30. This is the spectacular centerpiece of the magnificent Columbia River Gorge National Scenic Area. The falls, plunging 620 feet into the gorge, are the highest of the dozen or more in the area. A 1-mile trail, part of a network throughout the gorge, starts at the base. You can follow it across a bridge to a platform that affords a breathtaking view 660 feet straight down. The visitor center has exhibits on the area's geologic, natural, and human history. The Columbia River Scenic Highway (Rte. 30) west of here is a pleasant and picturesque alternative to the interstate. *Open year-round.*

40   Bonneville Lock and Dam

5 min. North on access road; follow signs. Bonneville was the first hydroelectric dam on the Columbia River and is now part of a system that supplies half of the total hydroelectric capacity in the U.S.A. At the visitor center on Bradford Island, look through underwater windows and see the fish ladders and salmon, trout, and other species migrating upstream. From an overlook on the shore, watch boats being raised and lowered in the locks, and visit the powerhouse, where the huge generators can be seen from a viewing platform. Exhibits in the visitor center recount the dramatic history of the Columbia River region and highlight local birds, animals, and fish. *Open daily except Thanksgiving Day, Christmas, and New Year's Day.*

62   Hood River Vineyards

5 min. Exit south, right on Country Club Rd., right on Post Canyon Rd., right on Westwood Dr. This small winery is perched atop a hill overlooking the picturesque orchards of the Hood River valley and the scenic Columbia River gorge. Despite its size, the family-run vineyard turns out a dozen different types of wines, ranging from dry to semisweet. On a tour through the vineyards, all stages of the art of wine making are personally explained by a vintner. *Open daily Mar.–Dec.*

84   Fort Dalles Museum

85

Exit 84: 2 mi./15 min. East on 2nd St., right on Union St., right on 10th St., left on Trevitt St., left on 15th St. Exit 85: 2 mi./15 min. West on 2nd St., left on Union St.; proceed as above. A varied collection of 19th- and early 20th-century Americana can be seen in this museum's displays. It was once the surgeon's quarters of Ft. Dalles, which in the mid-1800's was the only army post between Ft. Vancouver, Washington, and Ft. Laramie, Wyoming. One room is devoted to saddles and guns, the tools of the frontier soldier's trade. There's also a bedroom furnished in 1890's style and large collections of hand tools, surveying equipment, cartridge cases, kitchen utensils, and china, much of which was donated by first-generation descendants of pioneers. Another building houses a prairie schooner, a surrey, and other vehicles from the past. *Open Tues.–Sun. May–Sept.; Wed.–Sun. Oct.–Apr. except 2 weeks in Jan. Admission free but donations encouraged.*

28–35. *Each of Multnomah's two stages is the veritable essence of woodland waterfall.*

87. *Lewis and Clark would doubtless be astounded at the taming of the mighty Columbia.*

87 | The Dalles Dam and Lake Celilo

5 min. North on Rte. 197, right on NE Frontage Rd. Scenery, history, and technology are combined in a train ride and guided tour of 1½-mile-long The Dalles Dam, the huge powerhouse and navigation locks, with fish ladders where migrating salmon and steelhead trout can be seen. Indian petroglyphs have been moved here for display, and the visitor center offers exhibits on the Lewis and Clark expedition, the Columbia River and Basin, and the work of the U.S. Corps of Engineers. Allow an hour for the tour. Behind the dam 24-mile-long Lake Celilo attracts sailboarders, water-skiers, boaters, and fishermen. *Open daily mid-June–Labor Day.*

188 | Doll and Toy Museum

8 mi./15 min. North on Rte. 395. The major part of this excellent collection is composed of some 2,000 antique dolls, many dating back to the 1850's, including the first doll patented in America. Dolls representing characters as diverse as King Henry VIII, Winston Churchill, John Wayne, General Custer, and Chief Sitting Bull blend the past with the present. The doll buggy, dollhouse, and furniture displays include pieces dating back to the Civil War. For those whose interests run to guns and transportation, there are vintage cap pistols, BB guns, and toy cars and trains. *Open daily May–Oct. Admission charged.*

210 | Pendleton Woolen Mills

3 min. North on 10th St., right on SE Court Pl. The Pendleton Woolen Mills began making Indian blankets in 1909, and has since become famous for its woolen fabrics. On the factory tour you will see how raw wool is turned into finished blankets and bolts of cloth and watch the ingenious machinery that combs, divides, and works the wool into strands and spins them into yarn. In the weave room the Jacquard looms work the yarn into the colorful patterns that give the Pendleton blankets their distinctive character. *Open Mon.–Fri. except first 2 weeks in July and Christmas–New Year's Day.*

234 | Emigrant Springs State Park

2 min. Follow signs. Although the springs that attracted pioneers on the Oregon Trail to this pleasant site have long since dried up, it's still a worthwhile place to stop. The dangers and hardship encountered by the wagon trains are described in exhibits here, and there's a mile-long nature trail with some 40 signs identifying the trees, shrubs, and flowers that grow in this area near the summit of the Blue Mountains. In the spring the mountain meadows are carpeted with colorful wildflowers, and during the summer the temperature is 10 to 15 degrees cooler than in the lowlands. *Open daily mid-May–Oct., weather permitting.*

304 | Oregon Trail Regional Museum, Baker

5 min. West on Campbell St. This impressive brick structure, listed in *The National Register of Historic Places*, was built in 1920 as a natatorium (indoor swimming pool) and a community center with a ballroom. Today the expanding museum houses an extensive and outstanding collection of minerals, semiprecious stones, gemstones, petrified wood and ferns, ores, coral, and seashells. Notable displays include a half-ton cluster of Arkansas crystals and a blacklight room. There are also Indian artifacts, period clothing, early town memorabilia, and interesting items from the history of lumbering, mining, and farming in eastern Oregon. *Open daily mid-May–Sept. Admission free but donations encouraged.*

353 | Farewell Bend State Park

2 min. North on Rte. 30. Surrounded by dry hills of sagebrush and tumbleweed, this pleasant park is a tree-shaded oasis on a curve of the slow-moving Snake River here. The name harks back to pioneer days, when wagon trains, with the dangerous Indian territory behind them, split up at this bend as families headed for different destinations. The history of the Oregon Trail is highlighted in exhibits in the interpretive center. The geological diversity of this area attracts rockhounds in their quest for mineral varieties. *Open year-round.*

353. *Sturdy iron-bound wheels such as these were instrumental in populating the West.*

35   Lake Lowell Sector, Deer Flat National Wildlife Refuge

8 mi./10 min. West on Rte. 55, left on Lake Rd. From September to April this 9,000-acre lake is one of the major wintering and resting places for waterfowl along the Pacific Flyway. The refuge, established by President Theodore Roosevelt in 1909, attracts some 100,000 ducks and geese as well as bald eagles, red-tailed hawks, American kestrels, and prairie falcons. More than 190 species of birds have been seen here. Fishing, wildlife photography, and observation are permitted at various locations when they do not interfere with visiting birdlife. In the summer, sailboats and motorboats may be used during daylight. *Open daily except holidays.*

53   Boise, ID 83702

Convention & Visitors Bureau, 100 N. 9th St. (208) 344-7777. When French fur trappers first came to the site of modern-day Boise (pronounced *Boy*-see), they welcomed the greenery of the region and called its river *la rivière boisée* ("the wooded river"). When the town was platted in 1873, it was named for the river. A lively introduction to Idaho's capital and largest city is provided in summer by the 1890's-style Boise Tour Train, which leaves from the Idaho State Historical Society Museum (a significant attraction in itself) in Julia Davis Park for an hour-long excursion through the town. The park also accommodates the Boise Gallery of Art, Pioneer Village, a rose garden, tennis courts, boating, an amusement park, picnic grounds, and a zoo. Another attraction in downtown Boise is the impressive domed state capitol, a scaled-down version of the federal Capitol in Washington, D.C.

90 / 112   Bruneau Dunes State Park

Exit 90: 23 mi./30 min. South on Rtes. 51 and 78. Exit 112: 15 mi./20 min. South on Rte. 78. For some 15,000 to 30,000 years, wind-driven sand has collected here in a natural basin. Two large dunes, covering about 600 acres, are the major features of this park; the largest is 470 feet high. The park, in southern Idaho near the Snake River, also has

90–112. *Here in this most unlikely place are superb examples of sculptured sand dunes.*

several small lakes, where there's fishing for bass and bluegill. Hiking the sandy dunes is a favorite—and quite strenuous—pastime, and there's also a self-guiding 5-mile walk into the desert, around the lakes, and through the dunes. Eagles, hawks, and falcons are seen, as well as shorebirds and migrating ducks and geese. The visitor center features exhibits related to the flora, fauna, and fossils in this unique environment. *Open year-round. Admission charged.*

147   Malad Gorge State Park

2 min. South on access road. The stark beauty of this narrow gorge is hidden from view until you are almost at the edge of the rim, peering down into it. Complete with a waterfall and striking rock formations, the rugged 2½-mile-long chasm was formed a million years ago by a torrent of glacial meltwater that tore through the rocks. A footbridge that crosses the gorge at Devil's Washbowl provides the most spectacular view. At this spot the Malad River cascades 60 feet into a craggy basin, and the gorge is at its widest (140 feet) and deepest (250 feet). Hiking trails run along the rim, and signs recount the history of the area. *Open year-round.*

168   Jerome Bird Farm

2 mi./10 min. West on S. Lincoln St.; follow signs. The primary purpose of this 40-acre game farm is to improve hunting in Idaho by breeding and releasing pheasants, chukars, and other upland game birds. It also offers a rare opportunity to view at close range species that are at best only briefly glimpsed in the wild. Visitors can see thousands of birds at all stages of development, from eggs to chicks to fledglings to full-grown fowl. The farm stocks an astonishingly varied assortment of pheasants, including silvers, Mongolians, black-necks, ringed-necks, and goldens. In addition, it raises peacocks and numerous varieties of waterfowl. *Open year-round.*

173   Shoshone Falls, Twin Falls

10 mi./20 min. South on Rte. 93, left on Falls Ave., left on access road. Known as the Niagara of the West, this magnificent cascade that drops 212 feet into the Snake River is actually 52 feet higher than Niagara's Horseshoe Falls. It is a breathtaking example of nature's unrivaled ability to combine beauty and grace with power. The park offers excellent overlooks, along with a large picnic area and a boat ramp, and Dierkes Lake, half a mile from the falls, is popular with sailboarders, swimmers, and hikers. Although the spectacle is best in early spring, these thunderous falls are worth seeing in any season. *Open year-round. Admission charged in summer.*

I-86 Massacre Rocks State Park

28 mi./35 min. East on I-86 to Exit 28. Pioneers on the Oregon Trail called this area Gate of Death and Devil's Gate after a series of Shoshone Indian skirmishes left 10 immigrants dead. The ruts made by wagon trains still mark this 566-acre park, and a rock bears names inscribed by pioneers who passed through. The park's other attractions include a 20-station nature walk, magnificent desert scenery on the hiking trails, boating, and fishing on the Snake River. The arid climate supports a surprising 300 species of plants, and some 200 bird species have been sighted. The visitor center has Oregon Trail artifacts, along with displays related to trappers, Indians, and pioneers who passed through here. *Open year-round.*

26 Golden Spike National Historic Site

23 mi./25 min. South on Rte. 83, right on Promontory Rd., right on access road; follow signs. Laying the track for the first American transcontinental railroad across 1,776 miles of hostile wilderness in some 4 years was an unparalleled achievement. When the final spike was driven here at Promontory Summit on May 10, 1869, it firmly united West with East and marked the beginning of the end of the frontier. Only 400 feet wide in most parts, this 2,200-acre park stretches for 15 miles along the original trackbed. A self-guiding 9-mile auto tour follows the historic railroad grade. At the last spike site, working replicas of the original *Jupiter* and *No. 119* steam locomotives are on display from May through September, and in summer months, the operation of these locomotives is demonstrated every day. A ¾-mile hike at the tour's end passes the impressive remains of the Central Pacific's Big Fill. *Open daily except holidays. Admission charged Apr.–Oct.*

360 Willard Bay State Park

1 min. West from exit. A scant quarter-mile from the interstate, this park bustles with boaters, swimmers, and fishermen taking advantage of the 9,900-acre man-made lake. The freshwater lake, which has marinas and campgrounds at its north and south ends, was reclaimed from the salt marshes of the Great Salt Lake. On land, Russian olive, elm, and poplar trees shade camping areas. The area is a haven for birds, and more than 200 species have been sighted. Many can be spotted in early morning along the lake's dike. The sign at Exit 354 leads to the park's older, less interesting southern section. *North marina open year-round; south marina open Apr.–Oct. Admission charged.*

346 Ogden, UT 84401

Golden Spike Empire, 2501 Wall Ave. (801) 399-8288; (800) 255-8824 outside UT. The towns in which steam trains stopped usually prospered, and Ogden's Mediterranean-style station is an imposing monument to the commercial impact of the iron horse. It is now the centerpiece of the 25th Street Historic District, where commercial buildings of bygone days have been converted to modern use. Among the station's displays are model railroads, classic cars, a gem collection, firearms, and a gunsmith's shop. Fort Buenaventura State Park, a reconstruction of a fort established by pioneer Miles Goodyear, recalls the life and times of the mountain men. Visitors with a scientific bent will enjoy the local planetarium and the Natural Science Museum.

I-15 Lagoon Amusement Park and Pioneer Village

18 mi./20 min. South on I-15 to Exit 327, south on Lagoon Dr.; follow signs. This 100-year-old amusement park has everything from traditional arcade games to a merry-go-round with hand-carved animals, Dracula's Castle, gardens and fountains, and an opera house that features Broadway musicals. Rides include bumper cars, a Tilt-A-Whirl, and an 85-foot-high double-loop roller coaster. Pioneer Village, with century-old buildings, contains a jail, a two-story log cabin, a Pony Express station, and a narrow-gauge railroad. Guns, dolls, carriages, and Ute Indian beadwork are on display. *Open daily Memorial Day–Labor Day; weekends only Apr.–May and Sept. Admission charged.*

111 Devil's Slide

Heading west (only), drive 1 mi. past Devil's Slide exit (111) to roadside overlook. The name is not inappropriate for these two steep parallel rock outcrops about 10 feet apart and 800 feet long, with the sides of the chute projecting about 20 feet above the ground. Devil's Slide is a sedimentary formation of limestone. Although it can only be viewed from the road, it is unique, memorable, and worth photographing. *Open year-round.*

26. Jupiter *came from the west,* No. 119 *from the east on rails that spanned the continent.*

See N–S book, sec. 3.

5TH San Francisco, CA 94101

5th St. exit. Visitor Information Center, Hallidie Plaza, lower level, Powell and Market Sts. (415) 391-2000. The dramatic hills, superb harbor, one of the world's most beautiful bridges, and a local citizenry that obviously loves the place all help to make this one of America's favorite cities. The excellent public transportation system—with its buses, subways, and justly famous cable cars—serves all the major attractions, including Golden Gate Park, Fisherman's Wharf, Pier 39, Ghirardelli Square, Japantown, and Chinatown. For an unforgettable view of the city and the Golden Gate Bridge, drive to Vista Point at the north end of the bridge. Another perspective of the bridge and the city can be enjoyed from the various bay sightseeing cruises that leave from the Fisherman's Wharf area.

5TH. *A masterpiece of engineering worthy of its dramatic setting on the Golden Gate.*

UNIV Lawrence Hall of Science, Berkeley

University Ave. exit: 5 mi./14 min. East on University Ave., left on Oxford St., right on Hearst St., right on Gayley Rd., left on Rim Way, left on Centennial Dr.; follow signs. High on a hilltop overlooking the campus of the University of California at Berkeley, this science center is a memorial to Ernest O. Lawrence, inventor of the cyclotron and the university's first Nobel laureate. The center, recognized as a leader in the development of hands-on science exhibits, has a biology lab where you can hold gentle animals, and a wizard's lab where you can have fun with physics. There's also a planetarium, a dinosaur that howls at visitors as they enter the lobby, a full-scale replica of the nose section of the space shuttle *Challenger*, and Lawrence's original cyclotron. *Open daily except Thanksgiving Day, Christmas eve and day, and New Year's Day. Admission charged.*

ROUTE 37 Marine World–Africa U.S.A., Vallejo

3 min. West on Rte. 37. Visitors have an unusual relationship with the animals at this popular 65-acre wildlife park; many are so gentle and affectionate that they are allowed to roam around the grounds with their trainers. Among the attractions are dolphins and killer whales that catapult into the air, chimpanzees that ride bicycles, sea lions that kiss the visitors, and nearly 100 species of birds, many of which are rare or endangered. *Open daily Memorial Day–Labor Day; Wed.–Sun. Labor Day–Memorial Day except Thanksgiving Day and Christmas. Admission charged.* 禾 ♿

ROUTE 12 Western Railway Museum

12 mi./16 min. East on Rte. 12 (Beck Ave.). An open-air English trolley that resembles a boat, an electric locomotive used once to haul President Taft's personal train, and a faithfully restored 1903 "standard" passenger car with etched glass and a hand-carved wood interior are included with some of the more than 60 vintage trolleys on display at this outdoor museum. For the price of admission you can ride the museum's 1¼-mile line as many times as you like, enjoy a picnic beside a pond shaded by willows and inhabited by ducks, and visit one of the country's largest railway bookstores, where you can browse and buy an authentic copy of an engineer's cap. *Open weekends. Admission charged.* 禾

BUS Sacramento, CA 95814

Business exit: Convention and Visitors Bureau, 1421 K St. (916) 442-5542. The gold rush that made Sacramento a boomtown and the state capital is memorialized in the Old Sacramento Historic District and Sutter's Fort State Historic Park. The fort—the first to be restored in the U.S.A.—contains many original shops and historic artifacts. An Indian museum in the park features the handiwork of those who found their way to this region without the lure of gold. The Crocker Art Museum, with its opulent Victorian gallery, features old masters' drawings, Oriental art objects, contemporary paintings, and photographs. Car and rail buffs will enjoy the California Towe Ford Museum and the California State Historic Railroad Museum.

ROUTE 49 Marshall Gold Discovery State Historic Park

19 mi./40 min. South on Rte. 49. James Marshall, while building a sawmill for John Sutter on the American River here, discovered gold in 1848. They tried to keep the find secret; but word spread, and the California gold rush was on. Today a 280-acre park surrounds a working replica of the original mill. Exhibits and audiovisual presentations in the small museum illuminate the area's history. Trails lead through the town of Coloma past historic monuments, a winery, and ruins and relics that speak of a time when gold fever gripped the country. A recreational area along the river is a favorite spot for picnicking, swimming, trout fishing, white-water rafting, kayaking, and casual gold panning. *Open daily except Thanksgiving Day, Christmas, and New Year's Day. Admission charged.* 禾 🚶 🛶 🐟 ♿

ROUTE 174 Empire Mine State Historic Park

13 mi./25 min. North on Rte. 174. From its discovery in 1850 until it closed in 1957, the Empire Gold Mine was one of the most efficient in the nation, owing in large part to the importation of experienced hard-rock miners from Cornwall, England. Some of the mine's machinery is on view, and you can enter a short distance into the original tunnel and peer into a shaft that was once nearly a mile deep. Gold samples, interpretive exhibits, films, and slide shows are on view in the visitor center. A 90-minute tour includes the former owner's charming granite and redwood residence (circa 1900) and a scale model of the mine's 367 miles of tunnels. A formal garden with nearly 950 rosebushes, which traces the history of roses from Roman times to the 1920's, is most impressive. A checklist of plants and animals in this 784-acre preserve is available. *Open year-round; tours weekends only Dec.–Feb.; house and scale-model room open weekends only Apr.–Nov. Admission charged.*

ROUTE 267   Ponderosa Ranch

19 mi./20 min. South on Rte. 267, left on Rte. 28. Here high above Lake Tahoe in the Sierra Nevada, surrounded by fragrant pine forests, nestles a full-scale furnished replica of the famous Cartwright ranch house as depicted on television's *Bonanza* series. The surrounding park contains a museum of Western memorabilia; an extensive and well-documented collection of antique cars, steam-driven tractors, carriages, farm and logging equipment; and a frontier town complete with general store, an 1871 church, shops, and of course a saloon. Children will enjoy the shooting gallery, mystery mine, and petting farm. Scenic hiking and horseback treks through the 600-acre backcountry and breakfast hayrides are available in summer; and the Camera Trail offers spectacular views. *Open daily May–Oct. Admission charged.*

ROUTE 267   Lake Tahoe Nevada State Park

25 mi./30 min. South on Rte. 267, left on Rte. 28. The pristine beauty of Lake Tahoe, more than a mile high in the Sierra wilderness, is the distinguishing feature of this park. Along the three miles of shorefront are sandy beaches, shaded picnic areas, and Cave Rock, where fishermen try for Mackinaw and rainbow trout. Well-marked hiking trails, ranging from 1½ to 17 miles round-trip, lead to magnificent lake vistas, as well as meadows of wildflowers and aspen groves, golden in their

267. *Lake Tahoe and the snow-mantled Sierra Nevada as seen from the eastern shore.*

seasons. Mountain lions and bears forage in the 13,000 acres of backcountry but are rarely seen. Check with park rangers about guided nature walks, stargazes, and special activities for children. Primitive campsites are available in the backcountry. *Open year-round. Admission charged.*

13   Reno, NV 89501

Chamber of Commerce, 135 N. Sierra St. (702) 329-3558. Although it's probably best known for slot machines and easy divorces, this city has much more to offer. The Fleischmann Planetarium, located on the University of Nevada at Reno campus, features star shows, sky-viewing sessions, and movies of space and nature-related subjects on a 360° screen. Also on the campus is the Nevada Historical Society, which displays pioneer and mining memorabilia and Indian artifacts, including some exquisite Washo Indian basketwork. Near the university is the Wilbur D. May Museum, where Mr. May's remarkably eclectic collections, including more than 80 mounted animal heads, are shown. The Sierra Nevada Museum of Art, in its impressive neo-Georgian mansion, highlights Indian baskets, regional art, and changing exhibits.

15   Virginia City

25 mi./35 min. South on Rte. 395, left on Rte. 341. Between 1859 and 1878 millions of dollars' worth of silver and gold mined from the

Comstock Lode turned Virginia City into the world's richest boomtown. Today the residue of its colorful past is creating a boom of its own. Among the well-preserved structures on C Street is the Territorial Enterprise Building, where a young journalist named Sam Clemens began writing as Mark Twain. Other highlights in the town include some handsome old churches, an opera house, excellent museums, and a variety of architectural styles. You can take a half-hour narrated excursion on the historic Virginia and Truckee Railroad, tours of mines and mansions, a 20-minute informational trolley ride, or brochure-guided walking and driving tours. *Open year-round; most attractions open Memorial Day–Sept. Admission charged for some attractions.*

46   Lahontan State Recreation Area

25 mi./30 min. South on Alt. Rte. 95, left on Rte. 50. Isolated beaches, secluded coves, and the freedom to camp almost anywhere along 72 miles of shoreline enhance this picturesque park in rolling desert country. Formed by a dam on the Carson River, 17-mile-long Lake Lahontan Reservoir is shared in summer by swimmers, water-skiers, boaters, and anglers who try for walleyed pike, bass, crappie, and catfish. With some 34,000 acres to explore, bird-watching, photography, and backpacking are popular all year long. Campers should know that at night the temperature can drop by 50° F or more. *Open year-round. Admission charged.*

106 | Pershing County Courthouse, Lovelock

2 min. West on Main St. In the early 1900's the rivalry of Lovelock and Winnemucca was such that when Winnemucca put up a new courthouse, Lovelock had to go them one better. So in 1919 the town fathers built one with an imposing rotunda and a round courtroom. The courtroom can be seen if court is not in session. The surrounding park has a public swimming pool and picnic tables set among shady trees and flowering shrubs. In the 1840's and 1850's, pioneers on the Humboldt Trail stopped here to feed and water their livestock before heading west across 40 miles of desert. *Open year-round.*

106 | Tufa Park

6 mi./20 min. North on Central Ave. (becomes Meridian) left on Pitt Rd. for 2½ mi., right on wide gravel road for 1 mi. These strange formations, standing in the stark desert landscape like the fossilized remains of prehistoric beasts, are rocks, properly called tuffs, formed by the eruption of an ancient volcano. Paths wind around the sculpted forms, whose subtle shades of orange, yellow, and green coloring were created by mineral deposits and colonies of lichens. *Open year-round.*

106. *These weathered volcanic deposits could pass for fossilized giant clamshells.*

129 | Rye Patch State Recreation Area

2 min. West from exit. This oasis comes as a welcome relief to travelers weary of desert, sagebrush, and the heat of summer. Boating and waterskiing are popular in the 11,000-acre Rye Patch Reservoir, fed by the Humboldt River. The three picnic areas, a beach for swimming, and campgrounds on both river and reservoir are additional enticements.

The river is not a new attraction; digs have revealed 23,000-year-old bones of bison, elephants, and camels, as well as signs of human visits 8,000 years old. *Open year-round. Admission charged.*

176 | Humboldt Museum, Winnemucca
178

Exit 176: 5 min. East on Winnemucca Blvd., left on Malarky St., left on Jungo Rd. Exit 178: 5 min. West on Winnemucca Blvd., right on Malarky St., left on Jungo Rd. This small, eclectic museum focuses on regional history from the 1860's onward. Housed in a former church (circa 1907), the exhibits include musical instruments, Indian arrowheads, a long rifle, and a variety of pioneer, mining, railroad, and cowboy memorabilia. A second building features antique cars, Indian carvings, and a 1920 version of that classic of western transportation, the pickup truck. *Open daily except Sun.*

303 | Northeastern Nevada Museum, Elko

2 min. South from exit. In the history section there are exhibits of geology, mining, Indians, ranching, and railroading—all the major elements of pioneer life. Rolling stock includes stagecoaches, fire trucks, wagons, buggies, and such. The Shoshone Indian basket collection is one of Nevada's largest. There's also an exhibit on the Basques, who have a long history of sheepherding in the area. Pioneer days are represented with period rooms and an original Pony Express station. Bighorn sheep, bears, eagles, and other animals in the taxidermy display depict the wildlife of the state. In the art gallery the work of regional artists is shown. *Open daily except Thanksgiving Day, Christmas, and New Year's Day.*

351 | Angel Lake Campground

13 mi./25 min. South on Rte. 231; follow signs. Here's a fairly easy way to experience the rugged beauty of this state's high country. Angel Lake Campground, bordering a lovely man-made reservoir, is set in a spectacular mountain amphitheater. Surrounded by towering canyon walls, you can try for three kinds of trout just steps from the camp, or sample steep trails flanked with wildflowers in summer and colorful quaking aspens in fall. On your way to the campground you'll be treated to sweeping views of a picturesque valley, but the last 4 miles are a winding mountain road. *Open daily July–Sept.*

2 | Bonneville Speedway Museum, Wendover

2 min. South from exit. Sleek bullet-shaped cars, motorcycles in rocketlike cocoons, jet-powered vehicles, and other mechanical marvels have raced against the clock or other machines on the vast, hard, level expanse of the Bonneville salt flats. This unusual museum contains some of those vehicles, along with photographs and drivers' equipment. The museum has a surprising assortment of other things, including antique cars in mint condition, car-hood ornaments, famous guns, old tools, Pima Indian artifacts, musical instruments, motorcycles, old bottles, and a wooden three-wheel bicycle. The entire collection is well displayed and documented. *Open daily June–mid-Sept. Admission charged.*

104 | Saltair Beach

1 min. North from exit. As you approach the Great Salt Lake you'll see, stretching mirage-like into the distance, a large Moorish-temple-shaped building that seems to float on the water. This is Saltair Resort—the third. The first, built in 1893, was a splendid bathing resort complete with dance hall, restaurants, shops, arcades, and bathhouses. It burned in 1925 and was rebuilt the following year. In the 1950's a receding lake beached the resort, and it burned again in 1970. The present Saltair opened in 1983, only to be flooded the following spring, when the lake suddenly rose

NV | UT
60
102
See N–S book, sec. 7.
15
17   2   6
28
See E–W book, sec. 16.
84
UT | WY
78
2
104
310   I-15   128
156
80

I-15. *The purpose is profit, but the surprising by-product is a monumental work of art.*

12 feet. Swimming is popular here, and power- and sailboats can be rented for a closer look at the marooned building or a cruise on the lake. *Open year-round.*

310 Salt Lake City, UT 84101

Convention & Visitors Bureau, 180 S. West Temple. (801) 521-2822; (800) 831-4332 outside UT. No other city in America owes so much to one group of people. Since its founding in 1847 by Brigham Young, who told his hardy band of followers: "This is the place," Salt Lake City has been largely created by the Mormons (members of the Church of Jesus Christ of Latter-day Saints). The city is built around Temple Square, dominated by the Gothic-spired Temple. It is closed to the public, but visitors are welcome at the acoustically superb Tabernacle, where the famous choir can be heard Sunday mornings and Thursday nights. Organ recitals are given weekdays at noon and at 4 P.M. on Saturdays and Sundays. Other attractions include the state capitol, the Pioneer Memorial Museum, the Council Hall, the State Arboretum, and Liberty Park.

I-15 Bingham Canyon Mine

25 mi./30 min. South on I-15 to Exit 301, right on Rte. 48; follow signs. The world's first open-pit copper mine (and America's largest man-made excavation) is an awesome 2½ miles across at the top and half a mile deep; it covers almost 2,000 acres. From the visitor center on the mine's rim you can observe drilling, blasting, and loading, as well as the operation of electric shovels that lift 55 tons at a scoop into trucks as big as houses. Plaques show where explosives are placed, and a pamphlet explains how 12 pounds of copper are produced from 1 ton of ore. An audio program explains the day-to-day operations of the open pit mine. *Open daily mid-Apr.–Oct.*

128 Pioneer Trail State Park, Salt Lake City

5 min. North on Rte. 186, right on Sunnyside Ave. Pioneer Trail is a combination of attractions that make it one of Utah's most popular parks. Located at the mouth of Emigration Canyon, it includes portions of the last 35 miles of the difficult 2,000-mile route that brought the first Mormon settlers to their new home in Utah. The living-history museum, Old Deseret, with a dozen buildings erected between 1847 and 1869, including Brigham Young's farmhouse and furnishings, portrays the daily life of the pioneer farmers, blacksmiths, carpenters, and other craftsmen. Nearby, the "This is the place" monument commemorates the centennial of the arrival of the Mormons here in 1847. At the visitor center you'll find maps and brochures. *Park open year-round; Old Deseret open daily May–Sept. Admission charged.*

156 Rockport State Park

5 min. South on Rte. 189. Rockport Lake, formed by the Wanship Dam, is a prime water recreation area, attracting swimmers, sail- and motorboaters, sailboarders, and water-skiers in summer. The beach and the shoreline in this park on the lake's southern edge also offer pleasant spots to picnic. Fishermen take rainbow, brown, and cutthroat trout and smallmouth bass. The park provides scenic views of the lake and a chance to see the native wildlife. Boats and other sports equipment may be rented. Campers will find 250 sites on nine campgrounds during the summer. During the winter cross-country skiers and ice fishermen enjoy the park. *Open year-round. Admission charged.*

310. *The dominant man-made and natural features are the capitol and the Wasatch Range.*

34 Fort Bridger State Historic Site

5 min. Southeast on I-80 loop. This fascinating site played a variety of roles during the development of the western frontier. Jim Bridger, a famous trapper and mountain man, first built a post here in southwestern Wyoming in 1843 to serve pioneer wagon trains in their push westward. It was later bought by Mormons, who set it aflame before fleeing to the Salt Lake area under pressure from the military. It subsequently served as a military post, a Pony Express and overland stage station, and the Shoshone Indian Agency.

The 40-acre site now features Wyoming's first schoolhouse as well as several military structures dating back to the 1880's, including a guardhouse, a commissary, and a bandstand. Bridger's trading post and the commmanding officer's quarters have been reconstructed. Period furnishings and costumed personnel, who demonstrate crafts associated with the fort, bring the past vividly to life.

Along with the historic buildings and the demonstrations, an excellent museum illuminates four aspects of western history: Indian life, the fur trade, immigration and settlement, and military life. *Open daily mid-Apr.–mid-Oct.; weekends only Nov.–Mar.*

89 Sweetwater County Historical Museum, Green River

3 min. South on Flaming Gorge Way. Located in the county courthouse, this museum features small displays on natural history and the Shoshone and Ute Indians in Wyoming. It stresses the period from 1868 onward, when Green River became a major railroad center, and nearby Rock Springs developed an important coal-mining industry. Some 10,000 historic photos document this period in Sweetwater County's development. The Life in Chinatown exhibit, with items dating from 1875 to the 1920's, represents the sizable Chinese population that worked in the coal mines. You can also see examples of hand-carved furniture, guns, farm implements, Indian artifacts, glassware, and period clothing. *Open Mon.–Fri. and P.M. Sat. July–Aug.; Mon.–Fri. Sept.–June except holidays.*

211 215 Wyoming Frontier Prison, Rawlins

Exit 211: 5 min. East on Spruce St., left on 6th St. Exit 215: 5 min. West on Cedar St., right on 3rd St., left on Spruce St., right on 6th St. This maximum security prison was the scene of murders, attempted escapes, and executions. It originally held 70 inmates when it was opened in December 1901 but was filled to capacity with more than 400 prisoners when it was closed 80 years later. You'll hear many gruesome tales about the prison on a guided tour that begins with the turnkey office and search room and winds up with the death house and gas chamber. Along the way you'll see the cell blocks, kitchen, mess hall, library, and shower room. You'll also see items produced by the inmates, including blankets, doormats, and, of course, auto license plates. (Early license plates were made of leather.) *Open daily Memorial Day–Labor Day. Admission charged.*

235 Saratoga Hobo Pool

21 mi./25 min. South on Rte. 130, left on 1st St. Local Indians regarded these Wyoming hot springs as sacred, but when the waters failed to cure smallpox (brought by white men), they were considered bad medicine and shunned. Later, the springs were hailed as beneficial for a full spectrum of ailments, and the town of Warm Springs was born in 1900. (The name was later changed to Saratoga, after the city in New York State that is also famous for its springwater. "Hobo" refers to the fact that anyone can go there at any time, and it's free.) With temperatures ranging from 117° F to 128° F, the springs are popular year-round. Many come to fish and hunt. The North Platte River is one of Wyoming's two blue-ribbon trout streams, and the region abounds with grouse, deer, elk, and antelope. *Open year-round.*

3RD Laramie Plains Museum

3rd St. exit: 5 min. North on 3rd St., right on Ivinson Ave. The collections in this Laramie museum are housed in a classic Victorian mansion—something of a museum piece in

329. *The resistant parts of the granite are revealed by the sculpture it has become.*

itself—built in 1892 by the wealthy merchant and banker Edward Ivinson. After his wife's death he donated the house to the Episcopal Church, and it subsequently became a museum. The mansion is filled with regional artifacts and items that belonged to the Ivinsons. The latter include oyster plates hand-painted in Paris, Ivinson's banker's desk, and the clothes the couple wore on their 50th wedding anniversary. Several bedrooms contain collections representative of the Laramie area, including guns from Ft. Sanders, hats, toys, Indian beadwork, railroad memorabilia, relics of the sheep industry, and crafts created by inmates of the territorial prison. One of the most interesting outbuildings is a carriage house with saddles, harnesses, and old bicycles. *Open Mon.–Sat. June–Aug.; P.M. only Mon.–Sat. Sept.–May. Admission charged.*

3RD Geological Museum, University of Wyoming, Laramie

3rd St. exit: 5 min. North on 3rd St., right on Lewis St. This museum presents in an easily understood manner a graphic record of the wide variety of organisms that have existed over millions of years in the Rocky Mountain area. The centerpiece of the impressive collection of fossils is a complete skeleton of the genus *Apatosaurus* (formerly *Brontosaurus*), 70 feet long and 15 feet high at the shoulder.

The skeleton occupies most of the main floor, and its head extends into the balcony. Other fossils include the skeleton of a mosasaur, a giant marine lizard; the skull of a megaloceros, a primitive elk with antlers spanning 9½ feet; and the fossilized remains of camels, bison, mammoths, and rhinoceroses. *Open Mon.–Fri. except holidays.* ♿

329 Vedauwoo Picnic and Campground

2 min. North on Vedauwoo Rd. An Indian word that means "earthbound spirit," Vedauwoo captures that feeling in the striking pink-streaked granite formations created by the wind and rain. A cool breeze in summer draws climbers and hikers to the ancient formations and trails that are found in this 1-square-mile area. A mile away from them, a 60-foot granite pyramid commemorates the efforts of the Ames brothers—who manufactured shovels—to finance construction of the Union Pacific Railroad in the 1860's. *Open year-round but may be inaccessible during snow. Admission charged.*

362 Cheyenne, WY 82001

Chamber of Commerce, 301 W. 16th St. (307) 638-3388. The phrase "Cheyenne to Deadwood 1876" is still visible on the side of a

362. *The capital and the cowboy are two important symbols of the Equality State.*

weather-beaten stagecoach at the Cheyenne Frontier Days Old West Museum, where more than 30 horse-drawn vehicles colorfully recall the days before the automobile. Also shown are an ambulance, a hearse, and sightseeing coaches, along with fancy saddles, rodeo memorabilia, and exhibits on the advent of the railroad and the decline of the Plains Indian tribes. In Lions Park the solar-heated Cheyenne Botanic Gardens and a lake for swimming, boating, and fishing are especially popular. The Wyoming State Museum focuses on state history and frontier life. The exhibits recall the days of the Shoshone and Arapaho Indians, cowboys, pioneer women, and mountain men. Indian beadwork, guns owned by Buffalo Bill Cody, and a diorama of an 1880's cattle roundup are among the highlights.

55 59 Fort Sidney Officers' Quarters, Sidney

Exit 55: 5 mi./10 min. North on Rte. 19, right on Rte. 30, right on 6th Ave. Exit 59: 4 mi./6 min. North on 17J Link, left on Rte. 30, left on 6th Ave. This white clapboard duplex, which once housed two officers and their families, is now the home of the Cheyenne County Museum in Sidney. Here you'll see memorabilia of Ft. Sidney, as well as the county's evolution from raw frontier territory to a prosperous farming community. Other military displays range in time from the Spanish-American War to Vietnam. One room is outfitted as a gentleman's den, with an antique desk and typewriters, cigar tins, and whiskey bottles. Women of the day are represented by late-Victorian dresses, quilts, baby clothes, fans, and hair combs.

The nearby post commander's home, an elegant two-story structure, is furnished to reflect the period before 1894, when the fort was abandoned. The comfortable home has little sense of military rigor. A 19th-century grand piano occupies the parlor, and the simple kitchen contains a cast-iron cooking stove. The master bedroom displays women's dresses and period furnishings. *Officers' quarters open P.M. daily except Thanksgiving Day, Christmas, and New Year's Day; post commander's home open P.M. daily Memorial Day–Labor Day.*

126 Fantasyland, Ogallala

2 min. North on Rte. 61. Fairy tales and Mother Goose stories are brought to life at this roadside attraction for small children. Teddy bears and raccoons, Mother Goose, Woody Woodpecker, Old King Cole, Little Boy Blue, Pinocchio, Santa Claus, and many more childhood favorites have been animated and are accompanied by music. There's also a gypsy camp and an area called "The Forest of No Return," with demon-faced trees and the rumbling sound of thunder. *Open daily June–Sept. and Dec. except Christmas. Admission charged for those over 5.* ♿

126 Mansion on the Hill, Ogallala

5 min. North on Rte. 61. In 1887 a wealthy Ogallala citizen built this three-story brick house to welcome his bride-to-be (the bride, however, decided not to come). Today the mansion, furnished with the trappings of a bygone era, houses the eclectic collections of the Keith County Historical Society. Displays include fans, gloves, shoes, a sheriff's gun and blackjack, fossilized bones, photographs, posthole diggers, and delicate lacework. The second floor contains a collection of high school yearbooks, toys, and clothing; and the attic is a treasure trove of old radios, sewing machines, electric hair-curling machines, and other examples of earlier technology. *Open P.M. Fri.–Wed., Memorial Day–Labor Day.*

126 Lake Ogallala State Recreation Area

8 mi./13 min. North on Rte. 61. Lake Ogallala, 1½ miles long and a quarter-mile wide, is in fact a barrow pit dug when the North Platte River was dammed to create the adjacent Lake McConaughy reservoir. But its diminutive size and serenity are the essence of its appeal. Absent here are the crowds, the clamor, and the noisy motorboats to be found at "Big Mac," as the 26-mile-long Lake McConaughy reservoir is popularly known in these parts. Lake Ogallala's shoreline is low and reedy and offers plenty of peaceful places for picnics and camping. *Open year-round. Admission charged.*

177 Lincoln County Historical Museum, North Platte

5 mi./12 min. North on Rte. 83, left on Rte. 30, right on N. Buffalo Bill Ave. This town is known both as the home of Buffalo Bill and the site of a World War II railroad station canteen that served as many as 5,000 military personnel daily. Its current claim to fame is this large well-organized museum. Exhibits comprise a country store, a barbershop, a doctor's office, World War I military relics, Indian artifacts, telephones, farm equipment, a wide array of household items, and a remembrance of the popular canteen. *Open daily Memorial Day–Labor Day. Admission free but donations encouraged.*

177 Buffalo Bill Ranch State Historical Park, North Platte

5.5 mi./13 min. North on Rte. 83, left on Rte. 30, right on N. Buffalo Bill Ave. A fine old 1887 horse barn with rafters carved in the

177. *The home of the buffalo hunter and wild West character is unexpectedly stylish.*

shape of rifle stocks and adorned with Annie Oakley's logo (a heart-shaped bull's-eye with a bullet hole) dominates the tree-shaded grounds of the ranch that Buffalo Bill called Scout's Rest. His home, a three-story mansion built in 1886, when Cody's Wild West show was a big success, has large bay windows, a turreted third floor, and gingerbread trim.

Memorabilia include posters, photos, silver spurs, and Sitting Bull's ceremonial saddle blanket. On the grounds is an enclosure where buffalo still roam. *Open daily Memorial Day–Labor Day; Mon.–Fri. Apr.–May and Sept.–Oct. Admission charged.*

211 Pony Express Station, Gothenburg

5 min. North on Rte. 47; follow signs. This one-room log cabin with a shingled roof and a stone fireplace served as a Pony Express station in 1860–61, which represents the entire life span of that romantic form of fast mail delivery. At other times the cabin was a fur-trading post on the Oregon Trail and a stage station on the Overland Trail. A replica of the leather mailbag used by the hardy Pony Express riders is displayed, along with moccasins and stone arrowheads from the Indian territory they crossed. In summer you can take a carriage ride around the park and town. *Open daily May–Sept. Admission charged for rides.*

237 Dawson County Historical Museum, Lexington

3 mi./7 min. North on Rte. 283, right on 6th St., left on Taft St. Life in central Nebraska in the 1800's and early 1900's is recalled here with period rooms, a barbershop stocked with razors and lotions, a one-room schoolhouse, and a newspaper office. Early means of transportation on display include a Union Pacific locomotive and caboose, a 1923 Ford coupe auto, an 1882 penny-farthing bicycle, and the Emmett McCabe biplane, with its curiously bowed wings. The extensive collection also features a model train set, musical instruments, toys, guns, uniforms, antique cameras, and photographs from the Civil War through World War II. *Open Mon.–Sat. and P.M. Sun. Mar.–Nov.; Mon.–Sat. Nov.–Mar. except Easter, Thanksgiving Day, Christmas, and New Year's Day. Admission charged.*

257 Chevyland U.S.A.

3 min. North on Rte. 183, right on first access road; follow signs. Here you'll find one of the best collections of Chevrolets known to exist

in America. Models date from 1914 to 1975, and all are in running order. On display are a 1932 Roadster Deluxe; a 1957 Bel Air, the most expensive Chevy of its day; an assortment of Corvettes that trace the car's evolution since 1954; and a 1969 orange and white Camaro that is a replica of the pace car used at the 53rd Indianapolis 500. You'll also see some items not made by Chevrolet, such as a 1928 Whippet Cabriolet, a 1939 Ford pickup, an Indian Chief motorcycle, and a Harley-Davidson 1200 motorcycle with sidecar. Posters and hubcaps add their own nostalgic flavor to the collection. *Open daily Apr.–Oct. Admission charged.*

272 The Frank House, Kearney

4 mi./7 min. North on Rte. 44, left on Rte. 30, right on College Dr. This handsome mansion was built in 1889 by George Washington Frank, a wealthy New York entrepreneur who played a major role in the construction of the Kearney Canal. As a result of its superb craftsmanship and then-unusual amenities—such as electricity and steam heat—Frank's three-story home soon became the city's favorite showplace and social center. The exterior is enhanced by a full-length pillared veranda, a tile roof, and pinkish Colorado sandstone that was cut on-site. Inside you'll find a Grand Hall with Corinthian columns, a large stained-glass window by Louis Comfort Tiffany, six fireplaces, hand-carved oak woodwork, a master bedroom with unusual curved-glass windows, and 19th-century furnishings. *Open P.M. Tues.–Sun. June–Aug. Admission charged.*

272 / 279 Fort Kearny State Historical Park

Exit 272: 6 mi./8 min. South on Rte. 44, left on Rte. 50A. Exit 279: 6 mi./8 min. South on Rte. 10, right on Rte. 50A. As the first fort built by the U.S. Army on the famous Oregon Trail—the route of the great westward migration from the 1840's to the 1870's—Ft. Kearny was established to help protect travelers, settlers, and prospectors, and later housed troops to provide protection for workers on the Union Pacific Railroad. The fort was finally abandoned in 1871. A reconstruction of an old stockade now stands in a 40-acre park that is walled in by adjacent cornfields during the summer. Also on the grounds are a well-equipped blacksmith's shop and several antique wagons, including a covered wagon. *Fort open Memorial Day–Labor Day; grounds open year-round. Admission charged.* ⛓♿

279   Harold Warp Pioneer Village

12 mi./15 min. South on Rte. 10; follow signs. This astounding collection of Americana—more than 50,000 artifacts arranged in chronological order showing the nation's progress since 1830—represents virtually every field of human endeavor. Founded in 1953 by Harold Warp, a Nebraska native who became a Chicago plastics manufacturer, the 20-acre village contains 300 antique cars, including a 1903 Ford and a 1905 Buick, original Audubon prints and Currier and Ives prints, an antique steam-powered carousel (still 5 cents a ride), a Pony Express relay station, seven generations of authentically furnished rooms, an 1889 B & M locomotive, historic aircraft, including an early-model helicopter, and one of America's largest collections of antique farm machinery and horse-drawn vehicles. *Open year-round. Admission charged.*

312   Stuhr Museum of the Prairie Pioneer, Grand Island

4 mi./7 min. North on Rte. 281, right on Rte. 34. The life and times of the sodbusters and town builders who settled the Nebraska prairie are exceptionally well illustrated here. The main museum building was designed by architect Edward Durrell Stone and displays artifacts from 1860 to 1910, including dolls and toys, homemaker's equipment, period rooms, clocks, antique clothing, barbed wire, and Limoges dinnerware. A historical account of the pioneer era is narrated by the late Henry Fonda, a native of Grand Island. The cottage in which the Oscar-winning actor was born is one of the 60 restored structures in Railroad Town, an elaborate re-creation of a prairie community, where you can board the last working turn-of-the-century steam-engine train in Nebraska for a tour of the museum's

200 acres. In the town you can see log cabins, Indian artifacts, Civil War memorabilia, and antique farm machinery. *Museum open year-round; other exhibits and buildings open daily May–Sept. Admission charged.* ⛓.

353   Anna Bemis Palmer Museum, York

4 min. North on Rte. 81; follow signs. Named for a local teacher, author, and musician, this museum provides a glimpse into the collective memory of a small Nebraska town. On display are an old coin sorter once used by the bank, a Civil War drum, an 1880 cavalry supply wagon, a large-horned Edison phonograph, a spinning wheel, a sodbuster plow, and period furnishings and clothing. Also on exhibit are the pump organ and published works of James Asher Parks, a local composer who wrote "Santa Claus and Uncle Sam: A Merry Christmas Cantata." *Open Mon.–Fri. and A.M. Sat. except holidays.* ⛓♿

401   Lincoln, NE 68508

Convention & Visitors Bureau, 1221 N Street, Suite 320. (402) 476-7511; (800) 423-8212 outside NE. Regarded by experts as an outstanding example of public architecture, the state capitol has a 400-foot tower crowned with a 32-foot bronze statue called "The Sower." At the University of Nebraska State Museum you

can see remarkable displays on the natural history of the Great Plains, including a reconstruction of a gigantic prehistoric rhinoceros. Also on the campus is the Christlieb Collection of Western Art, which includes works by Frederic Remington and Charles Russell. The William Jennings Bryan home, Fairview, contains furnishings and memorabilia of the great orator. Among Lincoln's other attractions are the city parks, a children's zoo, and the unique National Museum of Roller Skating.

I-480   Omaha, NE 68183

Convention & Visitors Bureau, 1819 Farnam St., Suite 1200. (402) 444-4660. There's much more to Nebraska's largest city than the well-known grain and livestock business. The Joslyn Art Museum, an impressive art deco building clad in pink marble, houses fine regional and international collections. A replica of President Lincoln's funeral car, along with other railroad memorabilia, is on view at the Union Pacific Historical Museum. The Great Plains Black Museum features rare photos and displays on black American history, and the Omaha Children's Museum has hands-on exhibits. Gerald Ford's birth site includes exhibits, gardens, and a model of the original house. The Old Market has interesting shops, pubs, galleries, restaurants, and boutiques. Boys Town offers self-guiding and conducted tours.

401. *Nebraska's imposing state capitol dominates the city by night as well as day.*

80 | 452D | 454 | 3 | 46 | 57 | 29

452D | Fontenelle Forest Nature Center

4 mi./7 min. South on 13th St., left on Belle-vue Blvd. These heavily wooded ravines and ridges (created by vast windblown deposits of silt) occupy 1,300 acres on a bend in the Missouri River. It was named for Logan Fontenelle, whose mother was the daughter of an Omaha chief. An interpretive center provides a view of the area's use by Indians and fur traders. A self-guiding history trail leads to a depression left by a collapsed prehistoric Indian earth lodge; other trails follow the perimeter of the floodplain marshland and offer a chance to spot white-tailed deer, coyotes, and red foxes. For birders there are some 200 species to be on the lookout for. *Open daily except Thanksgiving Day, Christmas, and New Year's Day. Admission charged.*

454 | Sarpy County Historical Museum, Bellevue

7mi./15min. South on 13th St.; continue on Rte. 75, left on Galvin Rd., left on 24th Ave. This Nebraska county's development from the days of the Indians to the early 20th century is traced here in a variety of chronological exhibits. There is a model of an Omaha Indian earth lodge; a Jefferson peace medal marking a treaty between Indians and settlers; a model of a prairie schooner and an ox yoke; and plows, scythes, and other tools used by pioneers to farm. Re-created turn-of-the-century rooms contain such antique gadgets as an Aurora Acorn cookstove and a stereopticon. Models of a one-room schoolhouse, a sod house, and a 1918 Case steam tractor bring the exhibits to the 20th century. A fine collection of model trains has a Texas Zephyr streamlined diesel and a Mallet heavy freight locomotive. *Open daily except Thanksgiving Day, Christmas, and New Year's Day. Admission charged.*

3 | The Historic General Dodge House, Council Bluffs

3 mi./7 min. North on 6th St., right on 5th Ave., right on 3rd St. This three-story Victorian mansion, built in 1869 by Gen. Grenville Dodge, befits the man who once surveyed some 60,000 miles of track and later presided over 16 railroad companies. The house is ele-gantly detailed throughout; in the dining room, where two magnificent silver tea services are displayed, Dodge was host to five United States presidents and other luminaries. On the ground floor the front and back parlors are graced by fine lace curtains, Austrian crystal chandeliers, and pier mirrors at each end. On the second floor, Mrs. Dodge's bedroom has marble-topped furniture and Brussels lace curtains. A child's bedroom houses a fine exhibit of period toys and baby clothes as well as a four-story fully furnished dollhouse. The third-floor ballroom holds a square rosewood grand piano, a pump organ, and a large music box. *Open Tues.–Sat. and P.M. Sun. except Jan. Admission charged.*

3. *Christmas decorations add to the charming clutter typical of the Victorian era.*

46 | Prairie Rose State Park

8 mi./10 min. North on Rte. M47. Situated at the edge of loess hills, formed by the wind-blown silt of glacier deposits, this park's varied terrain encompasses a mature stand of bur oak, a new and established prairie, and a trail that follows the marshy and upland ground around a shallow lake. Named for the vanished village of Prairie Rose, the park shelters badgers, white-tailed deer, white pelicans, pheasant, and other wildlife. The large lake is fished for bass, channel catfish, crappie, and bluegill, and reedy inlets along its jagged east-ern shoreline ... numerous wat... *mission charge...*

57 | Pellett ...

5 mi./6 min. S... gravel road af... acres of woodl... change from the... trail winds thro... undergrowth in... opossums, racc... ants. Squirrels a... build their nest... round but impa...

I-35 | Walnut ...

7 mi./10 min. Sou... Rte. 5; follow sig... the Raccoon Rive... ing natural stand... North America. ... tower over a sto... lawns, lending the... al character. Picn... shaded grounds be... men concentrate o... and bridle trails invite further exploration. *Open year-round. Admission charged.*

I-235 | Des Moines, IA 50309

I-235 | *Convention & Visitors Bureau, 309 Court Ave., Suite 300 (800) 451-2625.* Across from the gold-domed capitol, the Iowa State Historical Building provides an introduction to the history and prehistory of the region. The governor's house, Terrace Hill, is a superb example of a mid-19th-century mansion, now opulently furnished as it was in the 1870's. Salisbury House is a remarkable 42-room replica of King's House in Salisbury, England. The vast interior spaces contain furnishings in the Tudor style and are highlighted by the rich colors of Oriental rugs and stained-glass windows. Modern tastes in art and architecture are displayed in the Des Moines Art Center.

155 | Trainland USA

4 min. North on Rte. 117. One of America's largest Lionel train layouts features a cross-country trip through elaborately detailed dioramas of the frontier, steam, and diesel eras. Scenes include an Old West gunfight, a three-ring circus in Arizona, and a moonshine still in Missouri. In the diesel display, visitors can activate a missile launch crane at the Florida Space Center, set a coal loader in motion in Kentucky, operate a ski lift in Colorado, and much more. It took 32 people 4½ years to build. The scope and craftsmanship must be seen to be believed. *Open daily Memorial Day–Labor Day; weekends in Sept.; P.M. Fri.–Sun. after Thanksgiving Day. Admission charged.*

164 | Jasper County Historical Museum, Newton

1 min. North on Rte. 14, right on S. 12th Ave. W., right on W. 18th St. S. Life in turn-of-the-century Jasper County is illustrated in a variety of spacious displays in this large museum. The re-created interiors of a Victorian home, a barn, and a one-room schoolhouse are com-plemented by an exhibit of farm implements and a collection of old wall clocks. Some coal-mining tools represent what was one of the area's major industries until Fred Maytag produced his first washing machine in 1907. The evolution of this labor-saving invention is documented with examples dating back to the old wringer models. *Open P.M. daily May–Sept. Admission charged.*

164 | Fred Maytag Park, Newton

3 mi./6 min. North on Rte. 14, right on Rte. 6, right on W. 4th St., left on 5th Ave., right on 3rd St. This small but attractive and well-appointed city park was founded by appliance manufacturer Fred Maytag in 1935. The terrain is hilly, well mown, and set with many mature shade trees and ornamental shrubs. The park has three picnic shelters, one an original log cabin that was moved to this site, and the Fred Maytag Bowl, a clamshell amphitheater with wooden bench seating. The park also has tennis courts, a playground with swings and slides, and a large swimming pool with a 170-foot water slide. *Open year-round. Fee charged for pool.*

173 | Rock Creek State Park

9 mi./17 min. North on Rte. 224, right on Rte. F27. The centerpiece of this pastoral 1,700-acre park is a large man-made lake, its irregular shoreline lightly wooded in places. Boats can be rented, and there are pleasant lakeside picnic and camping areas. Some of the surrounding meadow areas are reverting to a scrubby, prairielike state that contrasts with the efficiently farmed rolling hills beyond the park's boundaries. Hiking and snowmobile trails traverse the area. *Open year-round. Admission charged.*

220 | Amana Colonies

30-mi. loop tour. North on Rte. V77, right on Rte. 6, left on Rte. 220, right on Rte. 151/6; re-enter I-80 at Exit 225. This group of seven Iowa villages was settled in 1855 by 1,000 members of a pietist group of Lutherans who called themselves the Community of True Inspiration. They came from Germany by way of upstate New York in search of religious freedom. They became farmers, established themselves in the woolen, meat-smoking, and furniture industries, and lived communally until 1932, when the land and the businesses were incorporated. Today a peaceful atmosphere pervades these well-tended villages, which gently echo the past.

South Amana's Barn Museum has on display models of historic houses and barns, a shingle and sawmill complex, and a four-story granary. The Old Fashioned Store in High Amana, its interior unchanged for over a century, sells a large variety of traditional goods. The reconstructions, documents, antique tools, and other artifacts on view in the Museum of Amana History in the town of Amana illustrate life in the old colonies. The Amana Woolen Mill, which supplied fabric for Soviet army coats in World War II, has tours. *Barn Museum open daily Apr.–Oct.; Old Fashioned Store open daily except Christmas, New Year's Day, and Sun. in Jan.–Feb.; Museum of Amana History open daily mid-Apr.–mid-Nov.; Amana Woolen Mill open daily except holidays. Admission charged for Barn and Amana History museums.*

235–235. *Reflecting pool and modern sculpture are featured in the Civic Center's plaza.*

239 Kalona Historical Village

21 mi./25 min. South on Rte. 218, right on Rte. 22. A blend of old and new is immediately apparent in the Kalona region, home of the largest Amish community west of the Mississippi. Automobiles coexist with horse-drawn buggies on the streets of Kalona, where hitching posts are a familiar sight.

Kalona began as a railroad stop, and its historical village was conceived as a fitting site for the town's restored 1879 railroad depot, which now houses railroad memorabilia. Other buildings include the Wahl Museum, with fine collections of antique glassware; the Iowa Mennonite Museum and Archives; and a 19th-century log home. *Open daily except Thanksgiving Day, Christmas, and New Year's Day. Admission charged.*

246 Lake MacBride State Park

14 mi./20 min. North on Rte. 1, left on Rte. 382. Lake MacBride was created as part of a recreation area project completed in 1955. The state park surrounds the lake, while a nature recreation area is located to the south. The park provides a narrow swimming beach as well as facilities for camping and picnicking. In winter, trails are open for snowmobiling and cross-country skiing. The recreation area, administered by the University of Iowa, is more varied, its terrain wilder and less developed. The humane work of the Raptor Center is devoted to the rehabilitation of injured birds of prey. Hawks and owls can be observed in large open-air cages. *Open year-round. Admission charged for state park; admission free but donations encouraged at Raptor Center.*

254 Herbert Hoover National Historic Site, West Branch

1 min. North on Parkside Dr. (Rte. X30). The stock market crash of 1929 and the depression that ensued stigmatized the memory of Herbert Hoover, president from 1929 to 1933. This site serves to illuminate Hoover's long and distinguished career as a mining engineer, humanitarian, and statesman. (He remained a public servant until 1955.)

254. *From one white house to another—the birthplace of our 31st Chief Executive.*

Behind a picket fence on its original site sits the tiny cottage where Hoover was born. It attests to the humble beginnings of a man who became a millionaire as a mining engineer and later would not accept his presidential salary. Other 19th-century buildings include the Friends Meetinghouse (Hoover was a committed Quaker) and a schoolhouse.

The Presidential Library-Museum houses exhibits pertaining to Hoover's distinguished career. *Open daily except Thanksgiving Day, Christmas, and New Year's Day. Admission charged at both places.*

277 Wildcat Den State Park

13 mi./17 min. South on Rte. Y26. Wildcats once lived in dens within this complex and fascinating terrain of woods, ravines, and cliffs. Today the park features about 2 miles of trails rimmed with jewelweed and other varieties of blossoming shrubs, ferns, and wildflowers. Pine Creek, a small stream, follows the valley bottom to an old mill and to Pine Creek Bridge, constructed with wood planks on an iron frame in 1833. *Open year-round. Admission charged.*

I-74 The Children's Museum, Bettendorf

5 mi./6 min. East (south) on I-74 to Exit 4 (last Iowa exit), east on Mississippi Blvd. Despite its name, this museum isn't for children only. The Bettendorf Room, for example, is devoted to the history of a company that flourished here in the 1920's as a manufacturer of railroad-car wheel and axle assemblies. Included is a model of a 1930's Bettendorf boxcar. In another room, graphic exhibits portray developments in local history, including an influx of Armenians around 1913 and the establishment of dairy farming.

In the Time Machine section, young visitors can disassemble and play with a variety of small machines. There are also natural history exhibits, working traffic lights, and a hands-on TV studio for children, where they can practice using video equipment and hone their broadcasting skills. *Open Tues.–Sat. and P.M. Sun. except holidays. Admission free but donations encouraged.*

I-74 John Deere Administrative Center, Moline

I-74

I-74 exit: 12.5 mi./16 min. East (south) on I-74 to Exit 4B, east on John Deere Rd. (Rte. 5). I-74 exit: 14 mi./19 min. West on I-74 to Exit 4B, east on John Deere Rd. (Rte. 5). Visitors to these showcase headquarters, designed by Finnish-American architect Eero Saarinen, can tour the building and its atrium, see a film tracing the company's history from the invention of the steel plow by Vermont blacksmith John Deere in 1837 to the present, and browse in the display building, which includes a striking 180-foot mural by artist Alexander Girard that features actual three-dimensional objects such as pioneer tools and other memorabilia. *Display building open year-round; tours Mon.–Fri. except holidays.*

19 Bishop Hill

21 mi./30 min. South on Rte. 82, left on Rte. 570N, right on Rte. 1670E; follow signs. Swedish immigrants founded Bishop Hill as a religious colony in 1846 and endowed it with the simple elegance it still retains. The Steeple Building is a good place to begin your tour. It displays domestic articles that belonged to the first settlers and provides a detailed picture of their aspirations and lifestyle. The old Colony Church, also a museum, contains a wonderful collection of paintings by Olof Krans, a primitive artist who came to the colony as a boy in 1850. The restored Colony Hotel occasionally offers costumed demonstrations of 19th-century life. *Town open year-round; Steeple Building open daily Apr.–Dec.; Colony Church and Colony Hotel open daily except Thanksgiving Day, Christmas, and New Year's Day.*

33   Johnson Sauk Trail State Park

6 mi./8 min. South on Rte. 78. This 1,360-acre park lies at the southern edge of what was once the Great Willow Swamp. The area was famous for its abundant wildlife, and many Indian tribes, attracted by the wild game and fur-bearing animals, made their homes here. Wild creatures still inhabit the region and can sometimes be seen from the many hiking trails. The man-made lake tempts anglers, who come for the plentiful largemouth bass, bluegill, sunfish, crappie, and northern pike.

The lake is also a resting place for migrating water birds. *Open daily except Christmas and New Year's Day.*

75   "Time Was" Village Museum

8 mi./10 min. North on Rte. 251. Here is an intriguing array of the things our grandparents cherished, aspired to, or took for granted: dolls and Easter cards, Valentine cards and walking sticks, doorknobs and keys, trivets and watches, stuffed birds, chewing gum machines, and 419 potato mashers, each with a different design. Several period rooms contain the artifacts and evoke the atmosphere of their time and function. An extensive collection of antique carriages and automobiles includes an ornately carved Ringling Brothers circus bandwagon and a 1905 rear-engine Orient buckboard steered by a tiller. *Open daily May–Oct. Admission charged.*

81   La Salle County Historical Society Museum

4 min. South on Rte. 178. The museum occupies a long stone building constructed in 1848 as a warehouse on the Illinois and Michigan

Canal. Displays describe the productive years of the canal and help the visitor to browse through the area's earlier history. Models, paintings, and chronicles tell the story of the siege of Starved Rock and the Indian Creek massacre. A curious collection of hickory-nuthead dolls represents the Lincoln-Douglas debate in nearby Ottawa, and there are replicas of casts of Lincoln's face and hands. *Open Mon., Wed.–Fri., and P.M. Sat.–Sun. Apr.–Dec.; Wed.–Fri. and P.M. Sat.–Sun. Jan.–Mar. Admission charged.*

90   William Reddick Mansion, Ottawa

5 min. South on Rte. 23, left on Lafayette St. In the summer of 1858 a local crowd watched from the steps of this unusually handsome Italianate mansion as Abraham Lincoln and Stephen A. Douglas debated the issue of slavery in an adjacent park. The house, built a few years earlier by Ottawa businessman and politician William Reddick, served as the Reddick home for 30 years before becoming a library and then a national landmark. The unusual combination of cream Lemont limestone with red brick, the ornamental cornices and the marble fireplaces, the tin speaking tubes that allowed communication between the various parts of the house, and other features make this one of the most architecturally interesting antebellum homes in the state of Illinois. *Open Mon.–Fri. except holidays. Admission free but donations encouraged.*

112   Gebhard Woods State Park

5 min. South on Rte. 47; follow signs. One of several parks that flank the Illinois and Michigan Canal, where teams of mules once towed cargo-laden barges for miles between La Salle and Channahon, this park encompasses about 1 square mile of gently rolling terrain dignified by many old shade trees. The park's four ponds are stocked with trout. Fishing is also permitted in the canal or in Nettle Creek. Along the canal 1 mile to the west is the largest tree in the state: a 120-foot-tall eastern cottonwood with a trunk 27 feet around. Canoes can enter the canal from the park. *Open year-round.*

75. *All the objects in this farm kitchen are now cherished by collectors of antiques.*

See N–S book, sec. 21. | See N–S book, sec. 25. | See E–W book, sec. 13. | IL : IN | See N–S book, sec. 26. | See E–W book, sec. 6.

55   137   14   57   I-57   9   94   I-94   4   1   65   90   30   31   46   77

80   94

137   Pilcher Park, Joliet

4 mi./6 min. West on Rte. 30, right on Gougar Rd. Set along Hickory Creek, this extensive wooded park on Joliet's outskirts offers a variety of possibilities, including hikes through upland and lowland woods, ski and bike trails, picnic areas, and an interpretive nature center that has displays of native plants, birds, and mammals. Programs matched to the seasons include maple sugaring, bird-watching, fishing contests, ski races, and pond and woodland study trips. One of the various walks is a quarter-mile self-guiding trail marked with informative story boards. An artesian well here is popular with locals, who take its mineral water away by the bucketful. Also featured are a paved trail for the blind and handicapped and a greenhouse with four rooms that display trees, cacti, and flowers of the season. *Open year-round.*

I-57–I-94. Imagine the superb view from the 103rd floor of the world's tallest building.

I-57 I-94   Chicago, IL 60611

Tourism Council, 163 E. Pearson St. (312) 280-5740. This great cosmopolitan metropolis, beautifully situated on the southwestern shore of Lake Michigan, boasts a number of world-class attractions. The Art Institute is known for a wide-ranging permanent collection and creative special exhibitions. The Terra Museum, opened in 1987, has a superlative collection of American art; the John G. Shedd Aquarium, the world's largest such indoor facility, with more than 200 tanks, displays some 1,000 wonders of the deep. For an intimate sense of the city, take the El (the elevated railroad) around the Loop; and for a breathtaking overview of both the city and lake, try the observation area on the 103rd floor of the Sears Tower, at this writing the tallest building in the world.

1   Wolf Lake Park, Hammond

7 mi./25 min. North on Calumet Ave. Despite the unpromising surroundings of highways, high-tension lines, and gas storage tanks, this park, with its large lake, miniature golf course, and other recreational facilities, is an obvious success. Rental paddleboats, canoes, and sailboards are available, as is instruction on the last-named. The annual Augustfest, held during the first week of the month, brings some 300,000 people here for entertainment, food, and carnival attractions. A fishing pier and a boat ramp entice the angler to try for walleye, northern pike, or bass. *Open daily mid-June–mid-Sept. Admission charged.*

31   Wilbur H. Cummings Museum of Electronics, Valparaiso

15 mi./25 min. South on Rte. 49, right on Rte. 130. Electronics changes so quickly that yesterday's marvel soon becomes today's antique. This museum has electronic devices from the period of Edison and Marconi to the present, knowing that its latest state-of-the-art exhibits will soon be obsolescent. Among the highlights are a 1950's Seeburg jukebox that plays 78-r.p.m. records, Admiral Byrd's transmitter from a South Pole expedition, one of the first pinball machines, and radios by Atwater-Kent, Crosley, Philco, and other noted manufacturers. First-generation computers and VCR's, studio TV equipment, and other outmoded wonders are displayed and explained. The museum is on the campus of Valparaiso Technical Institute. Apply for free admission at the administration building. *Open year-round.*

31. *Consider the time it took the wind to deliver this pile of sand grain by grain.*

31   Indiana Dunes National Lakeshore

8.5 mi./13 min. North on Rte. 49, east on Rte. 12. These 1,800 acres of woodland trails and 3 miles of beach dominated by towering lakefront dunes evince an almost lyrical delicacy in an obviously industrial environment. A number of plants are relics of colder climates that existed here at the end of the Ice Age and left a remarkable diversity of vegetation. Arctic bearberries, alongside prickly-pear cacti and northern jack pines, share dune slopes with southern dogwoods. Though the dunes are large (Mt. Tom rises more than 190 feet) and are anchored against the wind by marram grass, sand cherries, cottonwoods, and other native plants, they are susceptible to erosion. A 2-mile trail leads through red oaks and sugar maples to the restored Bailly Homestead and Chellberg Farm. *Open year-round.*

77   Fort Joseph Museum, Niles

8.5 mi./15 min. North on Rte. 33 and Rte. 31/33. This Michigan fort, built by the French in 1691, commanded a key trade route between their holdings in Canada and Louisiana. In the French and Indian War it was held by the British, then briefly by Spain.

The documents, pictures, books, implements, and furniture in the 100,000-item museum, located in a Victorian carriage house, bring history to vivid life. Here, too, is a large collection of Sioux and other Indian artifacts, including pictographs of chiefs Sitting Bull and Rain-in-the-Face. *Open Tues.–Sun. Admission free but donations encouraged.*

77   Studebaker National Museum, South Bend

3 mi./9 min. South on Rte. 33, left on Jefferson Blvd. In the 1850's South Bend was known as the Wheel City, because of the scores of wagonmakers living and working here. Part of that tradition was created by the Studebaker Company, which in time went from building covered wagons to producing some of the most imaginative automobiles of the 20th century. You will see examples of these at Century Center (Jefferson Boulevard and St. Joseph Street). Among the highlights are Studebaker's 1902 electric car, the Dictator Series of the 1930's, and the bullet-nosed models so familiar in the 1950's. Dodge, Oliver, and Flanders are also represented. And not just cars: the 1923 Indestructo cabin trunk, for example, brings vivid reminders of those lost days when a trip abroad was the event of a lifetime. A short walk away, at the Archives Center (South Street and Lafayette Boulevard), more than 60 historic vehicles are on display. *Open daily June–Aug.; Tues.–Sun. Sept.–May. Admission charged.*

77   Potato Creek State Park

24 mi./30 min. South on Rte. 33 and Rte. 31 (business) through South Bend, right on Rte. 4. Fishermen come to Worster Lake for the bass, bluegill, brown trout, crappie, and channel catfish. The 300-acre reservoir was created in 1977, when Potato Creek was dammed, and

in parts of the lake the ghostly trunks of drowned trees can still be seen. The beach is large and boats are for rent. The landscape, with woodland and scrubby pasture, shows how former farmland reverts to its natural state. You can enjoy several trails, including a 3-mile bicycle trail that goes through many scenic areas. Bikes are rented at the same shop that rents boats. *Open year-round. Admission charged.*

101   The Old Bag Factory, Goshen

12 mi./19 min. South on Rte. 15, right on Rte. 33, right on Indiana Ave. In 1984, when Larion Swartzendruber moved his custom furniture business into this old factory building, he visualized a workplace and sales center for craftsmen. From an upstairs gallery you can see his Hardwood Creations being made. Here, too, are potters, doll and toy makers, a blacksmith's shop (the restoration of wood-burning stoves is a specialty), and an egg-decorating shop. Nearby is Quilt Design, an 1837 log cabin where quilts, sewn by Amish and Mennonite women in 20 states, are displayed and sold. *Open Mon.–Sat.*

121   Pigeon River State Fish and Wildlife Area

9 mi./12 min. South on Rte. 9, left on Rte. 120; follow signs. This wildlife area, which covers some 11,500 acres of woods, ponds, streams, and marshland, is home to deer, pheasants, and waterfowl as well as pike, bluegill, perch, and of course trout. The Curtis Creek Trout-Rearing Station, which is located in the wildlife area, successfully grows some 60,000 rainbow and brown trout per year. Although not native to Indiana, fingerlings 3 to 4 inches long are brought here from state hatcheries and raised in six 86-foot-long raceways. When 7 to 10 inches long, they are released in various streams and lakes. *Open year-round.*

156   Pokagon State Park

4 min. South on I-69 to Exit 154, west on Rte. 727. This park, named for Potawatomi chief Pokagon, has year-round appeal. In winter, thrill seekers head for the 1,780-foot refriger-

ated toboggan slide, where they can streak down and over hills at 45 miles per hour. The slide is open from Thanksgiving to March, and the toboggans, rented by the hour, can hold up to four passengers. Other attractions in this vast area include trails for hikers and cross-country skiers (rentals available), ice fishing, ice skating, sledding, and year-round camping. In summer, visitors come to fish, boat, and swim from Lake James's wide and sandy beaches. *Open year-round. Admission charged.*

2   Harrison Lake State Park
3

Exit 2: 20 mi./30 min. North on Rte. 15, right on Rte. 20, right on Rte. 27; follow signs. Exit 3: 20 mi./30 min. North on Rte. 108, left on Rte. 20, left on Rte. 66, right on Rte. M. The soggy black soil that once earned this region the nickname the Great Black Swamp today constitutes some of the most fertile farmland in the state of Ohio. Even amid vast fields of corn, oats, and soybeans, this 350-acre park sparkles with inviting greenery. Harrison Lake—framed by shaded picnic areas, lush meadows, and a hiking trail—provides water activities in every season and yields plenty of bluegill, crappie, and largemouth bass. In springtime vesper sparrows, brown thrashers, and yellowthroats are some of the songbirds to be heard and seen here. *Open year round.*

156. *Idyllic day at the park: out of school with friends, fish, and faithful dog.*

4 Fort Meigs State Memorial

3.5 mi./6 min. South on Rte. 20, right on Rte. 65; follow signs. Built on a bluff above the rapids of the Maumee River, Ft. Meigs played a key role in America's victory in the War of 1812. It was built in February 1813, and in May survived a siege and bombardment by the British; in July the British were repulsed again, paving the way for their defeat in the Battle of Lake Erie. The present fort is a reconstruction of the original; three of the seven blockhouses contain exhibits about the war and about the design and construction of forts. Within the stockade are the earthworks that sheltered the troops from cannon fire. *Open Wed.–Sat. and P.M. Sun. and holidays late May–early Sept.; Sat. and P.M. Sun. early Sept.–late Oct. Admission charged.*

I-280 Toledo, OH 43604

Office of Tourism & Conventions, 218 Huron St. (419) 243-8191. This major Great Lakes port is a city of iron and coal, where bicycle and wagon shops gave way to auto parts makers and a flourishing glass industry. The Toledo Museum of Art has magnificent glass displays and extensive collections in many periods of painting and sculpture. "Mad" Anthony Wayne won the Battle of Fallen Timbers here in 1794, at what is now Fort Industry Square. The Portside Festival Marketplace, on the waterfront, is a likely and lively focus for a visit, which could include a sightseeing cruise on the Maumee River and Lake Erie.

6 East Harbor State Park

15 mi./23 min. North on Rte. 53, right on Rte. 2, left on Rte. 269; follow signs. The park is Ohio's largest on Lake Erie, and one of its most popular. It lies on a limestone peninsula and embraces three sheltered harbors. One of these, Middle Harbor, is a wildlife refuge, and a trail along its southeastern shore leads to an observation blind from which waterfowl and shorebirds can be seen. For most people, though, the sandy beaches, boating, swimming, and fishing are the park's major attractions. *Open year-round.*

7 Edison Birthplace, Milan

5 min. South on Rte. 250, left on Rte. 113; follow signs. Thomas Edison was born in this modest but appealing house in 1847 and lived here until he was 7 years old. Some of the family furnishings are original—a high chair, a spinning wheel—and a collection of memorabilia includes several of his inventions: a 1901 mimeograph machine, a stock exchange printer, a 1929 model of his first light bulb (it used a strip of carbonized thread as a filament), a battery-powered miner's lamp, and Edison's first talking doll (1888). Just below the house is a marker for the canal that connected Milan with Lake Erie when Edison was a boy. *Open Tues.–Sat. and P.M. Sun. June–Labor Day; P.M. Tues.–Sun. Feb.–May and Labor Day–Nov. Admission charged.*

7 Firelands Museum, Norwalk

7 mi./10 min. South on Rte. 250, right on W. Main St. (Rte. 61), left on Case Ave. The museum is named for those lands that were given to residents of Connecticut to compensate them for property torched by the British during the Revolutionary War. Early maps of the district and surveyor's equipment are displayed, along with collections of firearms (including a Chinese hand-cannon dating from 1000 B.C.) and memorabilia of the Civil War (including cypress grave markers from the prison camp on Johnson's Island). Other items of interest range from authentic Indian arrowheads to a diorama of the Milan ship canal and a mammoth bass viol. The museum occupies a federal-style town house dating from 1835 and contains furnishings of that period. *Open Mon.–Sat. and P.M. Sun. July–Aug.; P.M. Tues.–Sun. May–June and Sept.–Oct.; P.M. Sat.–Sun. Apr. and Nov. Admission charged.*

7 8 Great Lakes Historical Society Museum, Vermilion

Exit 7: 25 mi./32 min. North on Rte. 250, right on Rte. 2, left on Rte. 60. Exit 8: 15 mi./20 min. North on Rte. 57, left on Rte. 2, right on Rte. 60. This lakeside museum provides a fascinating and colorful account of shipping on the Great Lakes. Excellent photographs of storms and wrecks show how dangerous these waters are, and there are models of the many kinds of ships and boats that ply the lakes. Displays of maritime equipment here include compass binnacles and steering wheels, radar units, an engine room console, and a complete steam engine. A comprehensive exhibit of safety and rescue equipment includes steam whistles and foghorns, shore beacons, and the light from a lighthouse on northern Lake Huron, gleaming like a precious chandelier of white and ruby crystal. *Open daily Apr.–Dec.; weekends only Jan.–Mar. Admission charged.*

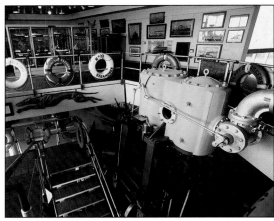

7–8. *With yellow steam chest, a steam engine is a key element in a shipshape setting.*

10 Cleveland, OH 44114

11 ***Convention & Visitors Bureau, 1301 E. 6th St. (216) 621-4110.*** The observation deck in the Terminal Tower gives the best bird's-eye introduction to the city. You can get a more intimate look on a trolley tour; and to see where some of America's great fortunes were founded, take a boat trip down the Cuyahoga River near the steel mills. You can also view the Flats entertainment district, with its waterfront restaurants and boutiques, or stroll through one of Cleveland's many parks and visit the renowned zoo.

The cultural attractions include the Cleveland Museum of Art, the Western Reserve Historical Society, and the Cleveland Museum of Natural History, where dinosaurs, fossils, and many artifacts are on display. An exhibit at the Health Education Museum depicts the workings of the human body.

Not to be missed is the downtown Arcade, where shops and restaurants are housed in a marvelous five-level skylit cast-iron fantasy—one of the largest such structures in the world.

11 12 Hale Farm and Village, Bath

Exit 11: 11 mi./16 min. South on Cleveland-Massillon Rd. (Rte. 21), left on Ira Rd., left on Oak Hill Rd.; follow signs. Exit 12: 15 mi./20 min. South on Rte. 8, right on Rte. 303, left on Riverview Rd., right on Ira Rd.; follow signs. Rural life in the mid-19th century is re-created in this engaging cluster of buildings in what was then the Western Reserve—the land "reserved" for settlers from Connecticut. Many of the buildings were moved to the site from other areas of Ohio. The federal-style farmhouse of Jonathan Hale is surprisingly elegant for an owner who had to hew his farm out of a wilderness. The village comprises a saltbox house, a meetinghouse, a log schoolhouse, a law office, a smithy, and a barn. Demonstrations of spinning and weaving, glassblowing, and smithing evoke life in earlier times. The farm and village are in the 32,000-acre Cuyahoga Valley National Recreation Area. *Open Tues.–Sat. and P.M. Sun. and holidays, mid-May–Oct. and Dec. Admission charged.*

11 12 Stan Hywet Hall and Gardens, Akron

Exit 11: 12 mi./20 min. South on Rte. 21; continue on I-77 to Ghent Rd. exit, east on Ghent Rd.; follow signs. Exit 12: 17 mi./25 min. South on Rte. 8, right on Talmadge Ave., right on Portage Path. This mansion is the largest private home in Ohio, a 65-room Tudor revival structure built in 1912–15 by Frank Seiberling, cofounder of the Goodyear Tire and Rubber Company. The flagstone corridors were artificially worn down to create an impression of age, and there are fan-vaulted ceilings, tapestries, linenfold paneling, and genuine Elizabethan furniture. In some of the rooms there are splendid Chinese wall hangings, Persian rugs, and 2,000-year-

old amphorae, while other rooms, like the Great Hall, with its 1-ton chandelier and polar bear rug, suggest a medieval barony. Surpassing authentic Elizabethan mansions, Stan Hywet (from the Anglo-Saxon word for "stone quarry") boasts a 40-foot indoor swimming pool. This vision of opulence is surrounded by gardens with shady walks, velvet lawns, and magnificent flower beds. *Open Tues.–Sat. and P.M. Sun. Admission charged.*

14 Nelson and Kennedy Ledges State Park

16 mi./19 min. Southwest on Rte. 5, right on Rte. 534, left on Rte. 422, left on Rte. 282. In this odd landscape a wooded hillside is crisscrossed by numerous small "canyons" from 10 to 30 feet wide. Trails follow the canyon rims or descend to their floors through crevices and between boulders; a woodland creek tumbles into a deep sinkhole with fern-covered walls. This strange setting seems to belong in an enchanted land. *Open year-round.*

I-76 Mill Creek Recreation Area

15 mi./20 min. West on I-76, left on Rte. 534, right on Rte. 224. This wide 2-mile peninsula jutting into Berlin Lake, a tremendous (3,600-acre) man-made body of water, contains nu-

merous campsites in wooded, grassland, and shoreline areas, as well as picnic spots and boat launch ramps. Created by a dam in a natural river, the lake has developed large fish populations, especially walleye and bass, and is popular with anglers. Water-skiing is also widely enjoyed, but boaters are advised to watch for shallow depths and underwater obstructions. Mill Creek also offers playgrounds, a nature trail, and all facilities, including 47 electricity hookups. *Open mid-May–Sept.*

I-79 McConnells Mill State Park

20 mi./30 min. South on I-79 to Exit 29, west on Rte. 422; follow signs. The handsome board-and-batten gristmill on a foundation of stone was built in 1868 and declared a national landmark in 1974. The full complement of milling machinery in it illustrates the life-giving process of turning grain into flour. One millstone has been restored for grinding. Just downstream from the mill is a covered bridge and the beginning of the Kildoo Trail, a 2-mile hike through a wooded ravine along Slippery Rock Creek. The trail is slippery (and steep) in places; wear appropriate footwear. *Park open year-round; mill open Thurs.–Mon. Memorial Day–Labor Day.*

I-79. *Note the burgeoning fall color, and how the man-made dams complement the rock forms.*

3 | Antique Music Museum

13 mi./15 min. North on Rte. 8. In this Pennsylvania building the sound of music—as it used to be—can be heard in remarkable variety. The nickelodeons (which play as many as 13 instruments), band organs used in skating rinks and merry-go-rounds, circus calliopes, and orchestrions are all marvels of mechanical ingenuity and eye-catching design. The monkey organs, music boxes, phonographs, and other melody makers in the collection are less grand in size but no less wondrous and nostalgic. The instruments are all in working order, and many are demonstrated for visitors. In addition to the musical wonders, there are signs, posters, advertisements, and scores of other antiques on display. *Open mid-Apr.–Nov. Admission charged.*

13 | Clear Creek State Park

11.5 mi./15 min. North on Rte. 36, right on Rte. 949. Masses of showy rhododendrons, flowering in late June and early July, attract travelers to this lovely woodland park with its rustic bridges, calm lake, and large old trees. Campsites for tents and trailers are prettily situated on the creek or scattered through the woods. Canoeing on the Clarion River is a soothing way to relax, as is fishing for bass and trout. Several trails lead through the park. *Open year-round.*

23 | Bald Eagle State Park

9 mi./15 min. North on Rte. 150. Named not for the bird but for an Indian chief, this verdant 6,000-acre park is best known for boating and fishing on Foster Joseph Sayres Dam, which covers more than 600 acres here. The dam, with a pleasant stretch of sandy beach, is nestled in the valley; the impressive Bald Eagle Mountains are to the south. Fishing equipment and boats, including sailboats and canoes, are available for rent at the marina. Some 200 picnic tables, set in a parklike meadowland with stands of shade trees, are conveniently near the playing fields. *Park open year-round; beach open Memorial Day–Labor Day.*

30 | Little League Baseball Museum, South Williamsport

16 mi./20 min. North on Rte. 15. This museum is a fascinating destination for young baseball players and fans. A series of well-organized displays illustrates the development of the Little League, shows how equipment is made, and promotes safety. There's a computerized quiz program on rules and regulations. In the Play Ball Lab, kids can pitch, bat, and check out their form on video playback. Major Leaguers' tips on how to play better are displayed, and a 30-minute documentary about Little League baseball is shown in a 100-seat theater. *Open daily except Easter, Thanksgiving Day, Christmas, and New Year's Day. Admission charged.*

34 | Bloomsburg National Historic District

5 min. South on Rte. 42, left on Rte. 11. Gracious homes and buildings in the center of this town provide a short course in the architectural history of the 19th century. An introductory tour of the district could begin with Columbia County Courthouse at Market and Second streets. This imposing building, with its high clock tower, was originally designed in the Greek revival style but in the 1890's was completed as Romanesque revival. Proceeding east and west on Second Street and then south on Market Street, you'll see some interesting examples of the Greek, colonial, and Georgian revival styles, among others. *Buildings open year-round.*

39 | Eckley Miners' Village
40 |

Exit 39: 10 mi./15 min. South on Rte. 309, left on Freeland-Drums Hwy. to Freeland, east on Rte. 940; follow signs. Exit 40: 9 mi./20 min. West on Rte. 940; follow signs. Eckley is a living-history museum and hopes to maintain this status. Established in 1854 as a planned company "patch," it became home to generations of immigrant coal miners and their families. Early-Victorian cottages, churches, mine buildings, and the company store stand today much as they were when shovels dug into the hillside and daily life was regulated by the steam whistle. More

39–40. Stairs, porch, and sloping cellar door add a homey touch to this house of God.

than 50 people remain, and the 58 buildings on this 100-acre site reveal the disciplined quality of life in a company town. The preserved cottages and a museum in the visitor center have informative displays that tell the story of the mine patches that are found throughout this region of northeastern Pennsylvania, noted for its anthracite coal. *Visitor center open daily May–Sept., daily except holidays Oct.–Apr.; village buildings open Memorial Day–Labor Day and weekends Sept.–Oct. Admission charged.*

48 | Quiet Valley Living Historical Farm

4 mi./7 min. South on Rte. 209, left on Hickory Valley Rd., right on Turkey Hill Rd., left on Quiet Valley Rd. Six generations of the Zepper family worked this farm from 1765 until 1913, and fortunately many of the tools and much of the equipment and furnishings have survived intact. As the farm activities are demonstrated by costumed guides, one can only marvel at the self-sufficiency that was attained by early-day farm families. Carding, spinning, weaving, and meat smoking are among the many household chores enacted, and in the mid-19th-century barn are some of the early machines designed to lighten the farmer's load. Everyone worked—including the family dog, which powered the treadmill to run the churn and washing machine. Children will enjoy the hay jumps in the barn and the animals that can be petted. *Open daily late June–Labor Day. Admission charged.*

25   Village of Waterloo

5 min. North on access road; follow signs. This charming village in a tranquil setting of lawns and shade trees was restored to its 18th- and 19th-century character in 1964. Here you'll find some splendid homes, many open to the public and a few privately owned, along with a working gristmill, a general store and tavern, and a blacksmith's shop.

The Ironmaster's House and the Stagecoach Inn date from the 1760's, when there was a forge. After the Morris Canal was opened in 1831, Waterloo became a major stop; the canal museum contains memorabilia of that era. In the homes and barns, such traditional crafts as candle dipping, broom making, and wheel-thrown pottery are demonstrated. *Open Tues.–Sun. Apr.–Dec. except Thanksgiving Day, Christmas, and New Year's Day. Also open holiday Mondays and closed the following Tuesday. Admission charged.*

43   Jockey Hollow Encampment Area, Morristown

15 mi./20 min. South on I-287 to Exit 26B, north on Rte. 202, left on Tempe Wick Rd.; follow signs. In these pleasant surroundings it requires an act of will to envision the hardship experienced here by some 13,000 soldiers of George Washington's Continental Army in the winter of 1779–80. It was the worst winter of the century. Six-foot snowdrifts blocked supply routes, and the troops had insufficient clothing—many had to wrap themselves in blankets. Illness and frostbite were rampant. General Washington besought the Continental Congress to provide funds for food and supplies—to no avail. Only a mutiny in 1781 forced the lawmakers to fulfill their obligation to the fighting men.

The farmhouse that served as headquarters for Gen. Arthur St. Clair is the main attraction. Much of the red clapboard structure is original, and some of the furnishings are of the period. You can tour the rest of Jockey Hollow on the park roads or on footpaths through the woods. *Open daily except Thanksgiving Day, Christmas, and New Year's Day.*

57   Lambert Castle Museum, Paterson
56

Exit 57 (headed east): 1 min. South on Rte. 20, right on Valley Rd. Exit 56 (headed west): 2 min. Make U-turn on ramps, east on I-80 to Exit 57; proceed as above. On the slope of Garret Mountain, with a panoramic view of the plain below and the Manhattan skyline in the distance, this brown and pink sandstone "castle," complete with crenellated towers, fully justifies its name—Belle Vista. Built by Paterson silk magnate Catholina Lambert in 1892, it now houses a museum run by the Passaic County Historical Society. The magnificent ceilings, inlaid floors, and intricately carved marble and wood fireplaces are beautifully preserved. In the ballroom gallery the museum presents collections that include paintings, furniture, textiles, and decorative art. Very impressive is the Koempel collection of souvenir spoons. About 1,000 of the 5,000-spoon collection are on display, including ones with enameled landscapes, cloisonné spoons from czarist Russia, and mother-of-pearl examples from China. *Open P.M. Wed.–Sun. except holidays. Admission charged.*

I-95   New York, NY 10019

11 mi./20 min. Convention and Visitors Bureau, 2 Columbus Circle. (212) 397-8222. This city's crowded diversity can be overwhelming, but even a short visit will be rewarding if you decide in advance what you want to see.

You might choose the spectacular views from the World Trade Center or Empire State Building; stroll on Fifth Avenue past Rockefeller Center, St. Patrick's Cathedral, and the intriguing shop windows. Central Park might beckon, or Chinatown, Greenwich Village, or the South Street Seaport. For museumgoers the choices are a challenge: will it be the Metropolitan, Guggenheim, Frick, or Whitney (all within walking distance of one another)? And there's also the American Museum of Natural History and the New-York Historical Society to consider. Other temptations are a boat ride in the harbor or to the Statue of Liberty or around the island of Manhattan. Be forewarned, however: the city is a difficult—and expensive—place to park a car.

I-95. *A necklace of beckoning lights on the Brooklyn Bridge leads to the captivating isle of Manhattan, where the skyline is dominated by the twin towers of the World Trade Center.*

17 Castle Rock Campground

5 min. Southeast on access road. Some 15 million years ago, volcanic ash, wind-borne from the nearby Tushar Mountains, settled here and formed rock. Slowly, the rock was carved by the elements into the buttes, pinnacles, and other formations for which the campground is named. A stream whose banks are lined with picturesque cottonwoods flows through the center of the campground. Other campsites are situated among the piñon pines and junipers on higher ground. The campground also serves as a trailhead for hikers bound for the rocky heights of the Tushar Mountains. *Open year-round.*

17 Fremont Indian State Park

5 min. North on access road, right on Park Rd. Mule deer, kit foxes, coyotes, and marmots now roam the red rocks and sage wilderness of Clear Creek Canyon, where Indians of the Fremont culture lived from A.D. 500 to 1400. The visitor center contains interpretive exhibits and some of the rich lode of Indian artifacts unearthed here, but the real adventure lies in exploring the canyon. You'll see petroglyphs along the quarter-mile Art Rock Trail, while the more rugged Discovery and Overlook

17. Indian farmers of the Fremont culture built pit houses like this reconstruction.

trails provide fascinating insights into the Fremonts' use of natural resources. A concessionaire offers horse-and-wagon and horseback-riding trips into the backcountry, and evening activities include cookouts. The creek's sparkling waters are favored by fishermen. *Open year-round. Admission charged.*

22 Big Rock Candy Mountain

7 mi./10 min. South on Rte. 89. This vivid yellow rock formation could well be the inspiration for the hobo song of the same name recorded by Burl Ives, about a fantasyland where "the bulldogs all have rubber teeth, and the hens lay hard-boiled eggs." Although you won't find the "lemonade springs where the whippoorwill sings," you can take the short trail from the mountain's base and get a close view of the interesting geologic confection of weathered volcanic rock tinted by minerals and hot springs. *Open year-round.*

24 Monrovian Park

10 mi./20 min. East on Rte. 118, right on Main St., left on Forest Rd.; follow signs. It comes as a pleasant surprise when the dark and narrow confines of Monroe Canyon suddenly widen, revealing the lush picnic area and a scattering of scrub oaks, narrowleaf cottonwoods, and vine maples. Wildflowers bloom in the shade of great cliff walls, and melodic birdsong mingles with the sound of water flowing over volcanic rocks. Anglers fish Monroe Creek in this delightful hidden park, which also serves as a trailhead for routes leading into Fishlake National Forest. *Open year-round but may be inaccessible due to snow and ice.*

54 Palisade State Park

23 mi./30 min. North on Rte. 89, right on Palisade Park Rd. When Daniel B. Funk settled in central Utah in the mid-1800's, he

---

If You Have Some Extra Time: Arches National Park

180 *27 mi./40 min.* The greatest works of mankind are reduced to insignificance by the arches, spires, columns, fins, cliffs, and buttes that nature created here through erosion on ancient sandstone. This park, which covers nearly 75,000 acres, is named for some 600 natural arches that can be seen in various stages of their timeless development—a process explained in detail near the visitor center. The most dramatic examples are Landscape Arch, believed to be the longest natural arch in the world, and Delicate Arch, a structure of surpassing grace poised at the edge of a great natural amphitheater in a setting of bare red sandstone. The air is marvelously clear, and there are spectacular views across the Colorado River gorge to the snow-capped La Sal Mountains on the horizon.

The relatively few trees that do well here, such as piñon pine and juniper, are those that have become efficient at taking up any available water and releasing it slowly. The desert is dotted with blackbrush, a plant that has both small leathery leaves and sharp spines on its branches. The wildflowers that brighten the landscape—evening primroses and the scarlet monkey flower—have short life cycles. Other wildflowers such as columbines and orchids as well as ferns, cattails, marsh grasses, tree frogs, and toads are found in the few places where water collects. Most of the animals, such as foxes, bobcats, and ringtails, come out primarily at night. During the day you may see jewellike hummingbirds as well as rabbits and scurrying chipmunks. Look also for eagles and hawks, who prey on the small animals.

Time spent among the sculptural forms of colorful sandstone in this unique landscape is not likely to be forgotten. *How to get there: south on Rte. 191; follow signs. Admission charged.*

found so few recreational facilities that he vowed to create a leisure-time area for everyone to enjoy. Mostly through his own efforts, he created a lake, built a dance hall, and planted shade and fruit trees; and in the mid-1870's Palisade State Park was opened.

The site Funk chose for the lake belonged to the Sanpitch Indians. Hoping to avoid trouble, he appealed to Brigham Young, the territorial governor, who helped him get a deed to the property. Today the park is popular for swimming, boating (canoes can be rented), fishing in the trout-stocked waters, and golfing. The annual Winterfest offers skating on the lower pond, sledding, cross-country skiing, and ice fishing. *Open year-round. Admission charged.*

129 / 147   San Rafael Reef

Headed east: drive past Exit 129 (Ranch exit) 10 mi. to roadside overlook. Headed west: drive past Exit 147 (Rte. 24 exit) 3 mi. to roadside overlook. Where the interstate penetrates the San Rafael Swell through Spotted Wolf Canyon, the scenery on both sides of this road is awesome. The San Rafael Reef is a sawtooth ridge along the eastern edge of the swell, a remnant of a 2,000-square-mile rock dome that bulged forth from the earth's surface 50 to 60 million years ago. The action of the elements over eons has eroded the sedimentary rock into a vast sea of frozen turbulence. The view area reveals spectacular panoramas of Mesozoic-era formations—towering pinnacles, winding canyons, and castlelike mesas. *Open year-round.*

160 / 165   Green River State Park

Exit 160: 5 min. East on Main St., right on River Blvd. Exit 165: 5 min. West on Main St., left on River Blvd. Located on the banks of the Green River and within the town of the same name, this campground and day-use area, nicely shaded by cottonwoods, is a pleasant oasis for a picnic or as a base for exploring the surrounding territory. The boat launch is a popular access point to the Green River, with its white-water rapids, serene stretches, and spectacular canyons.

Rock collectors will find jasper, agate, and petrified wood, and bird-watchers may spot an egret, a heron, or an ibis. *Open year-round. Admission charged.*

185   Sego Canyon Indian Rock Art

3 mi./30 min. North on Rte. 94 to a dry-wash crossing; walk 75 yd. to cliffs. The Archaic people, and later the Fremont people and the Ute Indians, who over the centuries have inhabited much of what is now Utah, were all hunters, farmers, and artists. Their enduring artistic creations, incised petroglyphs and painted pictographs, can be seen on the sandstone canyon walls. Some of the images represent desert bighorns and other indigenous wildlife, while the abstract shapes defy definition but stimulate the imagination. Unfortunately, some of the art has been marred by vandals who deface what they cannot comprehend, but the graffiti have not detracted from the significance of the site. *Open year-round but road may be flooded during rain.*

19   Colorado National Monument

4 min. South on Rte. 340. Stone monoliths rise from sheer-walled canyons 1,000 feet deep, while junipers and piñon pines cover lesser inclines in this 20,400-acre park. Rim Rock Drive twists through 23 miles of spectacular natural sculptures created by wind and water. Grand View, Redlands, and Cold Shivers Point are some of the aptly named scenic turnouts along the way. For hikers, easy trails along the rim afford many fine views, while longer trails with numerous switchbacks descend the canyon walls and link up with trails at the bottom. Bring water with you on all but the shortest trails. Indigenous animals include bighorn sheep, mountain lions, elk, and mule deer. *Open year-round. Admission charged.*

31   Museum of Western Colorado, Grand Junction

4 mi./12 min. Southwest on Horizon Dr., left on 12th St., right on Ute Ave. Mineral samples, Indian artifacts, and early settlers' tools displayed in this remodeled school building

19. *Juniper foliage and berries contrast beautifully with the sandstone monoliths.*

are among the items that illuminate the social and natural history of the region. Two blocks away, at the Dinosaur Valley branch of the museum, the exhibits focus on a much earlier time; there are fossils, a dinosaur skeleton, half-size animated models of dinosaurs, and photographs of historic paleontological digs in the area. In addition, the museum also operates the Cross Orchards Living History Farm, where costumed guides explain the development of fruit growing in the area. Directions to and hours of the dinosaur exhibit and the farm are available at the main museum. *Museum open Tues.–Sat. except holidays; Dinosaur Valley open daily Memorial Day–Sept., Tues.–Sun. Nov.–Memorial Day; farm open Wed.–Sat. mid-May–Oct. Admission charged for dinosaur exhibit and farm.*

70

43   47

26   90

60   116

176

27   203

2   205

23   228

16   244

47 Island Acres State Recreation Area

2 min. Follow signs. Picnicking on the lush lawn, camping, and winter eagle-watching are popular here, where the Colorado River is surrounded by the towering shale and sandstone walls of De Beque Canyon. A band of well-watered shoreline vegetation contrasts sharply with the bare rock above, and the riverside plants support a wide variety of wildlife, including two bison in a fenced pasture. Four ponds, one for swimming and three for fishing and nonmotorized boats, have recently been added. Skunks are frequently encountered, and visitors should admire them from a respectful distance. *Open year-round. Admission charged.*

90 Rifle Gap and Rifle Falls State Recreation Areas

14 mi./20 min. North on Rte. 13, right on Rte. 325; follow signs. This reservoir in western Colorado provides much-needed water for the surrounding country and also offers excellent boating, swimming (scuba diving is especially fine in the crystal-clear waters), and fishing. The shaded banks of East Rifle Creek support stands of cottonwoods and small growths of ferns and mosses. At Rifle Falls, 5 miles up Route 325, the creek drops over a wide natural cliff of travertine deposits that may have formed when a beaver dam slowed the creek enough for limestone deposits to create the outcrop and plateau. Rifle Box Canyon, located a mile from the falls, has steep, high walls overhung by limestone ledges. The nearby limestone caves are safe and easy to explore with the aid of a flashlight. *Open year-round. Admission charged.*

116 Hot Springs Pool

1 min. East from exit. This spa, surrounded by mountains, has one of the world's largest outdoor pools filled by mineral hot springs. The 400-foot-long outdoor pool, which can be visited even when there's snow on the mountain, is kept at a comfortable 90° F all year; temperatures in a smaller therapy pool climb to 104° F. Flowing at a rate of 2,500 gallons per minute, the springs completely replenish the pools every 8 hours. Called Yampa ("Big Medicine") Springs by the Ute Indians, the heated waters are still reputed to be therapeutic. *Open year-round except 2nd Wed. Sept.– May. Admission charged.*

203–205. The waning light at dusk brings a subtle blend of colors to the reservoir.

176 Colorado Ski Museum and Ski Hall of Fame, Vail

1 min. East on S. Frontage Rd. From "snowshoes" used more than 6,000 years ago for hunting and transportation to the sophisticated sports of today, the history of skiing is presented at the Colorado Ski Museum with films, videos, and displays. There are photographs of mailmen making their appointed rounds on long boards in the 1800's, Coloradoans' first ski races, and soldiers of the 10th Mountain Division with skis at the ready. The Hall of Fame displays photos of people who advanced the sport of skiing in the state. The museum is in a pedestrian mall. To reach it, park at the parking structure on the right, take the inner village bus, or walk two blocks west on East Meadow Drive. *Open P.M. Tues.–Sun. June–mid-Oct. and late Nov.–mid-Apr. except Christmas and New Year's Day.*

203 205 Scenic Overlook of Dillon Reservoir

Exit 203: 1 min. East from exit. Exit 205: 1 min. West from exit. From this heavily wooded site there is a magnificent alpine view of 3,300-acre Dillon Reservoir, with Grays and Torreys peaks towering in the distance. The water, stored here for the city of Denver, flows through a 23-mile tunnel bored through hard rock beneath the Continental Divide. The reservoir and its 25-mile shoreline and wooded areas provide inviting opportunities for fishing, boating, and water-skiing in summer and cross-country skiing and dogsledding in winter. *Open year-round.*

228 Georgetown–Silver Plume Historic Landmark District

3 min. South on Argentine St. More than 200 original buildings, many restored to their Victorian elegance, confirm picturesque Georgetown's early days as a booming mid-1800's Colorado silver-mining camp. Hamill House Museum, a silver baron's home, displays such luxuries as gaslight, a bathtub, and an outhouse topped with a cupola.

The Georgetown Loop Railroad was built in 1884 on narrow-gauge tracks, which enabled the steam train to maneuver the curves and trestles as it climbed the 700-foot grade from Georgetown to the Silver Plume mines. The train now carries passengers over this breathtaking reconstructed route. *Buildings open year-round; railroad operates daily Memorial Day–Labor Day, weekends only Labor Day–early Oct. Admission charged for train ride and mine tour.*

244 Central City Blackhawk National Historic District

12 mi./30 min. East on Rte. 6, left on Rte. 119. The diamond-dust-backed mirrors of the Teller House Hotel, now a museum, symbolize the luxury of what in its 1870's heyday was Colorado's largest and most famous mining boomtown. The Central City Gold Mine and Museum (in an aboveground building) shows the tools and explains the backbreaking labor that supported the splendor. There is still some gold in the piles of mine waste rock that line Gregory Gulch, and gold seekers still pan

See N–S book,
sec. 11.
🛣25

CO ┊ KS

8   32   36   61   96   59
[252]   [I-25]   [310]   [371]   [17]   🛣70

Clear Creek, seeking the glint that dominated early Colorado history. A pleasant half-mile ride on the old Colorado & Southern Railroad affords a view of Central City from the mountains. *Central City Gold Mine and Museum open daily June–Aug.; Teller House open daily June–Sept., weekends only Oct.–May. Admission charged.*   🍴 ⛺ 🚐 🧍 ♿

252 | Hiwan Homestead Museum, Evergreen

8 mi./15 min. West on Rte. 74, left on Douglas Park Rd., left on Meadow Dr. Begun as a summer retreat in the 1880's, this 17-room log structure evolved into a comfortable year-round house with twin octagonal towers and its own chapel. The last owners, who raised prize Herefords, gave it the name Hiwan, an Anglo-Saxon word meaning "a high, secluded place with enough for one ox to plow." Many rooms are restored to their 1915–30 style with a western motif. Displays involving local history and an extensive doll collection add to the charm of the house. The building is listed in *The National Register of Historic Places. Open P.M. Tues.–Sun. except holidays.*

I-25 | Denver, CO 80202

Convention & Visitors Bureau, 225 W. Colfax Ave. (303) 892-1112. There is a wealth of museums, parks, and shopping areas in the Mile-High City. The Denver Art Museum, covered with a million reflecting tiles, houses a superb American Indian collection, with many Mesoamerican pieces. Nearby is the U.S. Mint, where you can watch money being stamped. Among the old mansions on Capitol Hill is the popular Molly Brown House, former home of the "unsinkable" heroine of the *Titanic.* The flavor of Denver's past is preserved in Larimer Square, with its restored shops, arcades, and gaslights. The Denver Museum of Natural History has a state-of-the-art planetarium, and the Denver Zoo displays the animals in natural-habitat settings.

310 | Comanche Crossing Historical Society Museum, Strasburg

1 min. North on Strasburg Mile Dr., left on Rte. 36. Locals claim that it was here, a year after the driving of the golden spike at Promontory Point in northern Utah, that the first

U.S. transcontinental railroad was really completed. Many of the museum's displays focus on rooms from homes and businesses of the late 19th and early 20th centuries. Details catch the eye: the barbershop's handsome assortment of razors, the beauty parlor's electric curling machine, the post office's boxes, and an organ and wicker furniture in the parlor. An annex houses farm vehicles and fire trucks. Also part of the museum complex are a homesteader's cottage, two one-room schoolhouses, and a railroad depot with the stationmaster's living quarters. All are furnished in period style. *Open P.M. daily June–Aug.*   🍴

371 | Genoa Tower, Genoa

2 min. North on Rte. 109, left on Frontage Rd. This sprawling 20-room complex topped by a brightly painted tower was begun by C. W. Gregory, known as Colorado's P. T. Barnum. There's a touch of the circus carnival to it, with two-headed calves, an eight-legged pig, and a 75,000-year-old skeleton of a mammoth among its attractions. Other exhibits are an extraordinary hodgepodge of old bottles, bullets, Bibles, fiddles, and such. Many rooms are built of rocks with bottles embedded in the ceilings. A steep flight leads to the tower's deck, where you can see parts of six states. *Open year-round. Admission charged.*   🍴

17 | High Plains Museum, Goodland

2 min. North on Rte. 27, right on 16th St., right on Cherry St. This museum's pride and joy is a full-scale replica of what is claimed to be America's first patented helicopter—the circa 1910 Purvis-Wilson Flying Machine, the work of two Rock Island, Illinois, machinists. Press a button, and the blades will rotate. Another exhibit concentrates on the prairie rainmakers—companies such as the Interstate Artificial Rain Co. and solo operator Frank Melbourne ("The Rain Wizard"). Dioramas and displays, including musical instruments and a 1902 Holsman automobile, also capture the flavor of the region's past. *Open daily Memorial Day–Labor Day; Tues.–Sun. Labor Day–Memorial Day. Admission free but donations encouraged.*   🍴 ♿

228. *For this steep, twisting route the track is narrow-gauge and the engine powerful.*

70   Fick Fossil and History Museum, Oakley

5 mi./10 min. South on Rte. 83, left on 2nd St., left on Center St., left on 3rd St. It is not easy to visualize the dry Kansas plains as a watery realm of sharks, oysters, and prehistoric fish, but the evidence is here. The fossils, impressively displayed, were gathered locally by Mr. and Mrs. Earnest Fick and by Charles and George Sternberg. The sharks' teeth, some 11,000 in all, were arranged by Mrs. Fick in a remarkable variety of patterns and designs. The later history of the area is represented by historical exhibits, including a replica of a sod house, a railroad depot, a general store, an old horse-drawn farm wagon, a century-old Chandler Price printing press, and various local artifacts. *Open daily except Christmas and New Year's Day.*

135   Cedar Bluff State Park

13 mi./15 min. South on Rte. 147. This park is divided into two parts, one on the north and the other on the south shore of man-made Cedar Bluff Lake. In the northern area—the smaller of the two—there are inviting places to swim or picnic along the lakefront, where pink-blossomed tamarisks and cottonwoods grow at the water's edge. South of the dam the terrain changes dramatically to a desertlike environment with yucca and prickly poppy amid limestone bluffs. Park facilities include a marina and boat ramps. The quality of fishing depends largely on the water level. White bass, walleye, crappie, and catfish are most plentiful; bluegills, rainbow trout, and small-mouth, largemouth, and spotted bass are sparser. *Open daily mid-Apr.–mid-Oct. Admission charged.*

157   Fort Hays Frontier Historical Park

4 min. South on Rte. 183. Ft. Hays was built on the Smoky Hill stagecoach route in 1867 to protect settlers and railroad workers from Indian attack. As the white population in the area grew, the Plains Indians were forced to migrate, and in 1889 the fort was abandoned. Only 3 buildings of the original 45 still stand: the stone blockhouse, which doubled as a defensive outpost and camp headquarters; a guardhouse where prisoners were confined and guards quartered; and one officer's house. Exhibits include period furnishings, Indian and railroad memorabilia, frontier artillery, and a library with antique jigsaw puzzles. Mannequins add a sense of reality: a cell in the guardhouse holds one mournful-looking mannequin in period underwear while nearby hangs a 20-pound ball and chain. The visitor center displays models of the fort in its prime. *Open year-round.*

168   Cathedral of the Plains, Victoria

3 min. South on Rte. 255. The twin 141-foot rock spires of this beautifully crafted Roman Catholic church soar above the plains of Kansas. Officially named St. Fidelis Church but rechristened by William Jennings Bryan, this 220-foot-long, 110-foot-wide cruciform structure was built in 1911 of native Kansas stone, hand-quarried and carted in 50- to 100-pound slabs by devout Volga German parishioners. The Romanesque interior features an altarpiece portraying the martyrdom of St. Fidelis, stained glass windows, wood carvings depicting the stations of the cross, and 14 granite pillars topped by hand-carved capitals of Bedford limestone. A reproduction of the original dedication booklet includes such injunctions as "The bells are rung to get the people into the church on time, not to make work for the sacristan." *Open year-round.*

206   Wilson State Park

7 mi./11 min. North on Rte. 232. Hidden coves and inlets and miniature cliffs along the water's edge are among the enticements of this delightful park on Wilson Lake, where the water has exposed the sandstone underlying the surrounding prairie. The 927-acre park boasts a surprising variety of landscapes, with shiny-leaved cottonwoods along the shore giving way to prairie grass and wildflowers on the upland stretches. There are charming places for picnicking, and each of the six campgrounds has its own distinctive character. *Open year-round. Admission charged.*

206   Garden of Eden, Lucas

17 mi./22 min. North on Rte. 232, right on Rte. 18; follow signs. A monument to vigorous individuality if not outright eccentricity, this house and garden were created by a Civil War veteran named S.P. Dinsmoor. Among its attractions are what could be the only "log" cabin (circa 1907) built entirely of limestone; a sculpture garden whose various all-concrete pieces are a wondrous mix of biblical, socialist, and personal imagery; and a 40-foot-high mausoleum in which Dinsmoor's body lies, guarded by rather alarming concrete angels. Visitors to the house will see such curios as a weeping willow rocker, a handmade checkerboard table, and a painting of the horse upon which he and his first wife were married. Widowed, he was remarried at the age of 81 to his 20-year-old housekeeper. *Open year-round. Admission charged.*

225   Mushroom Rock State Park

238

Exit 225: 15 mi./24 min. South on Rte. 156, left on Rte. 111, left on Rte. 140, right on Rte. 141, right at sign. Exit 238: 18 mi./23 min. South toward Brookville, right on Rte. 140, left on Rte. 141, right at sign. This 5½-acre park is worth a stop just to marvel at the fascinating and awesome power of nature.

225–238. *It rather boggles the mind, but this is indeed nature's own creation.*

The curious rock formations are the remains of sandstone outcroppings worn away by the persistent winds sweeping across the prairie. The mushroom shapes were developed as soft lower layers eroded more quickly than harder ones above them. Some rocks are 25 feet tall, with caps 15 feet wide. Another interesting oddity is a 15-stripe American flag carved in rock, probably by westbound pioneers. *Open year-round.*

260   Indian Burial Pit

6 mi./9 min. South on Niles Rd., right on Rte. 140; follow signs. An unexpected benefit of the farmland erosion in the dust bowl years of the 1930's was the exposure of this resting place for prehistoric Indians. The 146 skeletal remains of men, women, and children lie as they were found, in layers, many with knees drawn up almost to their chests. Most are on their right sides and face east, probably oriented toward the rising sun. Such artifacts as flint knives, arrowheads, clamshell necklaces, and pendants abound at the site. Particularly poignant are the earrings and necklace placed near the remains of a small child. *Open year-round. Admission charged.*

275   Dwight D. Eisenhower Library, Abilene

2 mi./6 min. South on Rte. 15. Centered around the simple clapboard house that was his boyhood home, this museum-library complex celebrates the achievements of Dwight D. Eisenhower as supreme allied commander in Europe during World War II and as 34th president in the 1950's. The library houses papers, books, and other materials related to his career. In the museum guns, uniforms, and other military memorabilia trace Ike's rise from cadet to five-star general. Cartoons, posters, and buttons bring to life his presidential campaigns, and historic documents illuminate the White House years. Murals in the museum's lobby depict events in his life. The president, first lady, and a son are buried beneath plain marble slabs in the chapellike Place of Meditation. *Open daily except Thanksgiving Day, Christmas, and New Year's Day. Admission charged for museum.*

275. *Behind the severe facade is the human story of a president and great general.*

301   Fort Riley

3 min. North on Holbrook Ave.; follow signs. The U.S. cavalry played a key role in winning the West, and some of the buildings in this fort memorialize that achievement. At the museum in the former headquarters building, the story of these mounted troops is illustrated by uniforms, weapons, statues, and paintings (including originals by Frederic Remington). Nearby Custer House, named in honor of Gen. George Armstrong Custer, who lived at the fort, is fully furnished in 1880's style. You can take a self-guiding walking tour of the fort, which is the size of a small town and has many handsome structures built of native limestone. *Open daily except Easter, Thanksgiving Day, Christmas, and New Year's Day.*

362B   Topeka, KS 66603

Chamber of Commerce, 120 East 6th St. (913) 234-2644. Topeka's 160-acre Gage Park is the home of one of the world's finest zoos, which includes an exhibit of apes and a reconstructed Amazon rain forest complete with exotic vegetation, waterfalls, and free-flying birds. A swimming pool, picnic areas, and a botanical garden add to the attractive amenities of this city park. Topeka's impressive statehouse, in the French Renaissance revival style, is famous for its murals by John Steuart Curry; and the Kansas Museum of History features many period rooms and exhibits, including a 1912 airplane made in Topeka. Other points of interest are the Ward-Meade Historical Park and Botanical Gardens and Lake Shawnee.

202   Clinton State Park

7 mi./12 min. South on Rte. 59, right on Rte. 40, left on Rte. 13. Clinton Lake, an impressive body of water stretching for some 8 miles up the Wakarusa Valley, was built to control flooding and supply water to nearby Lawrence. It also offers many recreational possibilities, and this state park on its north shore takes full advantage of the site, with facilities for camping, boating, and swimming. Five other parks, run by the U.S. Army Corps of Engineers, also provide access to the lake. On the lake's east side a drive across the top of the embankment of the imposing 940-foot-long Clinton Dam affords fine views of the lake. *Open year-round. Admission charged.*

203   Perry State Park

21 mi./25 min. North on Rte. 59, left on Rte. 24, right on Rte. 237. Lovers of wide-open spaces will enjoy this pleasant park on the shore of Perry Lake. Formed in 1969 when the U.S. Army Corps of Engineers dammed the Delaware River as part of a flood control project, the lake has 160 miles of shoreline. A broad, sandy swimming beach backed by a meadow, lakeside camping and picnic facilities, and two boat ramps are the major attractions. Fishermen try for crappie, catfish, and bass. A public-use marina is located next to the park's Delaware Area. *Open year-round. Admission charged.*

203. *Catamarans are a popular mode of transportation on man-made Perry Lake.*

KS | MO 29 35 See N–S book, sec. 15 for I-29; sec. 18 for I-35.

70   17   224   11   2C 2D   8   NOL   20   78   98   50   148   22

224 Agricultural Hall of Fame and National Center

4 min. North on Rte. 7; follow signs. An important aspect of Americana is recalled here in this major national institution dedicated to American farmers. In the Hall of Rural Living, quaint displays re-create the parlor, sewing room, kitchen, and other elements of the country home of an imaginary grandmother. Her washing room has manual and early electric washers, and her "back-porch yard" overflows with canning equipment and glassware. In Ye Ol' Town, scenes of rural life include a general store, a telephone exchange, a dentist's office, and a wheelwright's shop. Also noteworthy are the Museum of Farming, an enormous warehouse filled with farm equipment; the National Farmers Memorial, with massive bronze-relief panels depicting farmers past, present, and future; and Farm Town U.S.A., with a 100-year-old railroad station, a blacksmith's shop, and a restored one-room schoolhouse. *Open daily Apr.–Nov. Admission charged.* ♿

224 Wyandotte County Historical Society and Museum

4 min. North on Rte. 7, right on access road; follow signs. History here in the heart of the Central Plains starts with the Indians, most notably the Wyandot, an educated people who emigrated from Ohio in 1843 and built a town complete with church, school, and council house. The exhibits in this museum trace life in the region from those days until well into this century. Other displays concentrate on local industries. Transportation is a popular theme, with memorabilia from the railroads and riverboats, which caused this strategic crossroads to boom, and from the trolley cars that once plied Kansas City's streets. A 1903 steam-driven fire truck is also on display. *Open Tues.–Sun. late Feb.–late Dec. except Thanksgiving Day.*

2C Kansas City, MO 64107

2D

Convention & Visitors Bureau, 1100 Main St., Suite 2550. (816) 221-5242; (800) 523-5953 outside MO. It may come as a surprise, but this beautifully planned city has more miles of boulevards than Paris, and, like Rome, has many handsome fountains. Its shopping centers, too, are noted for their appealing ambience. The Country Club Plaza has architectural echoes of Seville, Spain; Crown Center is an 85-acre city within a city; and at Westport Square some handsome Victorian structures have been converted into shops and restaurants. Among the museums here are the unique Miniature Museum and the Nelson-Atkins Museum of Art, known for the wide range of its holdings and its special emphasis on works from China and India. Swope Park, which contains the Kansas City Zoo and other attractions, is one of the nation's largest municipal parks.

NOL Independence, MO 64050

Nolan Rd. N. exit: Truman Home Ticket and Information Center, 223 N. Main St. (816) 254-9929. As might be expected, the man from Independence, our 33rd president, is well remembered here. There is in fact a Harry S Truman Historic District, a walking tour of which begins at the Truman home (the summer White House) and winds through a well-preserved neighborhood of brick sidewalks and stately homes. Elsewhere in the city is the Truman Library and Museum, which has a reproduction of his White House office among other exhibits. The restored office and courtroom where President Truman began his career is located in the Independence Square Courthouse. You can also see a 35-minute audiovisual presentation.

20 Fort Osage

17 mi./24 min. North on Rte. 7, right on Rte. 24, left on Rte. BB; follow signs. The fort built here in 1808 was the first outpost established in the lands acquired by the Louisiana Purchase. It served to protect the territory from intrusions by the Spanish and British, to enforce government licensing of white traders, and to establish friendly relations with 5,000 or so Osage Indians in the area. The present fort is a replica of the original, built on a promontory overlooking the Missouri River. Within a sturdy palisade are the blockhouses,

20. *They seem vulnerable today, but such fortifications were sufficient in their time.*

officers' and enlisted men's quarters, and the trading post. The museum's exhibits focus primarily on Indian culture and artifacts. *Open daily mid-Apr.–mid-Nov.; weekends only mid-Nov.–mid-Apr. Admission charged.* ⛲

98 Arrow Rock State Historic Site

13 mi./15 min. North on Rte. 41. A ferry across the Missouri River and steamboat traffic on the river helped establish this town as a trading center in the early 1800's. It was bypassed, however, by the railroad and fell into decline. In recent years local interest in restoration and preservation has made Arrow Rock something of a museum town. On a guided walking tour you will visit the small brick house of artist George Caleb Bingham, the Dr. John Sappington Memorial Building, where the medical concerns of the community are recalled by exhibits, and the Doctors' Museum, which houses a collection of medical instruments. The small clapboard courthouse and a printshop are also on the tour. There are a number of other historic structures to be seen, many of which are stores and gift shops. *Open year-round; tours daily June–Aug.; weekends only Sept.–Oct. and Apr.–May. Admission charged for tours.* ⛲ ⛺ 🚐

148 Audrain Historical and American Saddle Horse Museum, Mexico

17 mi./23 min. North on Rte. 54; follow signs. This distinguished clapboard mansion with its two-story porch and pediment is home to a museum dedicated to the American saddle horse, and features a number of rooms furnished and maintained by the local historical society in the style of the 1870–1900 period. The beautifully preserved rooms include the Ross Parlor, with its Aubusson carpet and a suite of fine rosewood furniture; the Period Bedroom, with a spool bed, cradle, and other accessories; and the Bride's Room, containing a display of antique wedding gowns. The Children's Room features a large collection of toys, dolls, and dollhouse furniture. Many original Currier and Ives prints grace the walls of the house. *Open P.M. Tues.–Sun., Feb.–Dec. Admission charged.*

148 Winston Churchill Memorial and Library, Fulton

8 mi./14 min. West on Rte. 54, left on Rte. F, left on Westminster Ave. One doesn't expect to see a 17th-century church built in London by Sir Christopher Wren sitting in a small town in Missouri—but here it is. The church, severely damaged by bombs in World War II, was slated for demolition. But it was brought here and rebuilt as a tribute to Sir Winston Churchill, who in 1946 had given his famous Iron Curtain speech at Westminster College in Fulton. The college raised funds by public subscription, and the building, renewed to past beauty, was dedicated in 1969. The Churchill Museum and Library are housed in the undercroft of the church. *Open daily except Thanksgiving Day, Christmas, and New Year's Day. Admission charged.* ♿

170 Graham Cave State Park

4 mi./6 min. North on Rte. 161, left on Rte. TT. Although this is a pleasant 365-acre recreational park, it is also gaining renown as an archeological dig. Excavations indicate that hunters and fishers lived in this area during the Dalton and Archaic periods from 8000 to 1000 B.C.—much earlier than had formerly been assumed. The early Indians were spear throwers; then, after a long time lapse, bow hunters and pottery makers inhabited this shelter. The cave is still undergoing excavation and cannot be entered, but there are signs and displays to identify notable discoveries. *Open year-round.* 🏕 ⛺ 🚐 🚶

210 / 228 Augusta A. Busch Memorial Wildlife Area

Exit 210: 11 mi./20 min. South on Rte. 40/61, right on Rte. 94, right on Rte. D. Exit 228: 14 mi./22 min. South on Rte. 94; right on Rte. D. The most striking features of this 7,000-acre preserve are the 32 man-made lakes with a surface area of 500 acres. Hunting and fishing are popular here. The lakes are stocked with bass, catfish, crappie, and pike, and boats may be rented for fishing. Private boats are not allowed. One lake is reserved as a refuge for waterfowl.

The area is mainly prairie and meadowland, with some forest land of predominantly oak and hickory. Where the land is cultivated, the farmers leave part of their crops unharvested to provide food for the wildlife. In addition to the waterfowl and other birds, the resident mammals are rabbits, coyotes, deer, raccoons, skunks, opossums, squirrels, and groundhogs. A 7.7-mile auto tour leads through the refuge, and a guidebook describes features along the way. *Open daily except Christmas.* 🏕 🎣

210–228. *Remarkably elegant digs for one so identified with the rigors of wilderness.*

210 / 228 Daniel Boone Home

Exit 210: 18 mi./30 min. South on Rte. 40/61, right on Rte. 94, right on Rte. F. Exit 228: 24 mi./36 min. South on Rte. 94, right on Rte. F. For those expecting to find that one of America's most famous frontiersmen lived in a log cabin or humble shack, this handsome four-story Georgian-style house, filled with attractive furnishings, will come as quite a surprise. One reminder of Boone's vocation is the powder horn he carved himself. Many of the furnishings were used by the Boone family; others are period pieces. As a trailblazer, scout, and Indian fighter, Boone lived by being well prepared. He was equally prepared for the other alternative and stored his coffin under the handsome four-poster bed in which he died. *Open daily mid-March–mid-Dec. Admission charged.* 🏕

ARCH St. Louis, MO 63102

Arch/Downtown exit: Convention and Visitors Commission, 10 S. Broadway. (314) 421-1023; (800) 247-9791 outside MO. The three spans across the Mississippi here dramatize the role of St. Louis as a jumping-off place to the West, and the magnificent 630-foot Gateway Arch commemorates the days of the wagon trains, when the only river crossings were by water. From the top of the arch one can contemplate the vast reaches so full of promise and danger in the days of the pioneers, an era graphically interpreted in the Museum of Westward Expansion located beneath the arch. St. Louis's excellent zoo has more than 2,500 animals and a miniature railroad to provide an easy introduction. Featured in the 79-acre botanical garden is the domed Climatron greenhouse and the largest Japanese garden in the United States.

63 Vandalia Statehouse State Historic Site

5 min. South on Rte. 51. Abraham Lincoln is not quite the hero in Vandalia that he is in the other parts of his adopted state. He led the effort to move the state capital from here, where it had been since 1820, to the more central location of Springfield. It was moved in 1839 after the local citizens had put up some $23,000 to erect a federal-style building that would serve as a capitol. Their efforts were in vain, and the building was demoted to the status of county courthouse. Now refurbished, it provides a fascinating reminder that in 1839 the corridors of power were heated with a battery of stoves, candles were used for light, and writing was done with quill pens. *Open daily except Thanksgiving Day, Christmas, and New Year's Day.* ♿

119. *Hand-hewn logs, dovetailed corners, and shake roof are true to the originals.*

119 Lincoln Log Cabin State Historic Site

10 mi./20 min. North on Rte. 130; follow signs. The volunteers in the living-history program, dressed in period costumes, plow, plant, and harvest, care for livestock, spin wool, and do the other chores that were required here at Goosenest Prairie in the mid-19th century. There are also first-person role players you can talk to about farm life and events of the era. They must feign ignorance of the world beyond their time and place. Abraham Lincoln's father and stepmother lived here during the mid-1800's in a cabin identical to this reproduction. The future president, then a young lawyer from Springfield, visited them at Goosenest Prairie on occasion. *Open daily except Thanksgiving Day, Christmas, and New Year's Day; interpretive programs daily June–Aug., weekends only May and Sept.*

119 Fox Ridge State Park

11 mi./22 min. North on Rte. 130. Hills, valleys, and woods come as a welcome surprise here on a plain that seems boundless. This oasis was not made accessible without the obvious labor of building boardwalks, bridges across steep little gorges, and steps up the hillsides for fine views of the forest canopy and the Embarras (pronounced *Am*-braw) River below. Be advised that the trails are on the arduous side, although there is one short trail for the handicapped. Free fishing boats suggest an outing on secluded 18-acre Ridge Lake. *Open daily except Christmas and New Year's Day.*

147 Lincoln Trail State Park

5 mi./10 min. South on Rte. 1. Part of the Lincoln Heritage Trail, which marks the nearly 1,000-mile route the Lincoln family took from Kentucky to Illinois, this beautiful park centers on a 146-acre lake with many coves and inlets. Photographs of triumphant anglers pinned to the wall of the store at the boat dock indicate that it's a good place to fish for stocked largemouth bass and channel catfish. In season the park is richly bedecked with wildflowers, honeysuckle, and other plants. Maple and American beech trees shade the many inviting ravines in Lincoln Trail. *Open daily except Christmas and New Year's Day.*

147 Twin Lakes Parks

16.5 mi./30 min. North on Rte. 1 through Paris. On the outskirts of the charming and grand-looking town of Paris, this pair of enjoyable community parks, which share a common main entrance, take their name from two lakes so elongated in shape that they might at first be mistaken for rivers. The shores of the lakes, which are partially edged by private homes, have tables nicely shaded by trees, a pleasant setting for a Sunday outing or picnic—despite the mystifying sign: "No beer, no liquor, no melons." *Open year-round.*

7 Early Wheels Museum, Terre Haute

3 mi./7 min. North on Rte. 41, right on Rte. 40. A superlative selection of vehicles is displayed in this fascinating museum. A prairie schooner represents the early days, followed by an 1898 Locomobile Steamer and an electric horseless buggy built in Indiana. There are many automobiles made between the turn of the century and World War II, including sleek European models, such as the 1921 Hispano Suiza and the 1921 Isotta Fraschini. Rounding out the collection are race cars and bicycles ranging from penny-farthing high-wheelers to modern lightweight racers. *Open Mon.–Fri. except holidays.*

11 Dobbs Park and Nature Center, Terre Haute

4 mi./7 min. North on Rte. 46, left on Rte. 42. The emphasis is on nature at this small, enticing park, which encompasses a surprising variety of habitats. Well-charted trails lead from plantations of pine and deciduous trees that harbor owls and deer through a mature forest of white oaks, tulip trees, sycamores, and beeches. In the nature center small animal exhibits and a tell-by-touch quiz attract children. A window looks out onto a bird-feeding station that flashes with the colors of cardinals, purple finches, and jays. Next to the center is a 3-acre lake where you can try for channel catfish, bluegill, and largemouth bass. *Park open year-round; nature center open Mon.–Sat. and P.M. Sun.*

37 Lieber State Recreation Area

3 mi./8 min. South on Rte. 243. This recreation area boasts hundreds of acres of lake and miles of inviting shoreline created by flood control projects on the Mississippi and Ohio rivers. A long sandy beach and a bathhouse invite swimmers to deep blue Cagles Mill Lake, and a marina with rental boats nestled in a quiet bay draws anglers for largemouth bass and bluegill. Exercise enthusiasts will appreciate the elaborate fitness trail; and the meadows and woodlands offer hiking, bird-watching, and berry and nut picking. The campground has more than 400 sites in all. Another popular attraction in this recreation area is Cataract Falls, which is the largest waterfall in Indiana. *Open year-round. Admission charged.*

79B Indianapolis, IN 46225

Convention & Visitors Association, 1 Hoosier Dome, Suite 100. (317) 639-4282. Almost everyone knows that every May, Indianapolis boasts one of the world's largest sports events, the "Indy 500." But there are other attractions worthy of note. Consider, for example, the Indianapolis Museum of Art, the Indiana State Museum, and the Children's Museum, one of the largest and most varied of its kind. You can visit the home of poet James Whitcomb Riley and President Benjamin Harrison's 16-room Victorian mansion. There's a new zoo and three large parks. In the heart of downtown, Festival Market Place in old Union Station, with its many shops and res-

79B. *Indiana's imposing war memorial bears the sculpture "Pro Patria" ("For Country").*

taurants, attracts crowds. And even if it isn't May, the Speedway is worth a visit. The Hall of Fame Museum displays antique and classic cars and more than 32 speedsters that have won the race since it was established in 1911; and you can get the feel of "the Brickyard" on a minibus ride around the circuit.

122 The Henry County Historical Museum, New Castle

5 mi./12 min. North on Rte. 3, right on Indiana Ave., right on S. 14th St. Dignified rather than opulent, this 1870 Victorian Italianate house still reflects the moderate tastes of its former owner, Maj. Gen. William Grose, one of Indiana's most notable Civil War military leaders. The impression of a family home is preserved by Grose family portraits, the general's intact master bedroom, a well-stocked summer kitchen, and 19th-century furnishings throughout the house. Besides Grose family and Henry County memorabilia, the museum has interesting collections of Victorian toys and playthings, day and evening attire, pocket watches, music boxes, and cooking, sewing, and farming implements. *Open P.M. Mon.–Sat. except holidays. Admission free but donations encouraged.*

137 Huddleston Farmhouse Inn Museum, Mt. Auburn

4 mi./15 min. South on Rte. 1, right on Rte. 40. Built between 1839 and 1841 by John Huddleston, this substantial three-story federal-style building with a barn and a smokehouse was not exactly an inn. It was in fact a private farmhouse that offered shelter to travelers on the National Road. For a fee a weary pioneer family could feed and water their horses, buy produce, then cook and bed down for the night in two ground-floor kitchens. This floor and another in the family's quarters upstairs have been restored with period furnishings, including a formal American empire-style parlor set, some fine examples of local chairmaking, and a family kitchen with the luxuries of an adjoining springhouse and herb garden. *Open Tues.–Fri. and P.M. Sun. May–Aug; Tues.–Fri. Sept.–Apr. Admission free but donations encouraged.*

156 Wayne County Historical Museum, Richmond

4 mi./10 min. West on Rte. 40; follow signs. Thanks to Julia Meek Gaar, its globe-trotting founder, this museum has a charmingly eclectic collection. A totem pole stands next to an ornate Italian cabinet; Victorian fans flank samurai armor; and the museum's showpiece

is a 3,500-year-old Egyptian mummy. Such delights as Lenci dolls, a perfect 1880's dollhouse, and Meissen china vie for attention with antique cars and re-creations of a pioneer kitchen and a general store. Outside, half a dozen preserved structures form a village square with displays related to local history. *Open Tues.–Fri. and P.M. weekends Feb.–Dec. Admission charged.*

I-75 Dayton, OH 45402

10 mi./18 min. Convention & Visitors Bureau, Chamber Plaza, 5th and Main Sts. (513) 226-8248 or (800) 221-8234; (800) 221-8235 outside OH. This river city seems to have invention in the air. The cash register, the electric starter, and the pull-tab tin-can top were devised by Daytonians. But the best-known local wizards were Orville and Wilbur Wright (see Carillon Park below). Arcade Square, a completely restored turn-of-the-century indoor farmers' market canopied by an enormous glass dome, contains some 50 specialty shops, restaurants, and boutiques. Other highlights in the city are the United States Air Force Museum, the home of black poet Paul Laurence Dunbar, and the baroque collections in the Dayton Art Institute.

I-75 Carillon Park, Dayton

11 mi./20 min. South on I-75 to Exit 51, east on Edwin Moses Blvd., right on the Stewart St. cross bridge, right on Patterson Blvd. Neatly fitted into this lovely park is a little town from yesteryear, re-created with a mixture of relocated original structures and exact replicas. Among others there's a 1796 log tavern, a blacksmith's shop, and a turn-of-the-century brick schoolhouse. But the emphasis is on transportation and Dayton's contributions to it, with a Wright *Flyer*, a railway station, the Wright brothers' cycle shop, a canal lock, and a fine collection of wagons, locomotives, trolleys, and antique cars. The bell tower that gives the park its name is a 150-foot limestone needle with a cascade of 40 bells that ring out in concert on Sundays during the months when the park is open. *Open Tues.–Sun. and Mon. holidays May–Oct.*

41 United States Air Force Museum, Dayton

8 mi./15 min. South on Rte. 4, left on Harshman Rd., right on Springfield Pike. "Where eagles rest" is the motto of this museum with an impressive array of military aircraft and related displays. Fighter biplanes from World War I still look sleek and deadly. World War II Messerschmitts, Spitfires, and Mustangs nestle under the wings of Flying Fortresses and Liberators. In the main hangar and nearby annex almost 200 planes and missiles are on display. They span the history of aviation from a reproduction of the Wright brothers' kitelike 1909 Military Flyer to a charred *Apollo 15* capsule that circled the moon. *Open daily except Christmas.*

62 Buck Creek State Park

4 mi./12 min. West on Rte. 40, right on Bird Rd. (becomes Buck Creek Ln.). In the midst of flat, rich farmlands, the large reservoir here is so unexpected that it seems at first to be a mirage. But it is a dream come true for anyone interested in water sports. For swimmers it offers a bathhouse and a half-mile-long sand beach that is raked daily. Boaters can launch their own or can rent row, sail, paddle, and power boats. Water-skiing, scuba diving, and fishing are also popular. The Corps of Engineers' visitor center has a nature display, and a nearby overlook affords a fine view over the reservoir. A restored federal-style homestead recalls the lifestyle of the early settlers. *Park open year-round; homestead open P.M. Sat. late May–Sept.*

97 Columbus, OH 43215

Convention & Visitors Bureau, 1 Columbus Building, 10 W. Broad St., Suite 1300. (614) 221-6623. The Ohio capitol (mid-1800's) is a noted Greek revival structure. Other architectural styles popular in the 19th century can be seen in Ohio Village at the Ohio Historical Center, which also features displays related to the area's prehistory and paleontology. A former German settlement has been re-created at German Village. Fans of the cartoonist and writer James Thurber can visit his boyhood home. At the Center of Science and Industry (COSI), children and adults can put their hands on displays pertaining to the technology and science in their daily lives. The Columbus Museum of Art has extensive holdings of European and American art, and Ohio State University offers regular tours of the galleries and gardens on the campus.

129 Mound Builders State Memorial

8 mi./15 min. North on Rte. 79. The Great Circle Earthworks is one of the most impressive of the huge geometric mounds that the Hopewell people built in this region close to 2,000 years ago. Now topped by stately trees and a sandy path for visitors, this great circular embankment measures some 1,200 feet in diameter and rises to 14 feet at its highest point. Exquisite pottery, figurines, and body ornaments of copper and mica in the visitor center leave one even more in awe of the complex and sophisticated civilization that mysteriously disappeared some 1,500 years ago. *Open daily Memorial Day–Labor Day; weekends Sept.–Oct. Admission charged.*

164 National Road–Zane Grey Museum

3 min. East on Rte. 22/40. The varied displays in this museum tell two tales. One concerns the great road that connected the new American nation to its western frontier. The other commemorates the noted Western novelist Zane Grey, who was born in Ohio and also wrote about this area's settlement. His great-grandfather, Ebenezer Zane, blazed the trail called Zane's Trace. Dioramas depict the development of the road, and lifelike tableaux re-create a tavern, a wheelwright's shop, and a blacksmith's forge. Historic vehicles on display include a Conestoga wagon and antique autos. *Open daily May–Sept.; Wed.–Sun. Mar.–Apr. and Oct.–Nov. except Thanksgiving Day. Admission charged.*

I-77 Salt Fork State Park

12.5 mi./20 min. North on I-77 to Exit 47, east on Rte. 22. In this 21,000-acre park the extensive lake is the centerpiece, with its many arms that provide sections for boats with unlimited power, no-wave zones for sailboats

97. *Bicentennial Park, overlooking the Scioto River, is a favorite gathering place in Columbus.*

OH | WV   WV | PA   79   See N–S book, sec. 38.   76   I-76 merges with I-70.

30   17   1   32   41   15   19   36

208   **1B**   **2A**   **I-79**   **I-76**   **9**   **10**   70 76

and other quiet craft, and sandy beaches for swimmers. You'll also find an 18-hole golf course, two marinas, boat rentals, and 26 miles of bridle paths through wooded rolling hills. *Open year-round.*

208   Barkcamp State Park

4 min. South on Rte. 149; follow signs. Set in rolling farmlands and wooded hills, this park has an atmosphere of spaciousness and seclusion. Numerous hiking trails meander through the countryside, where a variety of trees, shrubs, and wildflowers provide cover and food for the area's wildlife. Belmont Lake has facilities for swimmers and anglers, with a fishing pier for the handicapped. An antique barn contains an assortment of exhibits, including a boulder inscribed by frontiersman and sharpshooter Lewis Wetzel, that recall Ohio's rural past. *Open year-round. Admission charged.*

1B   Grave Creek Mound State Park, Moundsville

12 mi./17 min. South on Rte. 2; follow signs. The Adena people, first of the prehistoric Mound Builders, constructed this 69-foot-high conical hill as a burial site between 250 and 150 B.C. A path spirals to the top of the mound. In the Delf Norona Museum, dioramas and life-size models portray tribal life as it may have existed 2,000 years ago, and there are exhibits of tools, weapons, and other artifacts. Completely unauthenticated but intriguing is a replica of a small sandstone tablet written in "Iberic-Celtic" script. Where it came from is a mystery, but it is kept on display by popular demand. *Open Mon.–Sat. and P.M. Sun. except holidays. Admission charged.*

2A   Oglebay Park, Wheeling

5 min. Northeast on Rte. 88. This beautifully manicured 1,500-acre estate was given to the town by a Cleveland industrialist. Among the cultural and recreational facilities in the park, the Mansion Museum houses 18th- and 19th-century period rooms and outstanding examples of Wheeling's china and glass industries. Other attractions include a children's zoo,

formal gardens and an arboretum, three golf courses on rolling hills, tennis courts, and ski trails. *Grounds open year-round; museum open Mon.–Sat. and P.M. Sun. and holidays except Thanksgiving Day, Christmas, and New Year's Day.*

2A. *The Mansion Museum clearly defines the character of the Greek revival style.*

I-79   Arden Trolley Museum, Washington

5 mi./10 min. North on I-79 to Exit 8E, east on Pike St.; follow signs. Trolley buffs and children of all ages can savor the pleasure of a trolley ride on a 1920's car, smartly fitted with polished woodwork, chrome, and brass, along a 1-mile route in this indoor-outdoor museum. Twenty-five or more trolley cars, some in working order, others undergoing restoration, are exhibited in a large carbarn. The cars come from several towns in Pennsylvania and Boston, with one veteran of New Orleans' Desire line. *Open P.M. daily July 4–Labor Day; P.M. weekends only May–June and Sept.*

I-76   Bushy Run Battlefield, Jeannette

14 mi./25 min. West on I-76 to Exit 7, west on Rte. 30, right on Ash St., right on Pennsylvania Ave., left on Brush Hill Rd., right on Rte. 993. In August 1763 these tranquil woods and meadows on the Pennsylvania frontier were the scene of a desperate and crucial battle fought by the British to rescue Ft. Pitt from

siege by the Indians, whose combined forces were under the command of the great chief Pontiac. Guided and self-guiding tours from the visitor center lead to the sites of important episodes in this battle, which established the British on Indian territory after the French and Indian War. *Open Tues.–Sat., P.M. Sun., and Memorial Day, July 4, and Labor Day, but not other holidays. Admission charged.*

9   Fort Ligonier

12 mi./15 min. North on Rte. 711. Built in 1758 and now reconstructed, the fort still guards the frontier crossroads it defended when the British and Americans (including a militia unit commanded by young George Washington, then a colonel in King George's army) successfully held it against the French and the Indians in the mid-1700's. The stockade, which encircles the garrison's sparsely furnished log dwellings, is fiercely protected at the corners by an array of sharply pointed stakes. The visitor center and museum exhibits dioramas, weapons, utensils, and other 18th-century artifacts, as well as period rooms and objects from Ligonier's historic past. Colorful reenactments of battles and demonstrations of traditional handicrafts are featured during the summer months. *Open Apr.–Oct. Admission charged.*

10   Somerset Historical Center

4.5 mi./10 min. North on Rte. 601, left at fork on Rte. 985. A trim restored log house and several outbuildings evoke life in Pennsylvania's pioneer days. The well-furnished main house contains spinning wheels, quaint kitchen equipment, quilts, and other domestic necessities of the period. The visitor center has informative exhibits that explain skills such as preparing and spinning flax, woodworking, and fashioning utensils and tools that were once indispensable. In marked contrast, the technology of modern farming is illustrated by mid-20th-century machinery and implements. *Open Tues.–Sat. and P.M. Sun. and Memorial Day, July 4, and Labor Day, but not other holidays. Admission charged.*

11   Old Bedford Village

5 min. South on Rte. 220 (business); follow signs. In the 18th century, Ft. Bedford saw action in two wars and was the focus of a whiskey tax uprising that was suppressed by President George Washington and 13,000 federal soldiers. Today the village comprises more than 40 restored houses and shops that re-create rural Pennsylvania life around 1795. Authentically costumed staff members use antique tools and utensils to demonstrate the trades of baker, broom maker, blacksmith, bookbinder, and candlestick maker. *Open daily mid-Apr.–Oct. Admission charged.* 🪧 ♿

12   Crawford's Wildlife Exhibit, Breezewood

3 min. South on Rte. 30. Mr. and Mrs. Fred Crawford, natives of Breezewood, traveled extensively throughout the world and on their various safaris bagged some 300 species of wildlife. This collection is now in the museum, with several of the species portrayed in tableaux that re-create their natural habitats. Some of the animals in the exhibit—such as the snow leopard and black-spotted panther—are rare and seldom seen. Others are now extinct. *Open Mon.–Sat. and P.M. Sun. May–Oct. Admission charged.*

13   East Broad Top Railroad, Rockhill Furnace

14

Exit 13: 14 mi./22 min. North on Rte. 522. Exit 14: 18 mi./25 min. North on Rte. 75, left on Rte. 641, right on Rte. 522. Boarding at the charmingly detailed Orbisonia railroad depot, you can take a fascinating 10-mile round-trip on one of the oldest narrow-gauge railways in the U.S.A., through the scenic Aughwick Valley to the Colgate Grove picnic area. At the eight-stall roundhouse, visitors can inspect a steam engine, a gas-electric car, and the Armstrong turntable that rotates the engines. The Trolley Museum and trolley rides on the Shade Gap Electric Railway across the street offer other excursions into the past. *Train rides daily July–Labor Day, weekends only June and Sept.–Oct.; trolley rides weekends and holidays Memorial Day–Oct. Admission charged.* 🪧

22. *Across this rustic bridge is a foundry village little changed since the 19th century.*

14   Big Spring State Park

17 mi./24 min. North on Rte. 75, right on Rte. 274. This small park serves as a base for campers, hikers, hunters, and cross-country skiers who wish to explore and use the adjacent Tuscarora State Forest, which encompasses several mountain ranges typical of this part of the country. The forest can be explored on trails that lead over the great game-filled wooded ridges. One inviting hike traces the course of a stream in the Hemlock State Natural Area as it flows briskly from the ridge to the valley below. Pine trees tower over the picnic grounds. *Open year-round.* 🪧 🚶

16   Cumberland County Historical Society, Carlisle

4 mi./7 min. North on Rte. 11 (becomes Hanover St.), right on High St., right on Pitt St. An unpretentious brick building houses a surprising wealth of treasures and curiosities, from a 17th-century Jacobean settee to Schimmel and Mountz rooster carvings. The collection captures the very essence of Pennsylvania history with hand-illustrated texts, painted plank-bottom chairs, cast-iron mechanical banks, bookbinding presses, redware pottery, Revolutionary War weapons, samplers, a rich profusion of furniture, silverware, a "Grand Harmonicum," which is played by rubbing the edges of glass goblets, and local artifacts. *Open P.M. Tues.–Fri. and evenings Mon. except holidays.* ♿

17   Harrisburg, PA 17108

Chamber of Commerce, 114 Walnut St. (717) 232-4121. This capital city has a most impressive statehouse, with a dome based on St. Peter's in Rome and a grand interior staircase copied from the Paris Opéra. The nearby State Museum contains a wealth of regional artifacts from every era. The Museum of Scientific Discovery very successfully delivers on its name. The Susquehanna River's beauty can be enjoyed at Riverfront Park, a 5-mile esplanade. Also in the Riverfront District are handsome 18th- and 19th-century mansions.

19   Indian Echo Caverns, Hummelstown

10 mi./15 min. East on Rte. 283, left on Vine St. Over the course of 3 million to 5 million years, the constant dripping of mineral-laden water has shaped a large network of chambers and winding passageways, embellished by countless stalagmites and stalactites, all set against a backdrop of shimmering flowstone. Some formations look like humans, animals, and different kinds of plants. You'll also find a crystal-clear lake and a corallike mass of calcite. The temperature holds at 52° F. *Open daily Apr.–Oct.; weekends only Mar. and Nov. Admission charged.*

22   Hopewell Furnace National Historic Site

10 mi./16 min. South on Rte. 10, left on Rte. 23, left on Rte. 345. Hopewell was one of the pre-Revolution foundries that defied Britain's decree against producing finished products. It cast iron into cookware, stoves, and other essential products for a growing America and later provided armaments for the Revolution. In a walking tour of the historic village you'll learn about the process of smelting and casting iron. A film and demonstrations of sand casting and forging are scheduled regularly. *Open daily except Christmas and New Year's Day. Admission charged.*

24   Valley Forge National Historical Park

2 mi./6 min. North on Rte. 363. Valley Forge is an inspiring reminder of the American spirit during the Revolution. When the British captured Philadelphia in 1777, George Washington chose Valley Forge for his army's winter quarters. Owing to the crude housing, inadequate clothing, and poor rations, some 2,000 of the 12,000 men died here. But Washington's presence and the drill instruction volunteered by the Prussian officer Baron Friedrich von Steuben held the army together. The spring brought the offer of French assistance, and although five more years of conflict lay ahead, a critical turning point had been reached. These events are dramatically explained and exhibited at the visitor center and throughout the park. *Open daily except Christmas. Admission charged.*

24   Fort Washington State Park

11.5 mi./15 min. East on I-276 to Exit 26, west on Pennsylvania Ave., left on Bethlehem Pike. George Washington's army built a fort here shortly before moving to Valley Forge in the winter of 1777. The fort is long gone, leaving behind its name for this area, but a replica of the original may be visited on the same site on Fort Hill. The 483-acre park's unspoiled meadows and woods along the Wissahickon Creek are popular with visitors. A pamphlet for children describes plants and wildlife on a nature trail. Dogwoods lace the hills in spring. *Open year-round.*

24   The Mercer Museum, Doylestown

25 mi./35 min. East on I-276 to Exit 27, north on Rte. 611 to Doylestown exit; continue on S. Main St., right on E. Ashland St., right on Green St. Walk in through the heavy wooden doors, wander down the stone passageways and stairways and into the workshops—you might think you are in a medieval castle. This extensive museum, built from 1913 to 1916 by archeologist Henry Chapman Mercer, houses his fantastic collection of more than 40,000 preindustrial American artifacts. Old fishing boats, carriages, and even a Conestoga wagon hang from the walls and ceiling of a central gallery that soars to a height of six stories.

Lighting devices of various kinds, musical instruments, and whaling, barrel-making, and blacksmithing tools are just the beginning. *Open Mon.–Sat. and P.M. Sun. Mar.–Dec. Admission charged.*

39   Philadelphia, PA 19102

Visitors Center, 1625 JFK Blvd. (215) 636-1666. If you plan to stop in Philadelphia, it is advisable not to be in a rush. It takes time to do justice to Independence National Historical Park, which includes Independence Hall and other historic structures on Independence Square. In the park, which covers 42 acres, you'll see the Liberty Bell, Franklin Court, Carpenters' Hall, and several handsomely restored and furnished 18th-century houses.

The Philadelphia Museum of Art and the Franklin Institute Science Museum are justly renowned. The city's other museums are dedicated to such diverse subjects as Afro-American culture, antique toys, Jewish history, and the art of Norman Rockwell. There's also the American Swedish Museum, and the Please Touch Museum for Children.

24. *A winter like this and a supply shortage tested the spirit of America at Valley Forge in 1777.*

See N–S book, sec. 22 for I-55.

See E–W book, sec. 29 for I-70.

See N–S book, sec. 25.

IL ¦ IN

64

55 70

I-55

6

3

55

61

12

73

57

2

95

3

78

57

66

57

I-55   St. Louis, MO 63102

Convention and Visitors Commission, 10 S. Broadway. (314) 421-1023; (800) 247-9791 outside MO. The three spans crossing the Mississippi here dramatize the role of St. Louis as a jumping-off place to the West, and the magnificent 630-foot Gateway Arch commemorates the days of the wagon trains, when the only river crossings were by water. From the top of the arch you can contemplate the vast reaches offering such promise and danger in the days of the pioneers, an era graphically interpreted in the Museum of Westward Expansion. An excellent zoo has more than 2,500 animals and a miniature railroad to provide an easy introduction. Featured in the 79-acre botanical garden is the domed Climatron and the largest Japanese garden in the United States.

6   Cahokia Mounds State Historic Site, Collinsville

5 min. North on Rte. 111, right on Collinsville Rd. From A.D. 900 to 1250 a mighty society flourished on the Mississippi River. Cahokia, a major town built by the people of the Mississippian Indian culture, had 20,000 to 40,000 inhabitants, who farmed the surrounding land and traded with peoples as far away as the Atlantic and Gulf coasts. They also labored for centuries to build these impressive earthworks a basketful at a time. A few of the mounds were burial sites, but most were used for housing the elite or for ceremonial buildings. Woodhenge, a giant circle of cedar posts, was a sun calendar that determined the changing seasons. *Open daily except Thanksgiving Day, Christmas, and New Year's Day.* 🏕

61   Fairview Park, Centralia

12 mi./20 min. North on Rte. 51. This is a modest but pleasant stopping place for a swim in an Olympic-size pool, a picnic, or a game of catch or Frisbee. It also offers an opportunity to inspect two marvels of transportation: the steam locomotive (this one with stylish white wheels) and a jet plane of Korean War vintage. A 65-bell carillon, on which an occasional concert is given, stands in downtown Centralia. *Open year-round.* 🏕🏊

73   William Jennings Bryan Museum, Salem

22 mi./30 min. North on I-57 to Exit 116, east on Rte. 50, right on Rte. 37 (S. Broadway). Bryan, a former congressman, secretary of state, and three-time presidential nominee, was born in this simple frame house, where he lived for the first seven years of his life. He was a renowned orator, and his style is demonstrated in a recording of his celebrated cross of gold speech. Here, too, are his baby clothes, his Spanish-American War uniform, and political buttons and ribbons. The modest objects by which Bryan is remembered here are in poignant contrast with his accomplishments. *Open Fri.–Wed. except Thanksgiving Day, Christmas, and New Year's Day.*

95   Mitchell Museum, Mount Vernon

2 mi./10 min. East on Rte. 15 (becomes Broadway), left on 27th St., right on Richview Rd. The striking, windowless museum, surrounded by an elegantly proportioned colonnade, is on the parklike grounds of Cedarhurst, the 80-acre estate of the late John and Eleanor Mitchell. The structure embodies their dream of providing an art center for this part of Illinois. Exhibits include works by local residents as well as nationally touring shows that make stops here. The eclectic Mitchell collection of paintings, drawings, and sculpture, displayed in a nearby building, includes works by John Singer Sargent, Andrew Wyeth, Thomas Eakins, and other 19th- and 20th-century masters. The attractive wooded grounds contain a lake and two nature trails. *Open P.M. Tues.–Sun. except holidays.* 🚶♿

78   Wayne Fitzgerell State Park

15 mi./25 min. South on I-57 to Exit 77, west on Rte. 154 across first part of causeway over Rend Lake. As many as 2 million people per year seek recreation here, but the 19,000-acre Rend Lake and 21,000 adjacent acres of public land can easily accommodate them. (Stop at the visitor center for orientation.) Boating, hiking, swimming, and fishing are all popular, and there's a wildlife refuge with a viewing platform. During the tourist season interpretive programs are sponsored. *Park open year-round; visitor center open Apr.–Oct.*

🏕 ⛺ 🚐 🚶 🏊 🎣 ♿

12   New Harmony Historic District

10 mi./20 min. South on Rte. 165, right on Rte. 66. From the visitor center in the starkly modern Atheneum, walking and buggy tours take

57. *Reconstructed cabin shows the extensive hand-hewing required to build in pioneer times.*

you through this remarkably well-preserved town, which was founded by George Rapp and his followers as a utopian religious colony in 1814. Log houses, red brick dwellings, and community houses were once home to the first Harmonists, while the Workingmen's Institute reflects the intellectual bent of the next inhabitants, who were under the leadership of the Welsh social reformer Robert Owen. That 19th-century community was one of the first in the nation to establish a kindergarten, a free library, and a free public school. Near the so-called Roofless Church, the theologian Paul Tillich is buried. *Visitor center open daily Apr.–Oct., weekends only Nov.–Dec. and Mar. Admission charged for tours.*

25   Mesker Park Zoo, Evansville

18 mi./35 min. South on Rte. 41, right on Rte. 66, left on St. Joseph Ave.; follow signs. Giraffes and cranes in the same enclosure, a galleon crewed by squirrel monkeys, and peacocks residing with elephants give an aura of the wild to this appealing zoo. Lions, tapirs, arctic wolves, and other exotic animals live side by side with such natives as wild turkeys, otters, and geese. Visitors can ride a safari train around the park, maneuver paddle boats among the ducks and swans in the pond, and watch an elephant show. A special section contains goats, ducks, chickens, and rabbits for children to pet. The zoo also has two exhibits of free-flying tropical birds and one devoted to nocturnal animals. *Open daily except Christmas and New Year's Day. Admission charged.*

57   Lincoln Boyhood National Memorial, Lincoln City

9 mi./15 min. South on Rte. 231, left on Rte. 162. This simple working farm, situated within the Lincoln Boyhood National Memorial, commemorates the Lincoln family's 14-year sojourn in Indiana before they moved to their final home in Illinois. In the reconstructed log cabin, domestic items—such as a battling board, used to beat clothes on washdays, and long poles used to tear down the mud-and-wattle chimney when it caught fire—suggest some of the domestic challenges in pioneer days. A film at the visitor center portrays the life of America's 16th president while he lived in Indiana, and a nearby cemetery contains the grave of his mother. The adjacent Lincoln State Park has an 85-acre lake, pleasant woods and meadows, and an open-air theater where a dramatic presentation based on President Lincoln's boyhood is performed during summer months. *Memorial open daily except Thanksgiving Day, Christmas, and New Year's Day; park open year-round. Admission charged.*

105   Governor Hendricks' Headquarters, Corydon

3 mi./7 min. South on Rte. 135, left on Rte. 62 (becomes Walnut St.). The past is fondly remembered in this handsome federal house, which served as the home and headquarters of Governor William Hendricks from 1822 until 1825, when Indiana's state capital was moved to Indianapolis. The furnishings illustrate Indiana domestic life during three distinct periods from the 1820's to the 1880's. *Open Wed.–Sat. and P.M. Sun. and Tues. May–Sept.; Oct.–Apr. same as above except holidays. Admission free but donations encouraged.*

4   Louisville, KY 40202

5C

Visitors Information Center, 400 S. 1st St. (502) 584-2121. Since Churchill Downs is a primary attraction here, the grounds are open even when it's not racing season; and at the Kentucky Derby Museum at the Downs, various media are employed to give the feel of Derby Week. For visitors who have a little time to spend, the *Belle of Louisville,* an honest-to-goodness stern-wheeler, cruises the Ohio River in the leisurely style travelers were once accustomed to.

The J.B. Speed Art Museum adjacent to the University of Louisville comprises both contemporary and traditional art in a handsome neoclassical building; and the Museum of History and Science features natural history and aerospace exhibits, with emphasis on hands-on learning. Old Louisville (Victorian houses), Butchertown (a German neighborhood), and Portland (French and Irish) are among the lovingly restored city districts.

4–5C. *At Churchill Downs a horse creates a cloud of steam after a morning workout.*

5A   Howard Steamboat Museum, Jeffersonville

5B

3 mi./10 min. Exit 5A: north on I-65, east on Rte. 62, right on Spring St., left on Market St. Exit 5B: proceed as above. Overlooking the Ohio River, this 22-room mansion was built in the early 1890's by Edmunds Howard, whose shipyard produced some of the world's most elegant steamboats. The same superb craftsmanship lavished on the Howard vessels is evident in this luxurious Victorian home. Its hand-carved wooden archways, 36 chandeliers, and grand staircase are all modeled after those originally designed for steamboats. Also on display are scale models of famous boats, the mansion's original furniture in neo-Louis XV style, a $35,000 brass bed, and a steamboat pilot's wheel that's 9 feet wide. *Open Tues.–Sun. except holidays. Admission charged.*

53 58 Liberty Hall, Frankfort

Exit 53: 7 mi./10 min. North on Rte. 127, right on Rte. 60, left on Bridge St., left on Wapping St., right on Wilkinson Blvd. Exit 58: 6 mi./20 min. North on Rte. 60 (becomes E. Main St.) This historic mansion with soft rose-colored hand-made bricks and blue trim is graced by an elegant Palladian window. It was built by U.S. Senator John Brown in the late 1700's in a style that recalls an even earlier period and is named for his father's school. Impeccable antique Georgian furnishings and portraits fill the stately rooms once visited by such notables as James Monroe, Andrew Jackson, and the Marquis de Lafayette. Behind the house a formal garden with many of the ornamental trees and flowers of the period slopes down to the banks of the Kentucky River. Also here is the refurbished Orlando Brown House, built in the 1830's by the senator's son. *Open Tues.–Sat. and P.M. Sun. Mar.–Dec. except Thanksgiving Day and Christmas. Admission charged.*

NWT PAR Lexington, KY 40507

Newtown Pike exit; Paris Pike exit: Convention & Visitors Bureau, 430 W. Vine St. (606) 233-1221. For all the publicity about horses here in the bluegrass country, you don't have to be an equestrian to enjoy a visit. There are historic houses of note, two inviting university campuses, and some interesting renovated shopping areas.

In the Georgian-style Mary Todd Lincoln House, you can see furnishings that are similar to the originals the future First Lady lived with here as a girl. While the Todd House has an engaging charm, the Hunt-Morgan House, with its handsome 19th-century furnishings and woodwork, is a study in the restrained elegance of the federal style. Ashland, the handsome estate of the famous statesman Henry Clay, lies on the outskirts of town. The beautifully furnished Italianate house is surrounded by lawns and woodlands and also has an attractive formal garden.

The University of Kentucky campus offers an art museum, an anthropology museum, and a mile-long Tree Trail through the area.

53–58. *As exemplified here, beautiful proportions and materials are timeless in their appeal.*

94 Fort Boonesborough State Park

15 mi./25 min. South on Rte. 1958, right on Rte. 627, left on Rte. 388. In 1775 Daniel Boone had just established this vital frontier post on the banks of the Kentucky River when his young daughter was captured by Indians. With a few companions Boone set off after the marauders and, against all odds, recovered the girl. On a hill close to the original site, the log walls and blockhouses of Boone's fort have been lovingly reconstructed, as has the pioneer lifestyle itself. You'll see blacksmiths, spinners, toymakers, weavers, and candlemakers at their daily work. Elsewhere in the park you can swim in the river, fish for perch, catfish, and bass, launch a boat, picnic, and camp. Detailed information on the facilities is available at the visitor center. *Park open year-round; fort open daily Apr.–Sept.; Wed.–Sun. Sept.–Oct. Admission charged to fort.*

137 Rodburn Hollow Recreation Area

5 mi./12 min. East on Rte. 32, left on Rte. 60, left on Rodburn Hollow Rd. This wooded valley and the stream that traverses it provide a rest stop for hikers on the Sheltowee Trace, a 254-mile trail that passes through the land explored by Daniel Boone between 1769 and 1771. Sheltowee ("Big Turtle") was the name given to Boone by the Shawnee tribe. The Martin Brand Trail, starting at the ranger station, joins the Sheltowee Trace briefly. Picnic tables and grills are scattered throughout the recreation area, which also has a playing field and some primitive campsites. *Open daily late Apr.–mid-Oct.*

161 Carter Caves State Resort Park

5 mi./10 min. North on Rte. 60, left on Rte. 182. The craggy terrain here is endlessly varied. Cave tours range in difficulty from an easy walk past a 30-foot underground waterfall in magnificent Cascade Cave to a strenuous crawl through the tight passages of Bat Cave with your own flashlight and gear. Hiking trails aboveground wind over hills and into valleys past a huge natural bridge, a "wind tunnel," a box canyon, and carpets of wildflowers in spring. Saltpeter (used to make explosives) was mined here from 1812 to the Civil War. The park's modern amenities include a golf course, tennis courts, and riding stables. *Open year-round. Admission charged for sports.*

KY | WV

24   6   7   2   3   17   30   71

See N–S book,
sec. 36 for I-77;
sec. 38 for I-79.   77   79

161   185   191   6   8   11   28   58A   64

185 191 The Kentucky Highlands Museum, Ashland

Exit 185: 7 mi./12 min. Northeast on Rte. 60, right on Bath Ave. Exit 191: 8 mi./15 min. North on Rte. 23, left on 16th St. Built in 1917, this imposing limestone mansion with Renaissance-style porticoes houses a wide variety of items relating to eastern Kentucky's history. There are prehistoric Indian artifacts, models of blast furnaces, and a nostalgic collection of old-fashioned radios. The elegant staircase curves up from the first floor to the third-floor ballroom, which contains a stained-glass skylight that may evoke formally attired ghosts from a bygone era. *Open Tues.–Sat. and P.M. Sun. except holidays. Admission charged.* ♿

6 Camden Park, Huntington

5 min. North on 17th St., left on Rte. 60. All the familiar attractions can be found at this homey amusement park: two roller coasters, bumper cars, a haunted house, a carousel, a wet ride down a log chute, and a variety of sideshows. Roller skating, miniature golf, and an outdoor amphitheater with some famous names on the bill add to the festive atmosphere. A cruise along the Ohio River on the *Camden Queen*, a reproduction of an 1890 stern-wheeler, lets you experience the unique charm of the steamboat era. *Park open daily mid-Apr.–Labor Day; weekends only Apr. and Sept. Boat rides P.M. daily May–Labor Day. Admission charged.* ⛱

8 Huntington Museum of Art

3 mi./8 min. North on Rte. 527, right on Miller Rd.; follow signs. Special exhibitions at this museum have ranged from an extensive display about the Ohio River to a close look at a traditional Japanese house. The permanent collection includes paintings by Andrew Wyeth and John Singer Sargent, works by Millet and Boudin, and a particularly fine Dean gun collection. There's also a sculpture garden and nature trails flanked by oaks, beeches, ferns, and other wildlings. *Open Tues.–Sat. and P.M. Sun. except Christmas and New Year's Day. Admission charged.* 🚶♿

11 Beech Fork State Park, Barboursville

10 mi./20 min. East on Rte. 10, right on Green Valley Rd. After winding down the tortuous approach road and coming upon this serene and spacious area framed by wooded hills, you may feel like an explorer discovering a lost valley. The highlight of this 3,700-acre park, which is still under development, is its 760-acre lake, where canoes, paddleboats, and rowboats may be rented. Anglers can try for crappie, bass, pike, and channel catfish.

At the enticing little coves at the water's edge are 275 modern campsites with bathhouses and laundry facilities. Trails include a long nature trail and a physical fitness trail. There's also a camp store and a visitor center. *Open year-round.* ⛱ ⛺ 🚐 🚶 🎣 ♿

28 Blenko Glass Company, Milton

2 mi./8 min. South off exit, right on Rte. 60, left on Fairground Rd. Blenko stained glass graces such famous buildings as the Air Force Academy Chapel in Colorado, and Grant's Tomb, St. John the Divine, and St. Patrick's in New York City. The company's decorative glassware has been cherished by a number of First Ladies. The display area comprises an exhibit on the company's history and its current line of glassware. A museum contains historical glass along with the Designer's Corner, where state-of-the-art designs are exhibited by leading stained-glass studios.

Along the walkway to the factory itself, piles of jewellike broken glass await recycling. Inside the plant, you can watch from an observation deck as craftsmen fire and blow molten glass. Nearby, on the Mud River, you might see some of the 200 or so ducks and geese that make their home there. *Visitor center open Mon.–Sat. and P.M. Sun. except holidays; plant open Mon.–Fri. except July 1–15, Dec. 25–Jan. 1, and holidays.*

58A Sunrise Museums, Charleston

5 min. East on Oakwood Rd., right on MacCorkle Ave. (Rte. 61); bear right and go up C & O ramp, right on Bridge Rd., right on Myrtle Rd. The Children's Museum, housed in a former governor's mansion, captivates youngsters with "open us" discovery boxes of seashells and fossils, an exhibit that explains myths and legends of natural phenomena, a ray table that bends and bounces the light, a dollhouse, models of coaches and a circus wagon, and a 60-seat planetarium. The Art Museum has a fine collection of 17th- to 20th-century American art, along with etchings by Rembrandt and Picasso and engravings by Matisse and Dürer. *Open Tues.–Sat. and P.M. Sun. except holidays. Admission charged.* ♿

11. *In this forested realm, the only openings, such as this park, are man-made.*

58A Kanawha State Forest

8 mi./15 min. South on Rte. 119, left on Oakwood Rd.; follow signs. There are 17 trails to choose from amid these 9,250 forested acres in West Virginia—ranging from a steep climb over Overlook Rock Trail to a gentle stroll along Spotted Salamander Trail (designed for the handicapped). Joggers and bikers enjoy the paved road through this wilderness of pines, hemlocks, sycamores, and dogwoods. Beside the quiet lake there are wooden seats from which to view the scenic mountain backdrop; anglers try for bass, catfish, and bluegill. Deer, black bears, and raccoons inhabit the forest. *Open year-round. Fee charged for swimming.* ⛱ ⛺ 🚐 🚶 🦫 🎣 ♿

129 Grandview State Park

5 mi./8 min. Follow signs to park. Breathtaking views of the New River are a prime attraction here. At North Overlook you'll see the horseshoe bend in the river where hawks nest in a rocky gorge; and from Main Overlook the river and trains that run beside it are some 1,500 feet below. The steep hillsides, covered with mountain laurel, hemlock, dogwood, pink lady's slipper, and rhododendron, come alive with color in the spring and summer. On a self-guiding nature trail, you may see some of the turkey vultures, grouse, and wild turkeys that inhabit the park. *Open year-round.*

169 Organ Cave

8 mi./12 min. South on Rte. 219, left on Rte. 63. This gigantic West Virginia cavern stretches for 42 subterranean miles, making it one of the largest in America. Inside you'll find the million-year-old rock formation that gives the cave its name: a 40-foot-high limestone wall that looks like a church organ and has "pipes" that produce sounds when tapped with a wooden mallet. All trails in the cave afford fine views of frozen waterfalls and natural sculptures—including one bearing an eerie resemblance to Gen. Robert E. Lee. It is said that Thomas Jefferson discovered a dinosaur skeleton in the cavern in 1791. *Open daily Apr.–Oct.; by appointment rest of year: (304) 647-5551. Admission charged.*

8 Douthat State Park

6 mi./10 min. North on Rte. 629. Surrounded by George Washington National Forest, this 4,493-acre park is the habitat of a variety of wildlife. Deer amble through the deciduous forest, and industrious beavers build their dams nearby. Fishermen will enjoy 50-acre Douthat Lake, which is the home of bass and bluegill and is stocked weekly with rainbow trout. Rowboats and paddleboats are available for rent. Bird lovers may spot pileated woodpeckers, yellow warblers, screech owls, red-tailed hawks, and during migrations, a variety of waterfowl. The half-mile Buck Lick Trail is the shortest in a network of 24 hiking trails. Adjoining the office is a small museum featuring a topographical map of Virginia, local rocks and minerals, and a push-button nature quiz for children. *Open year-round. Admission charged.*

I-81 Natural Bridge

15 mi./20 min. South on I-81 to Exit 50, south on Rte. 11. Natural Bridge is a single block of solid limestone—90 feet long, up to 150 feet wide, and 215 feet high—that straddles Cedar Creek and joins two mountains in the Blue Ridge country. The Monacan Indians named this natural phenomenon the Bridge of God, but geologists credit millions of years of erosion by the creek as its sculptor. Look along the southeast wall of the bridge for the initials G. W., whittled by George Washington when he surveyed the site in 1750. It was once owned by Thomas Jefferson, who purchased it and 157 acres from King George III for 20 shillings. A sound-and-light show, "Drama of Creation," is presented at night. *Open year-round. Admission charged.*

I-81 Woodrow Wilson Birthplace, Staunton

4 mi./8 min. North on I-81 to Exit 57, west on Rte. 250, right on Coalter St. America's 28th president was born in this Greek revival Virginia town house on December 28, 1856. Today, 12 beautifully restored rooms display many of the original furnishings and family memorabilia. You'll see the Bible in which Reverend Joseph Ruggles Wilson, a Presbyterian minister, recorded his son's birth; a period quilt; antique dolls; a rolltop desk and a typewriter desk from Wilson's study at Princeton University, where he was president from 1902 to 1910; and two ornate brass oil lamps that he bought while he was a student at the University of Virginia. A Victorian garden and a carriage house containing Wilson's restored 1920 Pierce-Arrow presidential limousine add to the period atmosphere. A film about Wilson is shown at the reception center. *Open daily Mar.–Dec.; Mon.–Sat. Jan.–Feb. except Thanksgiving Day, Christmas, and New Year's Day. Admission charged.*

22 The University of Virginia, Charlottesville

5 mi./20 min. North on Rte. 29, right on Rte. 250 (business; becomes Ivy Blvd., then University Ave.). Located 20 miles east of the Blue Ridge Mountains, this 1,050-acre campus is a monument to the vision of Thomas Jefferson, who planned the university, designed its buildings, set the curriculum, recruited its first faculty, and served as its first rector. The original complex—with its academic and residential buildings, called pavilions, and hotels representing different European styles—was designated by the American Institute of Architects as an outstanding achievement of American architecture. The dominant structure is the 1826 rotunda, a scaled-down replica of the Roman Pantheon. *Grounds open year-round; rotunda open daily except Thanksgiving Day and mid-Dec.–early Jan.*

24 Monticello, Charlottesville

5 min. South on Rte. 20, left on Rte. 53. On his "little mountain," nestled between rolling farmland and the Blue Ridge Mountains, Thomas Jefferson began to build his dream house, Monticello, in 1768. For the next 40 years this versatile innovator supervised nearly every detail of its design and construction, drawing on his imagination to create one of America's architectural masterpieces. The gracious 21-room Palladian-style mansion—

24. *Thomas Jefferson's masterpiece is an important example of neoclassic architecture.*

crowned with the first dome ever built on an American house—reflects Jefferson's inventiveness and his lifelong love of collecting. It contains original domestic objects and a library with a nucleus of books that launched the Library of Congress. The gardens reflect his interest and skill in horticulture and landscape design. *Open year-round except Christmas. Admission charged.*

34 / 48 Kings Dominion

Exit 34: 24 mi./25 min. East on I-295, north on I-95 to Exit 40, right on Rte. 30. Exit 48: 29 mi./35 min. West on I-295, north on I-95; proceed as above. It's five theme parks in one. Shock-Wave, the stand-up roller coaster, begins with a 95-foot drop, races in a 360° loop, and ends with a triple corkscrew—just one of the more than 40 rides here. The less intrepid can get their feet wet on one of several spectacular water rides; stroll, snack, and shop along International Street; mingle with Yogi Bear and his pals; chime in for a sing-along; see some 50 species of wild animals from the Safari monorail; or look down on all the bustle from atop a replica of the Eiffel Tower. *Open daily June–Labor Day; weekends late Mar.–May, mid-Sept.–mid-Oct. Admission charged.*

I-95S Richmond, VA 23219

Convention and Visitors Bureau, 300 E. Main St. (804) 782-2777. Although the imperatives of the present day are stylishly acknowledged at Shockoe Slip and the Sixth Street Marketplace, proud memories of the Old South are found throughout this capital city, which was also the capital of the Confederacy. The handsome state capitol is a classic design selected by Thomas Jefferson. On Monument Avenue, paved with hand-laid brick, the statues of Confederate heroes vie for attention with the stately houses. Other historic highlights are St. John's Church, the John Marshall House, and the Wickham-Valentine House.

Among the attractions of more recent vintage are the Virginia Museum of Fine Arts, the Richmond Children's Museum, and the Science Museum of Virginia.

56. *The original inhabitants would still feel at home on Duke of Gloucester Street.*

56 Colonial Williamsburg

5 min. South on Rte. 132; follow signs. In this first and finest restoration of an early American town, one can come as close as is possible in the 20th century to experiencing the scope and character of colonial life in the 1700's. The main thoroughfare is the mile-long Duke of Gloucester Street, which runs from the Capitol to the College of William and Mary. Such artisans as weavers, cabinetmakers, gunsmiths, and many others explain their trades as they work. Sheep graze on the village green. The rhythmic clip-clop of carriage horses reinforces the illusion of a less complex and crowded time. *Open year-round. Admission charged.*

57A Busch Gardens, The Old Country, Williamsburg

4 min. Southwest on Rte. 199; follow signs. This enormous theme park—featuring reproductions of French, Italian, German, and English villages—brings the flavor of the Old World to America. You can enjoy a Renaissance fair, drive a replica of a Le Mans race car, and feast at one of the country's largest restaurants. Rides range from thrilling roller coasters to sedate river cruises, and craftsmen demonstrate everything from making fudge to carving a cuckoo clock. *Open daily mid-May–Labor Day; weekends only Apr.–mid-May, Sept.–Oct. Admission charged.*

62A The Mariners' Museum, Newport News

3 mi./7 min. South on J. Clyde Morris Blvd.; follow signs. The adventures, romance, and perils of the sea are dramatized in this outstanding collection of marine artifacts and vessels. Hundreds of items are on display: parts from the *Monitor* and the *Merrimack*, whose Civil War clash ushered in the era of ironclad warships; marine paintings dating back to the 17th century; replicas of Columbus's *Santa Maria*; full-size examples of a four-oar Norwegian rowboat and a Venetian gondola; and hand-carved figureheads, including a gilded eagle with a wingspan of 18½ feet that once adorned a U.S. Navy frigate. You'll also see the Crabtree Collection of miniature ships, carved with painstaking attention to detail. *Open Mon.–Sat. and P.M. Sun. except Christmas. Admission charged.*

BAR | California Desert Information Center

Barstow Rd. exit: 2 min. North on Barstow Rd.; follow signs. Whether you are about to cross the great Mojave Desert or have already done so, a stop here will enhance your appreciation of the region and its plant and animal life. Noteworthy among the displays are preserved specimens of desert rattlers (surprisingly small in size) and other creatures to watch out for when exploring on foot. Should you plan to venture onto desert roads in a four-wheel-drive vehicle, the center will provide you with a detailed map of the Mojave. On view part of the year is the Old Woman meteorite, the second largest ever found in the United States (the remainder of the year the Smithsonian has the real meteorite, while the center displays a replica). Weighing over 6,000 pounds, it was discovered in 1975 in the Old Woman Mountains in the eastern Mojave. Across the street from the information center you'll find a small, pleasant park with sheltered picnic tables. *Open daily except Christmas and New Year's Day.* ♿

ESS | Providence Mountains State Recreation Area

Essex Rd. exit: 16 mi./20 min. North on Essex Rd.; follow signs. This 6,000-acre recreation area, with sunbaked slopes ideally seen in spring, is a good place to explore the Mojave Desert. The visitor center at Mitchell Caverns is reached by a road that climbs imperceptibly over miles of rangeland before making an abrupt ascent into the mountains. On arrival, you'll find a spectacular vista encompassing more than 300 square miles of desert scenery, with the Providence Mountains to the west. The visitor center will provide you with trail maps and lists of the area's wildlife, including bighorn sheep and golden eagles. It is a half-mile walk to the refreshingly cool caverns, which are filled with unusual limestone structures. Also nearby is the Mary Beal Nature Study Trail. Miss Beal spent some 50 years in the Mojave collecting and identifying more than 1,000 specimens of desert flowers. *Recreation area open year-round; caverns and visitor center open mid-Sept.–mid-June. Admission charged for caverns.* ⛱ ⛺ 🚐 🚶

9 | London Bridge, Lake Havasu City

20 mi./25 min. South on Rte. 95, right on McCulloch Blvd.; follow signs. A bona fide old stone bridge from foggy London, England, relocated in a raw new city in the sunny Southwest? Incredible as it seems, the 140-year-old bridge was shipped stone by stone to Lake Havasu City, Arizona, in the 1960's. Purchased for about $2.5 million, it was brought here by an American real estate developer to attract visitors. The handsome arched bridge connects the city with Pittsburg Point, a large island in Lake Havasu. State-owned Pittsburg Point is devoted to recreation, and it offers parks, a swimming beach, and other facilities. Around the bridge on the mainland side there is a Tudor-style English village with pavilions, shops, and pubs flanking the water's edge. With pennants flying from the bridge, and sailboats and sightseeing steamers gliding under it, the scene is indeed festive. *Open year-round.* ⛱ 🚐 🚶 🛥 ♿

48 | Mohave Museum of History and Arts, Kingman

3 min. East onto W. Beale St. This excellent museum commemorates different periods of Kingman's past with a lively use of local color. Dioramas, artifacts, and a mural by Roy Purcell, a painter of the Southwest, vividly depict the everyday life of the Mohave and Hualapai Indians before and after the advent of the white man in the area. One room honors a favorite citizen, the late Hollywood star Andy Devine, who died in 1977. An early Shell gas pump is a reminder of old Route 66, a nearby section of which has been restored. Another attraction is a complete set of portraits of U.S. presidents and their wives. *Open Mon.–Fri. and P.M. weekends except Thanksgiving Day, Christmas, and New Year's Day. Admission free but donations encouraged.*

51 | Hualapai Mountain Park

11.5 mi./15 min. South on Stockton Hill Rd. (becomes Hualapai Mountain Rd.). Beautiful scenery and the pine-scented mountain air make this an ideal destination for a summer picnic. The park also has a number of stone and wood cabins for rent with wood-burning stoves or fireplaces. On weekends people congregate at the large rustic stone lodge, where there's a roaring blaze in the fireplace. Several miles of hiking trails cross the slopes to overlook points ranging in elevation from 6,000 to 8,000 feet or more, and eagles and hawks may be seen soaring overhead. *Open year-round.* ⛱ ⛺ 🚐 🚶

171 | Grand Canyon Deer Farm

2 min. Exit north, left on Deer Farm Rd.; follow signs. The deer farm's bright red barn with white trim is a friendly sight reminiscent of a child's picture book. And when you walk into the large fenced yard behind the barn, pet deer, goats, llamas, monkeys, shaggy miniature donkeys, and other small, friendly animals are ready to nuzzle you and take food from your hands. The farm usually has more than 100 deer and other creatures, many of which may be petted by children. Depending upon the time of year, fawns or other baby animals may be seen. *Open daily May–Sept.; Tues.–Sat. Oct.–Dec.; Wed.–Sat. Jan.–Mar. except Thanksgiving Day, Christmas Eve, and Christmas, weather permitting. Admission charged.* ⛱

195 | Slide Rock State Park

23 mi./30 min. South on I-17 to Exit 337, south on Rte. 89A. The park is in Oak Creek Canyon, one of the most beautiful spots in the Southwest and said to be the setting for Zane Grey's novel *Call of the Canyon.* About 13 miles south of Flagstaff the road suddenly enters the canyon, and for the next 16 miles it zigzags down between dramatic, pine-accented red rock cliffs and spires until you reach Sedona. Although the canyon is a recreation area, parking is difficult until you reach Slide Rock State Park. From the parking lot there, it's a short walk to Slide Rock itself, where the creek has worn a natural water slide over smooth red rocks made slick by moss. Children and adults alike enjoy slipping down the slide into a natural pool. Hiking and casting for rainbow trout are the other attractions. *Open daily. Admission charged.* ⛱ 🚶 🐟 ♿

195   Lowell Observatory, Flagstaff

3 mi./10 min. North on S. Milton Rd., left on Santa Fe Ave.; follow signs. With a certain old-fashioned charm, this observatory may strike you as too quaint to be involved in serious astronomical research. But ever since its founding by Percival Lowell in 1894, some important observations have been recorded here, including those that led to the discovery by Clyde Tombaugh of the planet Pluto in 1930—a discovery that was predicted by Lowell himself—and to the formulation of the theory of an expanding universe. The observatory has eight telescopes, among them the historic 24-inch Alvan Clark telescope, which is still in use. The telescopes are involved in gathering new data on everything from comets and nearby stars to distant galaxies and quasars. Near the dome is the mausoleum of Percival Lowell, perhaps best known for his studies of the planet Mars. The attractive

204. *No one knows why the Sinaguas chose to live in these cliffs—or why they left.*

grounds provide scenic views of the Flagstaff area. *Open Tues.–Sat. June–Aug.; open for 1:30 P.M. tour only, Sept.–May except holidays. For evening viewing call (602) 774-2096. Admission free but donations encouraged.*

195   Museum of Northern Arizona, Flagstaff

5 mi./20 min. North on S. Milton Rd., right on Santa Fe Ave., left on Humphreys St., left on Rte. 180. This museum has thousands of fascinating specimens and artifacts relating to the cultural and natural history of the region. The intriguing collection of Hopi kachina dolls, carved representations of deified ancestral spirits, is grouped according to the ceremonies with which they are associated. Examples of prehistoric baskets are shown along with exhibits of tools and the methods used to make them. Other crafts include Kayenta pottery and Navajo and Hopi weaving. One wing of the museum depicts the geologic history of the Colorado Plateau, featuring the skeleton of a huge 20,000-year-old sloth. The museum also boasts a lovely cloistered garden. *Open daily except Thanksgiving Day, Christmas, and New Year's Day. Admission charged.* ♿

204   Walnut Canyon National Monument

5 min. South on Walnut Canyon Rd.; follow signs. The entry road to this national monument whisks you away from the desert and into a forest scented by ponderosa pines and Douglas firs. The banana yuccas flourishing here open their large pale yellow blooms in the spring. Named for the black walnuts that grow within it, the deep canyon has walls of sandstone and limestone, where the Sinagua Indians made their home until about A.D. 1250. The Sinaguas were early hunters and gatherers until they finally turned to farming for survival. You can hike down a steep 240-step trail into the canyon and enter their cliffside homes or follow an easier trail along the rim that provides good views of the dwellings. Mule deer, pronghorns, elk, and other wildlife may be seen nearby, and bald eagles in winter. *Open daily except Thanksgiving Day and Christmas. Admission charged.* ⛢ 🚶 ♿

If You Have Some Extra Time:

Grand Canyon National Park

165   *60 mi./70 min.* We've all seen the dazzling photographs and read the glowing descriptions of its magnificence and unique evolution. But to stand on the South Rim is to be awed by the panorama of shapes and colors and challenged by the undeniable evidence of time that can only be counted in thousands of millions of years.

About 6 million years ago, the Colorado River began to carve the canyon in an area of land that had been slowly uplifted by movements in the earth's crust. Wind, ice, floods, and gravity also shaped the canyon's rock formations, creating this phenomenal conjunction of infinitely varied towers and walls with layers of limestone, shale, and sandstone left by ancient rivers, seas, and deserts.

It's about 10 miles across to the canyon's North Rim, and about 1 mile down to the Colorado River and the Vishnu schist, a 2-billion-year-old rock. Going from one canyon end to the other, the river twists so much that it is some 277 miles long. The 9-mile trail down to the river passes through four botanical zones; to see a comparable range of plant and animal life you would have to drive from the Mexican desert to northern forests. The canyon is like no other place on earth. If you have time, it's an experience that you'll never forget. *How to get there: Exit 165, north on Rte. 64 to park entrance. South Rim open year-round. Admission charged.*

285–311. *Former giants of the forest have been transformed to colorful solid stone.*

233 | Meteor Crater Natural Landmark

5 mi./8 min. South on Meteor Crater Rd. Anyone intrigued by space travel, science fiction, or astrogeology will be fascinated by this amazing site. Some 50,000 years ago a solid nickel-iron meteorite hurtled to Earth at the speed of about 45,000 miles per hour and slammed into the ground here. The result of the impact is a hole 570 feet deep, 4,100 feet wide, and over 3 miles in circumference. Almost nothing has been found of the meteorite—it is thought that most of it vaporized on impact—but the crater is the best preserved on our planet. Apollo astronauts trained here in the late 1960's because the moon is also pitted with meteoritic craters. In fact, from a platform below the rim, it is easy to imagine yourself on the moon. The museum offers exhibits on the history of the site and the study of earth and space sciences. *Open year-round. Admission charged.*

285 / 311 | Petrified Forest National Park

Exit 285: 21 mi./30 min. South on Rte. 180 to South Gate. Exit 311: 1 min. Exit north to North Gate. The park is famous for the Painted Desert (at the North Gate) and the Rainbow Forest (at the South Gate). A scenic 28-mile road connects the two. There are several stopping places, and an excellent park map explains the highlights along the way. In the Painted Desert Visitor Center, a film shows how wood becomes petrified. The Rainbow Forest Museum features exhibits on ancient reptiles and the region's human and geological history. A nearby trail leads past a jumble of 225-million-year-old fallen petrified trees. Some of the most magnificent vistas are at Blue Mesa, reached by a 3-mile loop road. Here the landscape is striated with smoky lavenders and rich blues. *Open daily except Christmas. Admission charged.*

26 | Red Rock State Park and Museum

4 mi./7 min. East on Rte. 66, left on Rte. 566; follow signs. Just east of Gallup, which is known as the Indian jewelry capital of the world, this park is an active Indian cultural center. In August the famous Intertribal Indian Ceremonial brings visitors here. But the year-round highlight of the park is the museum, whose modern terra-cotta building stands at the base of spectacular red-hued sandstone monoliths. In it you'll see outstanding examples of Pueblo pottery, Plains Indians beadwork, textiles, basketry, jewelry, and sand paintings. A garden displays some splendid sculptures of Indians carved from tree trunks. Nature trails are being developed that will lead visitors to petroglyph sites. *Park open year-round; museum open daily Memorial Day–Labor Day; Mon.–Fri. Labor Day–Memorial Day except Thanksgiving Day, Christmas, and New Year's Day. Admission free but donations encouraged.*

63 | Bluewater Lake State Park

7 mi./15 min. South on Rte. 412. The dazzling blue of the lake, a 7-mile-long reservoir in a deep valley, is a refreshing sight at the end of a drive through the piñon forest of the Zuni Mountains east of the Continental Divide. The chief attraction is the chance to fish for enormous, feisty rainbow trout and channel catfish. The record for both is 16 pounds. Ice fishing is popular in winter. In summer, the elevation (7,400 feet) and the breezes off the water provide relief from the searing heat of the valley below. *Open year-round. Admission charged.*

102 | Pueblo of Acoma

16 mi./20 min. South on Rte. 30, left on Rte. 32; follow signs. On its splendid sandstone mesa rising dramatically from the valley floor, Acoma, dating to about A.D. 1150, is called the oldest continuously inhabited community in the nation. In 1540, the first white visitor was the Spanish conquistador Francisco Vásquez de Coronado, who found ascending the mesa on foot so taxing that "we repented climbing to the top." Today visitors are taken to the village by bus. On the guided walking tour you can see the ancient houses, visit a mission chapel dating back to the 1600's, and enjoy the sweeping vistas. The visitor center has exhibits of pottery and jewelry and the history of Acoma. *Open daily except Easter weekend, July 10–13, and first weekend in Oct. Admission charged for tours.*

157A | Albuquerque, NM 87103

Convention & Visitors Bureau, 305 Romero St. NW. (505) 243-3696; (800) 284-2282 outside NM. The Spanish influence is pleasantly recalled in the Old Town area, with its plaza and the San Felipe de Neri Church (1706). The architecture on the University of New Mexico campus has been influenced by the Indian pueblos. Anthropology, geology, and the arts are featured in the city's museums. At the New Mexico Museum of Natural History you can step into a volcano or an Ice Age cave and admire a model of a flying quetzalcoatlus with its wingspan of 40 feet. World War II correspondent Ernie Pyle's home is open to the public. The Indian Pueblo Cultural Center details the culture and history of the Indian peoples of New Mexico.

I-25   Isleta Pueblo

16 mi./20 min. South on I-25 to Exit 213, south on Isleta Blvd., left on Rte. 147. One of the oldest communities in the U.S.A., Isleta was already a settled pueblo when Francisco Vásquez de Coronado passed by in 1540, looking for gold. Isleta's first mission church, begun in 1613, was abandoned during the Pueblo Indian revolt of 1680; it was restored in 1710 and the name changed to St. Augustine in 1720. Two stained-glass windows depict Pueblo Indians receiving the sacraments. The crosses on the church towers serve as landmarks for visitors trying to find their way through a maze of narrow streets to the plaza in the center of town, where pottery is fired and bread baked in beehive-shaped outdoor ovens. *Open year-round.*

I-25   Coronado State Park and State Monument

18 mi./20 min. North on I-25 to Exit 242B, west on Rte. 44. In 1540, Spanish explorers led by Francisco Vásquez de Coronado, in a futile search for gold, camped among Pueblo farmers at this oasis, still used by campers today, along the Rio Grande. Excavations of the Kuaua pueblo ruins revealed a subterranean room, or kiva, the walls of which were covered with murals that are outstanding examples of prehistoric art. Today these and other artifacts from the site are displayed in the monument's museum, and the partially restored village of 1,200 rooms is open for viewing. *Open daily except Thanksgiving Day, Christmas, and New Year's Day. Admission charged.*

164A / 167   National Atomic Museum, Albuquerque

Exit 164A: 5 min. South on Wyoming Blvd. Exit 167: 6 mi./9 min. West on Central Ave. (Rte. 66), left on Wyoming Blvd. A B-52 bomber used in the last atmospheric nuclear tests, a 280-mm. atomic cannon, and futuristic-looking surface-to-air missiles occupy the grounds outside this museum, which focuses on nuclear weaponry. Exhibits and films illustrate the history of the first atom bomb and include full-size models of its first

two designs. Also featured at the museum are planes and missiles created to carry atomic weapons, the development of the hydrogen bomb, advances in weapons technology, safety and testing, and demonstrations of peaceful uses of nuclear technology. *Open daily except Thanksgiving Day, Christmas, New Year's Day, and Easter.*

167   Sandia Peak Aerial Tramway, Albuquerque

11 mi./15 min. North on Tramway Blvd.; follow signs. One of the world's longest aerial tramways carries riders on a breathtaking trip of 2.7 miles, from Sandia Peak's desert base, over canyons and dense forests, to its verdant top. During the 15-minute ride, which covers a vertical rise of 3,800 feet, visitors may spot mule deer below and golden eagles circling overhead. From Sandia Peak, which is part of the Cibola National Forest, you can enjoy a spectacular view of more than 11,000 square miles. You'll also find hiking trails and areas for rock climbing and hang gliding. In winter the tram is a ski lift, giving access to 25 miles of trails. *Open daily Memorial Day–Labor Day; Thurs.–Tues. and P.M. Wed. Labor Day–Memorial Day. Admission charged.*

If You Have Some Extra Time: Canyon de Chelly National Monument

333   **65 mi./90 min.** Rising 30 to 1,000 feet above the valley floor, the vertical sandstone walls of this Arizona canyon are breathtaking, and the ruined cliff dwellings have varied cultural implications. The Anasazis ("Enemy Ancestors") lived here almost 1,000 years ago. They were primarily farmers dwelling in the valley near the Rio de Chelly, where they planted crops as the Navajo Indians do this day. The early Pueblo people built shelters in the high ledges of the valley walls. Today the ruins of these cliff dwellings evoke the spirit of an industrious and ingenious people.

This land now belongs to the Navajo Indians, and travel into Canyon de Chelly (pronounced "Shay") and its tributaries is allowed only with a park-ranger escort or in authorized groups. The only unguided walk is a trail (2½ miles round-trip) from an overlook on the South Rim Drive down to the ruins of the Whitehouse, a dwelling constructed in two sections, one on the canyon floor and the other in a cave directly over it.

The archeological museum at the visitor center presents the different Indian cultures that brought life to this dramatically forbidding landscape. *How to get there: Exit 333, north on Rte. 191 to Chinle, right on Indian Rte. 7; follow signs. Monument open year-round; visitor center open daily except Thanksgiving Day, Christmas, and New Year's Day. Admission charged.*

275 Rock Lake Trout Rearing Unit, Santa Rosa

4 mi./9 min. West on Will Rogers Dr. (becomes Parker Ave., then Coronado W.); cross bridge, left on River Rd. This state-run fish hatchery produces an estimated 33 million walleyed pike hatchlings each year for immediate release into lakes in New Mexico and other states. (If the pike are not released within a few days, they will eat each other.) It also raises 305,000 rainbow trout from fingerlings to lengths of 8–10 inches. Highly oxygenated water allows for considerable density of trout (which, unlike pike, are not cannibalistic) in the concrete ponds, where they feed from automatic food dispensers. *Open year-round.*

332. *An engaging array of artifacts, mostly related to the early days of railroading.*

275 Santa Rosa Dam, Lake and State Park

9 mi./15 min. West on Will Rogers Dr. (becomes Parker Ave.), right on 2nd St.; follow signs. Swimmers, water-skiers, and fishermen share Santa Rosa Lake with an abundance of migrating waterfowl. Hiking trails lead through the piñon and juniper trees and cacti that dot the surrounding wild high desert. The information center that overlooks the dam here on the Pecos River has exhibits on more than 250 archeological sites that reveal former habitation by early pueblo-dwelling Indian farmers, nomadic hunters, and the Comanche and Apache tribes. *Open year-round. Admission charged.*

329 Ute Lake State Park, Logan
356

Exit 329: 27 mi./30 min. Northeast on Rte. 54, left on Rte. 540. Exit 356: 25 mi./30 min. North on Rte. 39, left on Rte. 540. One of the largest lakes in New Mexico, Ute Lake is favored by fishermen, who flock from surrounding states to try for walleye, bass, crappie, and channel catfish. Scuba divers swim beneath the surface in pursuit of the biggest fish. Water-skiing, sailboarding, and swimming are other popular activities on this long, narrow lake, which was created by a dam on the Canadian River. *Open year-round. Admission charged.*

332 Tucumcari Historical Museum

5 min. North on Rte. 18, right on Tucumcari Blvd., left on Adams St. An early sheriff's office in this museum recalls the town's wild beginnings as a railroad construction camp called Six Shooter Siding. Other exhibits include Indian artifacts dating to 12,000 B.C., cowboy memorabilia, pioneer kitchens, and an early hospital. Outside there's a turn-of-the-century windmill, a chuck wagon, a Southern Pacific caboose, fossils, and farming and ranching implements. *Open Mon.–Sat. and P.M. Sun. Memorial Day–Labor Day; Tues.–Sat. and P.M. Sun. Labor Day–Memorial Day except Thanksgiving Day, Christmas, and New Year's Day. Admission charged.*

36 Cal Farley's Boys Ranch

21 mi./30 min. North on Rte. 385, right at sign north of Canadian River. This 10,000-acre ranch, founded by an Amarillo businessman in 1939 to help troubled boys, is now a community of nearly 400 students, complete with homelike dormitories, a chapel, and facilities for academic and vocational education through high school. The Old Tascosa Courthouse building, which housed the ranch's first six inhabitants, is now a museum of Panhandle culture and displays Indian artifacts, cowboy and pioneer memorabilia, and photos and documents that relate to Boys Ranch. Near the museum is a small zoo with local wildlife. *Open year-round.*

65 Don Harrington Discovery Center, Amarillo

3 min. North on Coulter Dr.; follow signs. This innovative center aims to generate a sense of wonder about science and the natural world. There are planetarium shows, an aquarium filled with piranhas and other exotic fish, displays that demonstrate the workings of the human body, and an ambitious schedule of special programs. The Black Hole exhibit demonstrates centrifugal force; a giant kaleidoscope and movie screens in the round deliver spectacular visual effects. *Open Tues.– Sat. and P.M. Sun. except holidays. Admission charged for planetarium shows.*

70 Wonderland Park, Amarillo

5 min. North on Buchanan St. (Rte. 287), left on NE 24th Ave. This family amusement park has 21 rides, including such thrillers as the Texas Tornado double-loop roller coaster, the Cyclone, the H_2O Raging Riptide water slide, the Scrambler, and the Big Splash log flume. Those who prefer gentler pursuits may try the carousel, miniature golf, or remote-controlled boats. In spacious Thompson Park, which surrounds Wonderland Park, picnic areas, a swimming pool, and a zoo add diversity. *Wonderland Park open P.M. daily late Apr.–Labor Day; P.M. weekends mid.-Mar.–late Apr. and Sept. Admission charged. Thompson Park open year-round.*

70. *Henry Ford's masterpiece, the Model T, in the Panhandle-Plains Museum.*

163. *The homey charm of the pioneers' kitchen was sacrificed for modern efficiency.*

70 | Panhandle–Plains Historical Museum, Canyon

20 mi./23 min. South on I-27 to Exit 106, west on Rte. 217. The ancient past of northwest Texas is imaginatively illustrated with marine fossils and dinosaur skeletons in this regional museum. Human settlement in the area is represented by artifacts from Southern Plains Indian tribes, a full-size 1925 oil drilling rig, and a ranching exhibit with guns, saddles, a chuck wagon, and vintage photographs. *Open Mon.–Sat. and P.M. Sun. except holidays. Admission free but donations encouraged.*   ♿

96 | Carson County Square House Museum

9 mi./15 min. North on Rte. 207. Exhibits on the history of the Texas Panhandle, from prehistoric Indian culture to space exploration, are presented in and around an 1880's square wood-frame house that, when built, was considered the embodiment of luxury on these treeless plains. Nearby, a dark, cramped dugout illustrates how less affluent settlers lived. (Not only was there no wood, but there were also no stoves and not enough water to make adobe bricks.) Other aspects of pioneer life are exemplified by a blacksmith's shop, a Santa Fe Railroad caboose, and a bank exhibit with a collection of cattle brands. There are

dioramas with aoudad sheep and other wildlife of the area, as well as one of the largest collections of paintings by Southwest Indians in the country. *Open Mon.–Sat. and P.M. Sun. except Thanksgiving Day, Christmas, and New Year's Day.*   ♿

163 | Pioneer West Museum, Shamrock

4 min. South on Rte. 83, left on 3rd St., right on Madden St. A favorite stop for traveling salesmen since its completion in 1928, the Reynolds Hotel has now become a museum, housing a wide variety of items that reflect Shamrock history. Plains Indian artifacts, cowboy memorabilia, and old weapons line several rooms. Carefully restored and re-created rooms—a doctor's office, a general store, a schoolroom, and a pioneer kitchen—evoke the past. *Open Mon.–Fri. except Thanksgiving Day, Christmas, and New Year's Day.*   ♿

38 | Old Town Museum Complex, Elk City

5 min. North on Rte. 6 (Main St.), left on Rte. 40 (business; becomes Van Buren Ave., then 3rd St.). Housed in a turn-of-the-century home with gingerbread trim, the museum features a mercantile display about original owner O. H. Young's business activities, rooms restored with late-Victorian period furnishings, a pioneer doctor's office, an antique wagon, and old photos and memorabilia from local rodeo impresarios. On the grounds a carefully restored one-room stone schoolhouse, built in 1894, and the Pioneer Chapel represent two formative influences on the lives of town homesteaders. *Open Tues.–Sat. and P.M. Sun. except holidays. Admission charged.*   ♿

53 | Foss Lake

7 mi./10 min. North on Rte. 44. At the south end of this 8,800-acre reservoir is Foss State Park, where swimmers and sunbathers enjoy the sandy beach, boaters and water-skiers cruise the water, and fishermen try for catfish, bass, walleyed pike, crappie, and bluegill. At the lake's northern end, the Washita National Wildlife Refuge accommodates thousands of migrating waterfowl and sandhill cranes. The birds and other wildlife are easily seen from roads, trails, and an observation platform. During the warm months scissor-tailed flycatchers perform their aerial acrobatics. *Open year-round.*

38. *Generous porches and a handsome gazebo provide welcome shade from the midday sun.*

212. *Traditional Seminole clothing is noted for its color and meticulous handwork.*

ROB Oklahoma City, OK 73102

Robinson Ave. exit: Convention and Tourism Bureau, 4 Santa Fe Plaza. (405) 278-8912. The highlights in this large city—more than 600 square miles in area and named from two Indian words meaning "Land of the Red People"—are widespread and varied. The National Cowboy Hall of Fame and Western Heritage Center attracts those interested in the lore and artifacts of the West, while the National Softball Hall of Fame appeals to sandlot ballplayers of all ages.

The state capitol is unique in that there are working oil wells on its grounds. Nearby, the State Museum presents the major events in the colorful history of the Indian Territory and Oklahoma. Kirkpatrick Center is a large museum complex featuring African, Oriental, and American Indian art, as well as photography and science displays, a planetarium, a greenhouse, and gardens. Oklahoma City's enormous zoo has some 4,000 animals as well as the Aquaticus, which features dolphin and sea lion shows and varied displays of aquatic life.

212 Seminole Nation Museum, Wewoka

17 mi./26 min. South on Rte. 56, left on 6th St. The museum effectively chronicles the Seminole Indians' way of life and their continuing struggle to adapt after forced relocation from the humid shores of Florida and the Gulf Coast to these dry, windy plains. Displays include 19th-century photos, an impressive collection of western sculpture and paintings, and a replica of an early Seminole chikee, a dwelling built on stilts and made of palmetto leaves, tree branches, and leather. The re-created Wewoka Trading Post recalls Oklahoma's pioneer days. *Open P.M. Tues.–Sun. Feb.–Dec. except Thanksgiving Day, Christmas Eve, and Christmas.*

240B Creek Council House Museum, Okmulgee

15 mi./25 min. North on Rte. 75/62, left on 6th St. This museum is housed in the former Creek national capitol, a handsome two-story stone building dating to 1878. It contains an interesting collection of Muskogee Creek and Yuchi Indian paintings, old photographs, historical maps, re-created rooms from territorial days, and tools, beadwork, hunting points, and other artifacts from the aboriginal period.

Until 1907 the Creek tribal council met in three rooms on the second floor, one of which has 48 chairs for the delegates from the 48 tribal towns. Another room displays Creek-made hanging rugs and tapestries along with historical costumes and clothing. *Open Tues.–Sat. except holidays.*

259 Fountainhead State Park

5 mi./8 min. South on Rte. 150. An oak and hickory forest contrasts with the prairies in this 2,800-acre park, which is actually a peninsula extending into Lake Eufaula (pronounced "you-*fall*-uh"). The huge man-made lake is famous for its largemouth and white bass fishing. The Nature Center features displays on the region's varied animals and plants, including bobcats, white-tailed deer, gray foxes, eagles, and owls, as well as the flowering dogwood and persimmon trees, blackberry bushes, and wild grapevines that provide both logs and food. Longhorn cattle and grazing elk can be viewed from an observation area, horses are available for guided scenic rides, and there are courses for full-scale and miniature golf. *Open year-round. Admission charged for sports activities.*

287 Greenleaf State Park
291

Exit 287: 13.5 mi./22 min. North on Rte. 100, left on Rte. 10. Exit 291: 14 mi./22 min. North on Rte. 10. This aptly named 565-acre park is situated in the beautiful oak-covered Cookson Hills. A 20-mile backpacking trail that circles 930-acre Greenleaf Lake provides striking views of the surrounding blue hills and the green Arkansas River valley. Boats are for rent at the lake, which has a swimming beach and offers excellent fishing for bass and catfish. Nearby Ft. Gibson Military Park, which was once a sprawling outpost at the edge of American civilization, has been rebuilt by the state of Oklahoma and is now open to visitors. *Open year-round.*

307 Spiro Mounds Archeological State Park, Spiro

29 mi./35 min. South on Rte. 59, left on Rte. 9, left on Lock and Dam Rd. No. 14. This small park encompasses 12 earthen mounds, dating from approximately A.D. 600 to 1600, which were used for Indian burial and religious ceremonies; a self-guiding walking tour leads to the largest. An audiovisual presentation at the Interpretive Center explains the sophisticated Spiro Indian culture and the area's importance as a trade center. "Grave goods" (possessions buried with their owners) and other artifacts excavated from the mounds are on display. *Open Tues.–Sat. and P.M. Sun. Apr.–Nov.; Wed.–Sat. and P.M. Sun. Dec.–Mar. except Christmas.*

7 Fort Smith National Historic Site and Old Fort Museum

13 mi./18 min. South on I-540 to Exit 8A, right on Rogers Ave. (Rte. 22). The main attraction here is the national historic site, and most notably the restored courtroom building

7. *Vintage pharmacy in Old Fort Museum has a fountain and the classic furniture.*

where, between 1875 and 1890, the "hanging judge," Isaac C. Parker, sentenced 160 Indian Territory outlaws to death. At the restored gallows nearby, as many as six men could be executed at one time. Although the site is surrounded by the Ft. Smith business district, its tree-lined grounds are evocative of the 19th-century frontier. Reservations for guided group tours must be made in advance by writing or calling the fort.

The Old Fort Museum, one block away, houses artifacts relating to Ft. Smith's military history. Ozarks craftspeople are occasionally on hand to demonstrate pioneer skills. *Historic site open daily except Christmas; museum open daily June–Aug.; Tues.–Sat. and P.M. Sun. Sept.–May except Thanksgiving Day, Christmas Eve, Christmas, and New Year's Day. Admission charged.* ♿

13 Lake Fort Smith State Park

13 mi./20 min. North on Rte. 71; follow signs. Surrounded by the grand peaks of the Boston Mountains, this wooded park is situated at the edge of a 650-acre lake known to fishermen for its bass, bream, crappie, and catfish. Skirting the lake, a 3½-mile stretch of the 140-mile Ozark Highlands Trail provides scenic views for hikers. An Olympic-size swimming pool, tennis courts, assorted playground equipment, and tree-shaded picnic sites combine to make the park a popular weekend retreat. Boats and canoes are available for rent. *Open year-round.*

81 Mount Nebo State Park, Dardanelle

15 mi./30 min. South on Rte. 7, right on Rte. 22, left on Rte. 155. From its elevation of 1,800 feet, the park affords dramatic views of the Arkansas River, Lake Dardanelle, and nearby peaks. The steep mountain road with its hairpin turns is especially scenic in the fall; in summer, picnickers in the park find a refuge from the heat below. Trails allow hikers to explore a cave, see several natural springs, and cross a natural stone bridge. Amenities include a swimming pool, tennis courts, a ballfield, playgrounds, and bicycles for rent. *Open year-round.*

108 Petit Jean Park and Museum of Automobiles

21 mi./30 min. South on Rte. 9, right on Rte. 154. A drive through this large park on Petit Jean Mountain offers majestic views of the Arkansas River valley. Scenic walking trails lead past waterfalls and along the rims of box canyons inscribed with Indian pictographs.

108. *Ledges tinged with lichen contrast with the deep green pines in Petit Jean Park.*

The many recreational opportunities include tennis courts and rental boats. The rotating collection of classic and antique automobiles at the museum, adjacent to the park, features a rare Arkansas-built Climber, Liberace's "solid gold" Cadillac, a 1914 popcorn wagon with a one-cylinder steam engine, a pink-and-pearl 1937 Packard Towncar that once belonged to Mae West, and several cars owned by Winthrop Rockefeller (former Arkansas governor), including his personal limousine: a seven-passenger 1967 Cadillac Fleetwood. *Park open year-round; museum open daily except Christmas. Admission charged for museum.*

125 Woolly Hollow State Park

18 mi./20 min. North on Rte. 65, right on Rte. 285. Lake Bennett is the focus of this picturesque 400-acre park in the Ozark foothills. The sandy beach is popular with swimmers, and the boat ramp and dock are used by sailboaters and those fishing for catfish, bass, bream, and crappie. Rental flat-bottomed fishing boats, pedal boats, and canoes are well suited to the quiet waters of the lake. A tree-shaded picnic area and a playground overlook the lake, and nearby is a restored 1882 one-room log house. A nature trail that skirts the lake offers colorful views in the fall. *Open year-round.*

129 Toad Suck Ferry Lock and Dam Park

7 mi./14 min. West on Rte. 286. The origin of the name Toad Suck is uncertain, but one theory involves an antebellum tavern frequented by hard-drinking steamboat passengers who sucked down whiskey until they swelled up like toads.

A ferry operated here until 1970, when a lock and a dam were completed as part of an Arkansas River navigation project. The park straddles the river, which is primarily used for boating and fishing for bass and catfish. There are picnic areas and campgrounds, along with a ballfield and a playground. On the east bank one of the old ferryboats is on view. *Park open year-round; park office open Mon.–Fri.*

147   Pinnacle Mountain State Park

10 mi./20 min. South on I-430 to Exit 9, west on Rte. 10, right on Pinnacle Valley Rd. Thousand-foot-high Pinnacle Mountain, surrounded by the forested lowlands of this 1,770-acre park, is the first elevation of consequence encountered along this interstate (driving west from the Mississippi River), and as such affords some fine scenic vistas of the area.

147. *Cypress knees, part of the root system, create a surreal scene in the water.*

The park is a favorite of bird-watchers and is known for its abundance of flora and fauna, as well as its fine natural history exhibits and interpretive programs. A number of well-marked hiking trails explore the terrain, including one for the handicapped and a rugged one that's of mountaineering caliber.

Several shaded picnic grounds, fishing and boating on the Big and Little Maumelle rivers, and a playground round out the park's recreational facilities. *Open Mon.–Sat. and P.M. Sun.*

I-30   Little Rock, AR 72201

Convention & Visitors Bureau, Markham St. and Broadway. (501) 376-4781. The very rock that gave the city its name can be seen in Riverfront Park. And if this park doesn't suit your fancy, there are more than 50 others in Little Rock and in North Little Rock, just across the Arkansas River. The city grew rapidly at the turn of the century, which accounts for the Victorian and related styles of many homes to be seen in the Quapaw Quarter and other historic areas. Some 14 restored buildings dating from the early 1800's to the 1850's still stand in the Arkansas Territorial Restoration, and self-guiding auto and walking tours of the historic areas are available. The Old State House, which currently serves as a museum of Arkansas history, has an intriguing touch-and-see display in Granny's Attic. The grounds of the present state capitol feature an extensive rose garden. Other popular attractions are the Arkansas Arts Center, the Decorative Arts Museum, the Arkansas Museum of Science and History, and the excellent zoo.

242   Village Creek State Park

13 mi./20 min. North on Rte. 284. This huge (7,000-acre) nature park was created to preserve and make available to visitors some of the natural features peculiar to Crowley's Ridge. The ridge is a mantle of windblown silt, up to 10 miles wide and 500 feet high in parts, that wanders for 150 miles through the otherwise flat Mississippi River valley in eastern Arkansas. Its unspoiled upland forests stand in relief against miles of cultivated fields. And most of what you'll see—from the soil and trees to the fish and other varieties of wildlife—is not found elsewhere in the state. Resident naturalists are happy to expound upon this phenomenon. Nature trails meander through the forest and alongside the park's creeks and small lakes. Lakeside picnics, swimming, fishing in stocked waters, and camping are favorite activities. The park is noted for its flowers in spring and foliage color in fall. Flocks of migratory birds punctuate the autumn landscape. *Open year-round.*

1   Memphis, TN 38103

1D

Visitors Information Center, 207 Beale St. (901) 526-4880. King Cotton still plays a major role in the city's economy, Beale Street and W.C. Handy are appropriately memorialized, and a riverboat still plies the mighty Mississippi; but the best-known attraction is Graceland, home of Elvis Presley, the King of Rock and Roll. Tours are so popular that reservations are suggested. Call (901) 332-3322, or (800) 238-2000 from out of state.

The river that brought life to Memphis is honored at Mud Island by a scale model of the Mississippi from Cairo, Illinois, to New Orleans and the Gulf of Mexico. The Memphis Pink Palace Museum and Planetarium features exhibits on natural history, pioneer life, and the Civil War. The National Ornamental Metal Museum has a working blacksmith on the premises, and for nature lovers there is a zoo with an aquarium and a botanic garden.

56   Hatchie National Wildlife Refuge

1 min. South on Rte. 76. Preserved as a feeding and resting area for migrating and wintering waterfowl, these 11,556 acres are a prime example of this region's natural terrain. A bottomland periodically flooded by the meandering Hatchie River, it is densely forested with water-tolerant oak. But the woods regularly give way to airy stretches of open water, which are now dotted with nesting boxes for wood ducks. A wide variety of songbirds also breed here, while mallards and black ducks are winter visitors. Red-shouldered hawks, barred owls, and wild turkeys thrive in the refuge. *Open year-round.*

80A   Casey Jones Home and Railroad Museum, Jackson

2 min. South on Bypass 45; follow signs. Down to the shaving mug and straight razor in the bathroom and the green mason jars in the kitchen, the furnishings in this simple white clapboard house give the impression that it was only yesterday that Casey Jones left for his fateful journey on the *Cannonball Express.* The glories of the railroad age are commemorated in displays of lanterns, switch

1–1D. *A Mud Island model of the Mississippi includes the meanders and oxbow lakes.*

keys, uniforms, and other memorabilia, including copies of the music for the 1909 hit that immortalized Jones. Near the house is a sister engine to the one in which Jones met his end. *Open daily except Thanksgiving Day, Christmas, and Easter. Admission charged.*

116 | Natchez Trace State Park

5 min. South on Rte. 114. In the 1930's, after a century of farming and erosion, the terrain here was a wasteland of washed-out gullies and bare ridges. But thanks to a government reclamation project, the area today is as well forested and supportive of wildlife as it was when early 19th-century travelers passed through on the trail (then called a trace) that gave the park its name. It is also a spacious, full-scale state park with hiking trails and lakes for swimming, fishing, and boating. There's a self-guiding car tour on several

miles of winding, well-paved roads; a highlight is an ancient 106-foot-high pecan tree, reputedly grown from a nut left by one of Andrew Jackson's men on his way home from the Battle of New Orleans. *Open year-round.*

143 | Loretta Lynn's Ranch

6 mi./12 min. North on Rte. 13. Touring the ground floor of the columned white plantation house where the legendary singer lives is a major attraction; but this pleasant, 7,000-acre ranch offers a number of other diversions. For campers there's a swimming pool, a miniature golf course, tennis courts, and a creek with rainbow trout. Day visitors will be interested in the 100-year-old gristmill that has been turned into a museum commemorating Loretta Lynn's career. On display are an impressive number of gold records, some of her early costumes, plaques, citations, and commendations. Photographs of her parents and old mining artifacts prove that she is indeed a coal miner's daughter. *Open Apr.–Oct. Admission charged for museum.*

172 | Montgomery Bell State Resort Park

12 mi./25 min. North on Rte. 46, right on Rte. 70. When America was young, rich deposits of iron ore drew settlers to these rolling hills. One of the early ironmasters to come to the South was Montgomery Bell, who forged cannonballs for the Battle of New Orleans. Along the hiking trails of this extensive 3,800-acre park, you can still see the remains of ore pits and smelting furnaces. Lakes nestled in the woods offer swimming, boating, and fishing. *Open year-round.*

192 | Warner Parks, Nashville

5 mi./10 min. South on McCrory Ln., left on Rte. 100; follow signs. Establishing an elaborate city park in the midst of open country may have seemed the height of folly in the 1930's. But Percy Warner, his brother Edwin, and his son-in-law Luke Lea revealed remarkable foresight in preserving these 2,600 acres of meadows and wooded hills that are now sur-

rounded by suburban Nashville. The Percy Warner Park has 28 miles of scenic roads with stone bridges and drywalls. The smaller Edwin Warner Park has a nature center with a wildflower garden. *Open year-round.*

I-265 | Nashville, TN 37213

I-65 | *Tourist Information Center, James Robertson Pkwy. (615) 242-5606.* The city's renown as the headquarters of country music tends to obscure the many other rewarding aspects of this gracious state capital. Tribute is paid to antiquity in the splendid Greek revival capitol and in the Parthenon, an exact-size replica of the ancient temple in Athens containing a museum and an art gallery. Exhibits in the Tennessee State Museum depict life in the area from prehistoric times through the Civil War, and at Ft. Nashborough, a replica of a 1779 frontier fort, the cabins, stockaded walls, and artifacts recall the days of the pioneers. There's a Country Music Hall of Fame and other music-related museums. The Grand Ole Opry and the extensive Opryland Showpark further celebrate Nashville's musical heritage.

I-65 | The Carter House, Franklin

20 mi./27 min. South on I-65 to Exit 65, west on Rte. 96; follow signs. The pockmarks and bullet holes on the house and smokehouse here recall the Battle of Franklin, one of the bloodiest engagements of the Civil War. On November 30, 1864, Confederate general John B. Hood launched a desperate attack against the Union forces that were entrenched around the house and its outbuildings. Among the more than 1,700 Confederate fatalities was Capt. Theodrick "Tod" Carter, whose father and sisters found him mortally wounded less than 200 yards from the family home.

The visitor center houses a small museum; there's a slide show and an elaborate model of the battlefield. The modest but handsome house, its doorway flanked by hand-poured glass windows and Doric columns, is furnished with original family possessions and other antiques. *Open Mon.–Sat. and P.M. Sun. except holidays. Admission charged.*

215 | Opryland U.S.A., Nashville

7 mi./12 min. North on Rte. 155 (Briley Pkwy.); follow signs. This 120-acre stage show and park complex combines the Grand Ole Opry, the legendary country music showcase, with numerous other attractions. Amusement park rides, some with names based upon musical themes, such as "The Old Mill Scream," appeal to both adults and children; and the stage shows reflect a variety of musical tastes.

Also part of Opryland are the Roy Acuff Museum, which houses a fine collection of memorabilia from the early days of country music, and the *General Jackson*, a paddle-wheel showboat that offers cruises on the Cumberland River during the day and in the evening. *Open daily Memorial Day–Labor Day; weekends Mar.–May and Sept.–Oct. Admission charged.*

221 | The Hermitage

4 mi./8 min. North on Rte. 45; follow signs. Andrew Jackson—war hero, Tennessee gentleman, and seventh president of the United States—is fittingly remembered at this 625-acre historic site, where two of his homes have been faithfully restored. The "early Hermitage" is a simple log cabin in which Jackson lived happily with his wife, Rachel, from 1804 to 1819; the Hermitage, their second home, is a gracious mansion with wide verandas and Doric columns. Most of the furnishings belonged to the Jackson family, including the crystal, the fine banquet table, mirrors, and a number of impressive family portraits. The garden, landscaped for Rachel in 1819, contains more than 50 varieties of herbs and flowers, as well as the hickory-shaded Palladian tomb of the president and his wife. *Open daily except Thanksgiving Day and Christmas. Admission charged.*

238 | Cedars of Lebanon State Park

6 mi./10 min. South on Rte. 231. More than 20 miles of hiking and bridle paths wind through the cedars in this 9,000-acre facility. (The cedars are not actually cedars of Lebanon, but eastern red cedars.) Along the trails you'll find limestone glades, caves, sinkholes, prickly-pear cacti, and the rare Tennessee purple coneflowers. Park facilities include campsites, cabins, a large swimming pool, and acres of picnic tables. During the summer, programs and guided tours are conducted by the park staff. *Open year-round.*

268 | Edgar Evins State Park

5 min. South on Rte. 96. This 6,000-acre park, established in 1975, takes full advantage of one of the loveliest places in Tennessee: Center Hill Lake. Created by the U.S. Army Corps of Engineers in 1948, the lake is surrounded by the hills of the Cumberland Plateau; its miles of indented shoreline, accessible from the park's marina, are edged with rocky bluffs. The lake attracts water-skiers as well as fishermen in search of record-breaking bass.

Campsites here overlook the water, and a village of cabins has its own swimming pool. There are also abundant picnic shelters and tables by the lake. Meandering along the bluffs is the Highland Rim Trail, a favorite of hikers. *Open daily except Christmas Eve– New Year's Day.*

273 | Joe L. Evins Appalachian Center for Crafts

6 mi./10 min. South on Rte. 56; cross Hurricane Bridge, left on Center Dr. The scenic road winding its way through the mountainous woodlands of Tennessee's Center Hill Lake region to this Appalachian crafts center is in itself worth the trip. The center, set on a promontory overlooking the lake, is a division of Tennessee Tech University, a school where the students learn a number of traditional and nontraditional techniques in various crafts, including woodworking, sculpture, ceramics, glassblowing, and silver and steel jewelry. A gallery, featuring changing exhibits, serves as a showcase for the handiwork of students, faculty, and area artisans. Attached to the gallery is a shop that sells some of the creations of the students. *Open daily except Thanksgiving Day, Christmas–New Year's week, and last 2 days in June.*

317 | Cumberland Mountain State Park

8.5 mi./20 min. South on Rte. 127. This 1,720-acre park, the legacy of 1930's federal government projects, is located around pleasant

407. *Falling water defines the power that drives the mill's wheels and machinery.*

See N–S book, sec. 32.

75

11   20   14

376A   387   407

75   See N–S book, sec. 32.

See N–S book, sec. 41.

81

TN | NC

88

I-81

0   3   20

50   50B   53A

40

Cumberland Mountain Lake in the wooded hills of the Cumberland Plateau. A lodge and other rough-hewn buildings are made of Crab Orchard stone, an attractive rose-colored sandstone that is quarried in this region. *Open year-round.*

356 / 376A American Museum of Science and Energy, Oak Ridge

13 mi./ 25 min. Exit 356: northeast on Rte. 58; continue on Rte. 95. Exit 376A: northwest on Rte. 162, left on Rte. 62; follow signs. The secret life of Oak Ridge, Tennessee, changed the course of world history. It was an important part of the World War II Manhattan Project and produced the uranium required for the first atom bomb in 1945. Oak Ridge has remained in the forefront of nuclear research and production ever since.

The purpose of the museum is to inform the visitor of contemporary energy requirements and methods of generation, as well as the history of energy use in the United States and alternatives for the future. The exhibits are dynamic, inviting participation wherever possible. Models demonstrate the principles of gravity, thermodynamics, aerodynamics, and magnetism, and a small area is devoted to Oak Ridge's role in the development of the atom bomb. *Open daily except Thanksgiving Day, Christmas, and New Year's Day.*

387 Knoxville, TN 37902

Convention and Visitors Bureau, 500 Henley St. (615) 523-2316. Mid-April, when the dogwoods are in bloom, is the most colorful time of the year in Knoxville; but the historic houses, the museums, and the excellent zoo are of interest year-round. Early colonial days are recalled at the Gen. James White Fort with stockade. The territorial era (1790–96) is represented by the handsome two-story clapboard home of the then governor, William Blount. At the Armstrong-Lockett House, built in 1834, there are notable collections of old silver and furniture, and the Civil War era is recalled at Confederate Memorial Hall. The Knoxville Museum of Art, located on the 1982 World's Fair site, features a popular display of period rooms in miniature.

407 The Old Mill of Pigeon Forge

16 mi./35 min. South on Rte. 66, right on Rte. 441, left at first light. Since its construction in 1830, the charming Old Mill of Pigeon Forge has been working continuously. Powered by the Little Pigeon River, the mill's rumbling 24-foot water wheel and two tub wheels drive the original 2-ton millstones cut from buhrstone. During the Civil War water-powered looms on the second floor helped clothe Confederate soldiers. A gift shop features stoneground grains, and guided tours are frequent. *Open Mon.–Sat. except Thanksgiving Day and Christmas. Admission charged.*

I-81 The Crockett Tavern Museum, Morristown

8 mi./15 min. North on I-81 to Exit 8, north on Rte. 25, west on Rte. 11E; follow signs. Davy Crockett was a boy of 10 when his parents built and ran a four-room log tavern and hostelry here along one of the first roads that led west. The tavern was burned after being used as a smallpox hospital after the Civil War, but this reconstruction conveys the atmosphere of the original. All the furniture and the pots and kettles are authentic relics from the days when America was slowly pushing west. *Open Mon.–Sat. and P.M. Sun. May–Oct. Admission charged.*

50 / 50B Biltmore Estate, Asheville

2 min. North on Rte. 25; follow signs. A thousand men spent 5 years building this majestic mansion with 250 rooms for George Vanderbilt, grandson of the prominent 19th-century New York shipping and railroad magnate Cornelius Vanderbilt. When the mansion was completed on Christmas Eve, 1895, it became one of America's largest privately owned houses—a distinction it still holds. Overlooking the French Broad River valley and the Blue Ridge Mountains, this French Renaissance-style château contains a 20,000-volume library, an ivory chess table once owned by Napoleon, 16th-century Flemish tapestries, paintings by Whistler and Renoir, one of the first heated indoor swimming pools, and one of the oldest existing bowling

50–50B. *The detailing of just one section implies the grandeur of the whole.*

alleys. The beautifully landscaped grounds—highlighted by a 4-acre English garden considered the finest of its kind in America—are the work of Frederick Law Olmsted, the 19th-century architect famous for his design of New York City's Central Park. *Open daily except Thanksgiving Day, Christmas, and New Year's Day. Admission charged.*

53A Folk Art Center, Asheville

3.5 mi./6 min. East on Rte. 74, left on Blue Ridge Pkwy. Fine craftsmanship is a tradition hereabouts, as a walk through the center's spacious Folk Art Museum quickly reveals. Isolation in the early days demanded that mountain folk create their own tools, pottery, woodwork, woven and leather goods, jewelry, and musical instruments. The tradition still lives, and visitors here can usually see a potter, a wood-carver, or a weaver in action, offering step-by-step demonstrations as the work progresses. *Open daily except Thanksgiving Day, Christmas, and New Year's Day.*

73 | Mountain Gateway Museum, Old Fort

1 min. North on Catawba Ave.; follow signs. During the summer of 1776, Gen. Griffith Rutherford stationed some 500 men at the Old Fort Plantation, which was once located here, to protect the frontier while he led a campaign against the Cherokees, who were suspected of being allies of the British. As settlers traveled westward after the Revolution, the area surrounding the Old Fort became a gateway to the Blue Ridge Mountains. The history of the region in general and the fort in particular is preserved in this handsome stone building, constructed by the Works Progress Administration (WPA) during the 1930's. The items on display—each one a reminder that pioneer life called for determination, hard work, and ingenuity—include tin candle holders, photos of moonshine stills, homemade axes, and several musical instruments, including a so-called ukelin, a cross between a ukelele and a violin. *Open daily except Thanksgiving Day, Christmas, and Easter.*

CHR | Historic Bethabara Park, Winston-Salem

Cherry St. exit: 5.5 mi./11 min. North on Cherry St., left on University Pkwy., left on Bethabara Rd. A group of immigrant Germans from Saxony, who were members of an evangelical Protestant denomination called the United Brethren (or the Moravians), settled here in 1753, founding Bethabara, the community that today is called Winston-Salem. At this park you will find an archeological site of the original community in addition to three restored buildings and a reconstructed fort. In the 1788 parish house, which contains the minister's quarters, you'll see period furnishings and unusual tile stoves. The 1782 potter's house displays samples of bowls, plates, and other ceramic objects found at this important site of colonial craftsmanship. On view at the 1803 brewer's house are 18th-century German books. The new visitor center contains a slide show and exhibits on the history of the Moravians, the early Bethabara settlement and its trades, and the archeology of the site. *Grounds open year-round; buildings open daily Apr.–mid-Dec.*

270. *A flowering cherry tree and beds of tulips—the very essence of springtime.*

210 | 217B | High Point Museum

Exit 210: 12 mi./19 min. South on Rte. 68, left on Centennial St., left on Rte. 70A (Lexington Ave). Exit 217B: 10.5 mi./17 min. West on Rte. 70A (Lexington Ave). The city of High Point, named for the distinction of being the highest point along the railroad line between Goldsboro and Charlotte, is now noted as one of America's leading producers of furniture and hosiery. This museum traces the Piedmont area's history over three centuries, with changing displays of toys, telephones, firearms, textiles, and an exhibit on the community's black heritage. On the grounds are two log buildings where costumed guides demonstrate candlemaking, spinning, weaving, and open-hearth cooking on weekends. *Open Tues.–Sat. and P.M. Sun.*

126 | Hagan-Stone Park

8 mi./12 min. South on Rte. 421, right on Hagan-Stone Park Rd. The crucial role of tobacco farming in the development of the region is always in evidence as you explore this 409-acre park, named for two well-known local citizens. At the Lorillard tobacco exhibit, photos and periodicals explain the planting, picking, and curing processes. Even the park's office, a log cabin from the Civil War era, once served as a storage barn for tobacco leaves. Nature lovers will find several inviting trails, including one that leads to a reconstructed 1846 wood-frame schoolhouse. A 23-acre lake offers paddleboating, rowboating, and fishing. *Open year-round.*

266 | 270 | North Carolina Botanical Garden, Chapel Hill

Exit 266: 7 mi./12 min. South on Rte. 86, north on Rte. 15/501, right on Laurel Hill Rd. Exit 270: 10 mi./16 min. South on Rte. 15/501, left on Laurel Hill Rd. The white ash tree, which furnishes the wood for most baseball bats, and the hardy witch hazel shrub, with a bark, twigs, and leaves that supply the essentials for a classic American skin lotion and flowers that appear in autumn after its leaves have fallen, are only two of the numerous species you'll find at this orderly 500-acre complex of trees, shrubs, and small plants. There are also sections devoted to herb gardens and poisonous plants, as well as one of the best collections of carnivorous plants in the country. Two miles of informative, well-marked trails show the way. *Open daily except Thanksgiving Day, Christmas, and New Year's Day.*

270 | Sarah P. Duke Gardens, Durham

5 mi./9 min. North on Rte. 15/501 and Bypass 15/501, south on Rte. 751; follow signs. Nearly every part of these serene gardens, located on Duke University's west campus, is a minor masterpiece of design. You can follow one of three descending paths past a riot of chrysanthemums to a rose garden of formal elegance. In the H.L. Blomquist Garden, step carefully across the native-plants pool on a series of old millstones and enjoy the bleeding hearts, rhododendrons, and hundreds of other rare and native plants shaded by vines and magnolias. The view from the wisteria-covered pergola will further delight the eye and soothe the spirit. *Open year-round.*

140

4

See N–S book, sec. 49.

95

138

12

266 270

408

ROUTE 132

End I-40

408 Moores Creek National Battlefield

14 mi./20 min. West on Rte. 210; follow signs. In February 1776 the quiet of this stretch of woods and rolling meadows was dramatically shattered when a band of patriots successfully ambushed 1,600 kilted Highlanders and area Loyalists who had been recruited by the royal governor. This small victory resulted in North Carolina's vote for independence in Philadelphia a few months later.

Today the informative visitor center illustrates the skirmish with original weapons and an audiovisual program. The History Trail leads through the battleground and along the creek, and a nature trail features plants that were important to the economy of the 18th century. *Open daily except Christmas and New Year's Day.*

408 U.S.S. North Carolina Battleship Memorial

16 mi./20 min. West on Rte. 210, left on Rte. 421; follow signs. This impressive memorial to the 10,000 North Carolinians who died in

408. *Although outmoded, this World War II battlewagon is still an impressive sight.*

World War II faithfully re-creates what military life was like on one of the most powerful battleships of its time. A self-guiding tour lets visitors explore the pilothouse and engine rooms, see how meals were prepared, inspect the quarters of the 2,000-man crew, climb up and down ladders and into a gun turret, examine a Kingfisher floatplane, and aim antiaircraft guns. A summertime sound-and-light show with simulated battle effects illustrates the ship's proud history. *Open year-round. Admission charged.*

ROUTE 132 New Hanover County Museum of Lower Cape Fear, Wilmington

5 mi./15 min. Continue on Rte. 132, right on Rte. 17 (becomes Market St.). A beautifully crafted model of Wilmington's busy harbor in 1863 serves as a centerpiece in this museum, which focuses on the city as a major southern port in the 19th century. The collection also includes artifacts from the Lower Cape Fear Indians, Civil War weapons, samples of early exports and imports, historic photos, antique clothing and furnishings, and a variety of domestic items and tools. Such historical displays, along with the knowledgeable staff, make the museum an especially fine place to begin a visit to Wilmington, where you will find many other historic houses, museums, and gardens. *Open Tues.–Sat. and P.M. Sun. except holidays.*

ROUTE 132 Carolina Beach State Park

14 mi./25 min. Continue on Rte. 132 and Rte. 421. Essentially a large sand dune topped with live oaks, this small park on the Cape Fear River also comprises grasslands and thick, swampy vegetation in its remarkably varied terrain. Ferns, mosses, pines, grasses, even insect-digesting plants such as the sundew, bladderwort, and Venus's-flytrap (found only within a 60-mile radius)—all these grow along the well-marked nature trails. Songbirds as well as ospreys and laughing gulls swoop overhead, and white-tailed deer, marsh rabbits, and raccoons may occasionally be seen. A marina on the river provides launching ramps and boating supplies. *Open daily except Christmas.*

132. *Open and closed leaves attest to the deadly efficiency of the Venus's-flytrap.*

ROUTE 132 Fort Fisher State Historic Site

22 mi./30 min. Continue on Rte. 132 and on Rte. 421. The massive earthworks erected here at the outset of the Civil War gave Confederate forces control of the Cape Fear River and kept Wilmington's port open to supplies for General Lee's army. Visitors today can stroll through the remains of the mounds and fortifications and a restored palisade. The museum uses old photos, drawings, and supplies recovered from sunken blockade-running ships to explain the fortifications and the battles that took place. *Open Mon.–Sat. and P.M. Sun. Apr.–Oct.; Tues.–Sat. and P.M. Sun. Nov.–Mar.*

ROUTE 132 North Carolina Aquarium at Fort Fisher

22.5 mi./30 min. Continue on Rte. 132 and Rte. 421. Nestled in dunes and surrounded by nature trails, this aquarium complex features intriguing exhibits and films about marine life and coastal ecology. More than 15 aquariums hold sharks, lobsters, endangered sea turtles, tropical reef fishes, and other local sea life. One tank has clams, crabs, and whelks that visitors may handle. The humpback whale is thoroughly analyzed in exhibits on whale behavior, and you can view a 49-foot replica of this marine mammal. *Open Mon.–Sat. and P.M. Sun. except Thanksgiving Day, Christmas, and New Year's Day. Admission free but donations encouraged.*

86. *The few plants that have gained a foothold here stand out in the vastness of the dunes.*

42 | West of the Pecos Museum

5 min. North on Rte. 285. In the late 19th century, law "west of the Pecos" meant almost no law at all; and this museum, which is set in and around a turn-of-the-century hotel, tells the story of the Old West at its wildest. In the saloon of the Orient Hotel you can see the spot where a local man dispatched two outlaws. Step outside the museum proper and you'll see the grave of gunfighter Clay Allison, a hanging tree, a jail, and a reproduction of the famous Jersey Lilly Saloon, where Judge Roy Bean dispensed frontier justice. The less violent side of cowboy life is illustrated with displays about ranching and rodeos, reconstructed rooms from a school and a church, and the restored hotel bridal suite. *Open Mon.–Sat. and P.M. Sun. Admission charged.*

86 | Monahans Sandhills State Park

1 min. North on Park Rd. 41. Sand dunes, some 70 feet high, cover this 3,840-acre park. Some dunes shift when blown by the wind, but others are secured by scrubby growths of Harvard shin oak and sagebrush. An interpretive center provides information on the park's animals, plants, history, and geology; the center's large windows look out on the feeding and watering stations that attract wildlife. The past is evoked by an 1880's windmill and a railroad section house from the days when the Texas & Pacific Railroad made a water stop here. A working oil well demonstrates a modern industry in operation. *Open year-round. Admission charged.*

116 | The Presidential Museum, Odessa

2 mi./6 min. Northwest on Rte. 385 (Grant Ave.), left on 7th St. Created after the assassination of President John F. Kennedy, this sophisticated museum honors the office of the presidency and the men who have occupied it. The collection includes portraits and autographs of former presidents, campaign buttons and other memorabilia, excellent reproductions of the Inauguration gowns worn by First Ladies, and an exhibit on the changes in political campaigning brought about by radio and television. Broader topics of American history are presented in changing exhibits. *Open Tues.–Sat. except holidays.*

126 | Water Wonderland, Odessa

5 min. North on Rte. 1788, left on Rte. 80. More than 20 rides and attractions entice the adventurous to hurl down steep water slides, negotiate simulated mountain rapids in a tube, and ride a 30-mile-an-hour water toboggan. A wave pool with 4-foot swells, a beach for sunbathing, and coves for small children are especially popular. A miniature golf course and electronic video games are among the non-aquatic attractions. *Open Memorial Day–Labor Day. Admission charged.*

136 | Petroleum Museum, Library, and Hall of Fame, Midland

2 min. North on Rte. 349, left on N. Frontage Rd. The dramatic history of the oil industry is presented in this well-endowed museum. An immense diorama of the floor of the Permian sea that once covered the area shows replicas of the thousands of underwater creatures whose remains formed the organic substance we call oil. Among the other excellent displays you can see are a re-created street corner of a 1920's West Texas boomtown, polished rock cores that were taken from oil wells, a simulated view of an oil pipeline from a patrol plane, and the fiery spectacle of an oil well blowout. On the grounds outside the museum, the collection of oil rigs ranges from a 1910 cable tool model to modern pumping units. *Open Mon.–Sat. and P.M. Sun. except Thanksgiving Day, Christmas Eve, and Christmas. Admission charged.*

136 | The Museum of the Southwest, Midland

5 min. North on Rte. 349, left on Missouri St. Housed in an elegant brick mansion built in 1934, this fine collection includes paintings by the Taos Society of Artists, a bronze sculpture by western artist Frederic Remington, and a mural-size sand painting. The cultural history of the Southwest is represented by wood carvings, pottery, textiles, tools, Indian baskets, and a tepee. Sharing the grounds with this museum is a children's museum with hands-on exhibits and a planetarium, and there's a research center. *Open Tues.–Sat. and P.M. Sun. except holidays.*

177   Heritage Museum, Big Spring

3 min. South on Rte. 87, left on 6th St. For some 12,000 years Indians, pioneers, travelers, cattle ranchers, and a variety of animals have been attracted to the watering hole for which the town is named—a colorful history that is recalled here with artifacts and mural-size pictures. The arrival of the Texas & Pacific Railroad in 1881 is represented by the Iron Horse steam whistle in the transportation room, which sounds at the press of a button. Ranching is illustrated by guns, saddles, branding irons, and 54 pairs of horns (some spanning as much as 10 feet) that were once proudly carried by the famous Texas longhorn cattle. Re-created period rooms and a collection of old photographs recall pioneer days. *Open Tues.–Sat. except holidays.*   ♿

177   Big Spring State Recreation Area

4 mi./8 min. South on Rte. 87, right on Rte. FM700. Scenic Mountain, a limestone-capped mesa 200 feet high, is the setting for this urban park. A 2½-mile road carved from its steep sides provides panoramic views of the city of Big Spring and the Texas plains. On the informative nature trail, markers identify the native vegetation, and hikers are likely to see jackrabbits, cottontails, ground squirrels, and many species of birds. Highlights include a

136. *These mechanical monsters were created to bring forth the riches of oil.*

prairie-dog town and bluffs marked with graffiti done by travelers who have stopped here from the 1870's to the present. *Open year-round. Admission charged.*   🚻 🚶 ♿

210   Lake Colorado City State Recreation Area

6 mi./10 min. South on Rte. FM2836. Since Lake Colorado City is warmer than other area lakes (its water circulates through Colorado City's electric power plant), it offers a longer season for water-skiing and swimming, and anglers catch bigger catfish and bass because the warmer water gives the fish an extended growing season. Mesquite, short grasses, and shrubs provide a habitat for many varieties of songbirds. In winter the lake attracts flocks of migratory waterfowl. *Open year-round. Admission charged.*   🚻 ⛺ 🚐 🛶 🎣 ♿

244   Pioneer City-County Museum, Sweetwater

4 min. North on Rte. 70, right on Rte. 80, left on Ragland St. This spacious house, built in 1906, contains Indian artifacts, early ranching and farming implements, photos of pioneers, and other items that have figured in the area's past. History is brought to life by re-creations of an old courtroom, a pioneer schoolroom, and a leather and saddle shop. There are displays of antique toys and dolls and late 19th-century women's fashions. A unique exhibit focuses on the Women Airforce Service Pilots, who trained at nearby Avenger Airfield to ferry aircraft to World War II battle zones. *Open P.M. Tues.–Sat. except holidays.*

283A   Buffalo Gap Historic Village

16 mi./25 min. South on Rte. 83/277; continue on Rte. 89, right on Elm St. This charmingly restored frontier village has an interesting history. Underground water produced unusually lush vegetation, which in turn attracted herds of buffalo; they were followed by buffalo hunters, and in 1874 the area's first permanent residents settled here. The sandstone courthouse and jail, constructed in 1878 when Buffalo Gap was the county seat, has gunports and fortresslike walls designed to withstand possible Comanche attacks. It is surrounded

by 15 original and re-created buildings of the period. A railroad station, physician's office, barbershop, wagon barn, cabinet mill, blacksmith's shop, and other structures are furnished with items in daily use in the late 1800's. *Open daily mid-Mar.–mid-Nov.; weekends in winter except Thanksgiving Day and Christmas. Admission charged.*   🚻

290. *The photographer seems to be as interesting to the giraffes as they to him.*

290   Abilene Zoological Gardens

5 min. South on Rte. 322; follow signs. This excellent zoo enables visitors to compare the wild turkeys, pronghorns, bison, javelinas, and coyotes of the Texas plains with animals that share a similar environment in the African veld: gnus, zebras, elephants, lions, ostriches, hyenas, and antelopes. A bridge over the giraffe area offers the viewer the unusual experience of seeing these towering animals from above. Other creatures here include sea lions, bears, primates, and alligators, as well as unusual birds and snakes. Native plants and wildflowers help to make the zoo resemble a natural environment. *Open daily except Thanksgiving Day, Christmas, and New Year's Day. Admission charged.*   🚻 ♿

370   Stephenville Historical House Museum

25 mi./30 min. South on Rte. 108, left on Washington St. A steep-roofed limestone cottage built for a former Confederate colonel in 1869 is surrounded by a collection of 19th-century structures. They include log cabins, houses, a barn, and a schoolhouse, all carefully restored and outfitted with furnishings of the time. Indian artifacts, minerals, and tools are displayed in the Carriage House. The Chapel on the Bosque, a Presbyterian church with Gothic windows and a spire adorned with fish-scale shingles, contains an exhibit that illustrates spiritual growth in the region. *Open P.M. Fri.–Sun. Apply at Chamber of Commerce for admission.*

370. *Gothic architecture with gingerbread trim reveals the colonel's eclectic taste.*

386   Lake Mineral Wells State Park

19 mi./28 min. North on Rte. 281, right on Rte. 180. Small oaks and mesquite cover the rolling hills of this park and frame the 646-acre lake, which attracts boaters, swimmers, and fishermen. Steep-walled gulches in the sandstone and shale are a challenge to rock climbers. Hikers enjoy the 5 miles of trails through bottomland groves of pecan, cottonwood, cedar elm, and red oak. The park provides an excellent habitat for many animals, including white-tailed deer, wild turkeys, opossums, armadillos, and coyotes. *Open year-round. Admission charged.*

409   Holland Lake Park, Weatherford

1 min. North on Santa Fe Dr., right on Holland Lake Dr. The graceful woods and cattails reflected in tranquil Holland Lake serve as a contrast to a garden of cacti and other plants native to the arid Texas plains. The park is a pleasant place for a picnic and a walk on a nature trail. Local history is evoked by two restored 19th-century log cabins, which are connected by a single roof and contain pioneer furnishings and tools. The bullet-scarred walls of one cabin attest to the killing of George McClesky by Indians in 1873. *Open year-round.*

437B   Fort Worth, TX 76109

Convention and Visitors Bureau, 123 E. Exchange Ave. (817) 624-4741. Although a large modern city, Fort Worth has not forgotten the Texas of song and story. Activities at the Stockyards Historical District on the north side include cattle trading and shopping for rodeo gear and western wear. But the city also boasts three world-famous art museums: the Kimbell, which displays works dating from pre-Columbian times to the present day; the Amon Carter, which has a fine collection of sculpture, photographs, and paintings featuring, but not limited to, the American West; and the Modern Art Museum of Fort Worth, noted for its 20th-century art. The Museum of Science and History offers imaginative exhibits for children and adults. The terraced Water Gardens enhance the city center.

467A   Dallas, TX 75202

Convention & Visitors Bureau, 400 S. Houston St. (lobby of Union Station). (214) 746-6700. Highlights of life in Dallas include the Cotton Bowl, Neiman-Marcus, banking, business, glass-walled skyscrapers, and the $50 million Dallas Museum of Art. At Fair Park the old and the new are combined with a steam train museum, a science museum, gardens, and an aquarium. In Old City Park a bit of 19th-century Dallas is preserved. There's a justly famous zoo and some unusual theme museums, such as the Biblical Arts Center and the Telephone Pioneer Museum. Although they recall a time of trauma, the John F. Kennedy Memorial Plaza and the Texas School Book Depository attract many visitors.

556   Tyler Municipal Rose Garden

12 mi./24 min. South on Rte. 69, right on Front St. W. Hundreds of varieties of roses grow among archways, camellia bushes, fountains, pavilions, and around an ornamental pond, creating an ambience of beauty and fragrance. More than 38,000 rosebushes, a tribute to the region that produces one-third of the commercially grown rosebushes in America, bloom in this 22-acre garden from May through October. A large greenhouse is filled year-round with such tropical plants as the red passion vine, lavender bougainvillea, Amazon lily, hibiscus, and bird-of-paradise. *Garden open year-round; greenhouse open daily except holidays.*

617   Franks Antique Doll Museum, Marshall

5 mi./12 min. North on Rte. 59, left on Grand Ave. This delightful collection of 1,600 antique and unusual dolls includes exquisite French and German bisque dolls, milliner's models, Shirley Temple dolls, dolls made by Limoges and Dresden china companies, Gibson girls, Kewpie dolls, mechanical dolls, and character babies, all outfitted in costumes authentic in their periods. The museum is located behind the grand late-Victorian house of Clara and Francis Franks; it also features buggies, miniature furniture, iron and tin toys, dishes, trunks, and of course dollhouses. *Open by chance, or for appointment call (214) 935-3065. Admission charged.*

633   T. C. Lindsey & Co., Jonesville

3 min. North on Rte. 134. This tin-roofed old-time country general store and post office has been in business since 1847. Veteran clerks boast that the emporium is second to none in its stock of one- and two-gallon overalls, sunbonnets, walking sticks, mint-condition wood cookstoves, bullwhips, wringer washing machines, mule collars, and jawbreakers. The

467A. *As the oil wells went deeper, the Dallas skyline they helped to finance went higher.*

goods for sale are displayed among mounted sets of longhorns, deer heads, butter churns, and thousands of antiques. The store has been used as a set for several movies. *Open Mon.– Sat. except holidays.*

18A | R. W. Norton Art Gallery, Shreveport

3 mi./15 min. South on Line Ave., left on Thora Blvd. This outstanding collection is best known for its works by Old West artists Charles M. Russell and Frederic Remington. However, the nearly four centuries of sculpture, painting, and decorative European and American art represented here include such diverse works as 16th-century Flemish tapestries, sculptures by Rodin, and the work of silversmith and patriot Paul Revere. Each spring visitors come to see a different kind of artistic display: a rainbow of azaleas blooming beneath the stately pines. *Open P.M. Tues.– Sun. except holidays.*

19A | Hamel's Amusement Park, Shreveport

6 mi./12 min. Northwest on Spring St., right on Lake St., right on Clyde Fant Pkwy., right on E. 70th St. North Louisiana's largest roller coaster and such other favorites as the Tilt-A-Whirl, Scrambler, bumper cars, and a water-splashed log ride delight visitors of all ages. For small children, a merry-go-round and additional rides are housed in the Kiddie Barn. A train that travels the 15-acre park's perimeter reveals the various attractions and manicured grounds, and from the top of the Ferris wheel you can see the Red River and beyond. *Open Wed.–Fri. evenings and P.M. weekends June–Aug.; P.M. weekends Sept.–Oct. and Mar.–May. Admission charged.*

19A | Barnwell Garden and Art Center, Shreveport

3 min. Northwest on Spring St., right on Crockett St. A large glassed-in botanical conservatory is filled with tropical and exotic trees, native shrubs, and seasonal flowers, while another wing that is part of the same building displays visiting and permanent exhibits of works by local artists. Barnwell's beautiful grounds contain a sculpture garden as well as a reflecting pool. Interspersed among towering sycamore and cottonwood trees are scenic overlooks from which visitors can enjoy a panoramic view of the Red River. *Open Mon.–Fri. and P.M. weekends.*

33 | Lake Bistineau State Park
47 |

Exit 33: 13 mi./27 min. South on Rte. 157, left on Rte. 3227, right on Rte. 164, right on Rte. 163. Exit 47: 13 mi./25 min. South on Rte. 7, right on Rte. 164, left on Rte. 163. A hint of wilderness pervades Lake Bistineau, which was formed by the damming of a serpentine Louisiana bayou. There's a boat ramp and rental boats for fishermen, who try for largemouth and yellow bass, black crappie, bluegill, bullheads, and sunfish. The large beach is popular with swimmers. The picnic grounds and a play area are set among venerable pines. Visitors come to see the hardwood trees draped with Spanish moss, for which the 750-acre park is known. *Open year-round. Admission charged.*

47 | Germantown Colony Museum, Minden

10 mi./25 min. North on Lee St., right on Broadway, left on Elm St., right on Germantown Rd.; follow signs. Small clusters of original and restored pioneer log houses and their outbuildings form the remnants of a communal colony of German settlers established here in 1835. Tools and other items displayed in the blacksmith's shop and smokehouse testify to the labors of the settlers, while the tombstones in the hillside graveyard tell of many lives cut short. Ancient mulberry, persimmon, and pear trees on the grounds attract a colorful assortment of birds. *Open Wed.–Sat. and P.M. Sun. Admission charged.*

67 | Lake Claiborne State Park, Homer

16 mi./30 min. North on Rte. 9, right on Rte. 518, right on Rte. 146. This 6,400-acre lake surrounded by rolling pine-covered hills is a favorite with water-skiers. In the quieter stretches of the lake, fishermen try for channel catfish, largemouth and striped bass, black crappie, and bream. Clear water attracts swimmers to the park's sandy beach; nearby there are boats for rent. More than a hundred picnic sites are scattered throughout the countryside and along the lakeshore under fine old hardwood trees. *Open year-round. Admission charged.*

84 Louisiana Tech Horticultural and Equine Centers, Ruston

5 min. South on Tech Dr., right on Rte. 80, left on Tech Farm Rd. Visitors to this university are free to browse through the spacious greenhouses filled with fig, banana, and pencil trees, night-blooming cereus, poinsettias, orchids, and tropical ferns. Seasonal shows include a candlelight Christmas walk (the first two weeks of December) that features thousands of poinsettias. The stables, barns, and paddocks of the equine center can also be toured. Owners bring their horses here for breeding, training, and other activities. *Horticultural center open Mon.–Fri. except holidays and last two weeks in Dec.; equine center open daily except holidays.* ⚊♿

118 Louisiana Purchase Gardens and Zoo, Monroe

7 min. South on Rte. 165 Bypass, right on Tichelli Rd. The zoo, built on a swamp with the waterways incorporated in the design, contains a large collection of rare African and Asian animals and is known for its Old World primates, particularly its lemurs. Many of the exhibits can be seen from a tour boat, which winds lazily through the gardens, shaded by Spanish moss-draped cypresses and oaks. A train with a coal-fired steam engine also carries passengers through the park and sometimes has to wait for a free-ranging antelope or bison to move off the tracks. Pelicans, flamingos, ducks, deer, and other native creatures find refuge here. Flowering plants are scattered throughout the park, named for the U.S's great 1803 real estate bargain. *Open daily except Thanksgiving Day, Christmas, and New Year's Day. Admission charged.* ⚊

153 Poverty Point State Commemorative Area

18 mi./30 min. North on Rte. 17, right on Rte. 134, left on Rte. 577. Archeologists can only guess at the purpose of these mounds and ridges created along Bayou Macon about 3,000 years ago through long and arduous labor by the inhabitants of Poverty Point. Excavations have turned up thousands of artifacts, including beads, stone tools, spears, and numerous baked-clay objects that were used for cooking. The 400-acre site can be toured by car, but for a closer look visitors can take a tram to the largest mound, where many climb to the top. If an archeological dig is in progress, this too may be seen. Audiovisual programs and artifacts are displayed at the visitor center, where an observation tower provides an overall view of the mounds. *Open daily except holidays. Admission charged.* ⚊♿

118. *Azaleas brighten the winding route of the tour boat through the gardens and the zoo.*

4B Vicksburg National Military Park

2 min. West on Clay St. As a major Confederate strongpoint on the Mississippi, Vicksburg resisted a number of attacks, but a 47-day siege in 1863 finally forced the city to surrender, thus opening the river to Union forces and northern shipping. Markers and monuments in a profusion of kinds and sizes line the paved 16-mile drive through the park and the cemetery. The 17,000 Union graves are mute reminders of the human cost of war. At one end of the park the U.S.S. *Cairo* Museum displays artifacts and the recovered remains of the ironclad Union gunboat *Cairo,* the first ship to be sunk by mines detonated by electricity. At the other end the visitor center offers artifacts, life-size exhibits, and an 18-minute film on the Vicksburg siege. Civil War books, maps, and other materials can be purchased at the center. *Park open year-round; visitor center and museum open daily except Christmas. Admission charged.* ⚊♿

46 The Mississippi Agriculture and Forestry Museum, Jackson

5 mi./10 min. North on I-55 to Exit 98B (Lakeland Dr.), east on Lakeland Dr. Life-size tableaux, complete with sound effects and voices, show vivid re-creations of loggers in action, workers hauling bales of cotton, and life in a sharecropper's cottage. Themes include logging days, "the rail age" (including early steam-driven farm machinery), and "the era of roads." Individual exhibits explain cotton processing (there is an authentic Bisland cotton gin), the impact of electricity, and the economics of farm life.

Also here is the National Agricultural Aviation Museum, which focuses on the 20th-century fight against the boll weevil, featuring crop-dusting planes from the 1930's to the present. Some strange boll-weevil catchers of pre-spraying days are also on display.

If you cross the road to the Fortenberry-Parkman Farm, you can see workers in 1920-period dress and talk to them about rural life in the South during the early 20th century. *Open Tues.–Sat. and P.M. Sun. except Thanksgiving Day, Christmas, and New Year's Day. Admission charged.* ⚊

4B. *Monument commemorates the role of the Union navy in taking Vicksburg in 1863.*

46   Jackson, MS 39216

Visitor Information Center, 1180 Lakeland Dr. (601) 960-1800. Jackson's importance as a state capital and rail center brought destruction during the Civil War, but it has also helped to make this the state's leading city today; and the sense of history here is still strong. The mansion where 40 state governors have lived, which briefly served as headquarters for Union general Ulysses S. Grant, is open to the public and furnished with excellent period pieces. The State Historical Museum in the 1839 Greek revival Old State Capitol features dioramas illustrating the history of the state; the Museum of Natural Science also uses dioramas to good effect. The homes of two former Jackson mayors are of interest: The Oaks, an antebellum wood-frame cottage hand-hewn in 1846, and the Manship House, a charming Gothic revival structure built about 10 years later. The history and culture of blacks in Mississippi is featured in the Smith-Robertson Museum and Cultural Center.

77   Roosevelt State Park

5 min. North on Rte. 13; follow signs. Built around Shadow Lake in the 1930's and named for the president at the time, Franklin Roosevelt, this pleasant, well-planned park is deservedly popular. The swimming area boasts a tall wooden diving tower and wide docks for sunbathing. Other attractions include boating, tennis, miniature golf, and softball.

Some exceptional hiking trails with views of the lake meander through a dense oak forest and past magnolias, kudzu vines, and a wide variety of wildflowers. Flocks of geese can at times be seen roaming the roads in the park. *Open year-round. Admission charged.*

150   Okatibbee Lake

8 mi./15 min. North on Rte. 11, left on Rte. 19; follow signs. Created as part of a flood control project for the upper Chickasawhay River in 1962, Okatibbee Lake has developed into an extensive recreational area. There are miles of access to the lake's irregular shoreline, six swimming beaches, picnic grounds sheltered by tall pines, boat launches, campgrounds, basketball courts, softball fields, and a water park with swimming pool and elaborate water slides. The Lake Resource Center at Damsite West provides information about the best places for fishing and bird-watching. An island (visible from atop Okatibbee Dam) is home to the largest egret rookery in Mississippi. *Open year-round.*

150 / 153   Jimmie Rodgers Museum, Meridian

Exit 150: 3 mi./10 min. North on Rte. 11, right on 8th St., left on 39th Ave., left on Jimmie Rodgers Dr. Exit 153: 6 mi./25 min. North on 22nd Ave., left on 8th St., right on 39th Ave.; left on Jimmie Rodgers Dr. In the 1920's, fans knew him as "the singing brakeman" and "the blue yodeler," and he became the first country music superstar. Born in Meridian in 1897, Jimmie Rodgers really did become a railroad man, and this small museum tells his story. It has records, sheet music, family photos, railroad memorabilia, his boots, and his guitar. He was the first artist in Nashville's Country Music Hall of Fame. Each May, country music stars from all over the nation gather for a week-long Jimmie Rodgers Memorial Festival. The museum is located in an authentic turn-of-the-century park. *Open Mon.–Sat. and P.M. Sun. except Thanksgiving Day, Christmas, and New Year's Day. Admission charged.*

150 / 153   Merrehope Mansion, Meridian

Exit 150: 3 mi./10 min. North on Rte. 11, right on 8th St., left on Martin Luther King, Jr. Dr.; follow signs. Exit 153: 3 mi./12 min. North on 22nd Ave., left on 8th St., right on Martin Luther King, Jr. Dr.; follow signs. This 20-room modified Greek revival mansion, with a 1968 name formed from the words *Meridian, restoration,* and *hope,* started out as a small cottage. That original structure was one of the few buildings left standing when Gen. William T. Sherman's Union troops set fire to the town in February 1864. Elegant details abound: the deep ruby glass framing the front door, crystal chandeliers, elaborately carved moldings, high canopy beds, even the small mirrors set between table legs that gave ladies a chance to check their petticoat hems. The "Trees of Christmas" exhibit (early December) affords visitors a look at the seasonal decorations of different cultures and various periods. *Open Mon.–Sat. and P.M. Sun. except July 4, Thanksgiving Day, Christmas Eve and Day, and New Year's Eve and Day. Admission charged.*

153   Clarkco State Park

20 mi./25 min. South on Rte. 45; follow signs. The calm, warm waters of Clarkco Lake make this park a favorite of water-skiers and fishermen. There are boats and canoes for rent, and a sun deck and sandy beach attract swimmers. The short nature trail or the longer backpacking trail passes through the lovely woods of oak, pine, and holly. Look for the "double tree," which is a natural combination of a pine and a sweet gum—an amazing amalgam of needles and leaves. *Open year-round. Admission charged.*

71A   Mound State Monument

14 mi./16 min. South on Rte. 69 to Mound-
ville; follow signs. Scattered across a meadow
on the Black Warrior River are 20 remarkably
intact earthen mounds, dating from a time
when as many as 3,000 Mississippian Indians
lived in the area (A.D.1000–1500). A museum,
built over two burial sites, provides a memorable perspective of an ancient culture. Here in
their burial position are skeletons and objects
intended for the afterlife, undiscovered for
more than 500 years. Other displays interpret
the findings; and outdoors, the main ceremonial mound, topped with a re-creation of a
temple, can be climbed for an overview of the
site. There is also a reconstructed Indian village, with life-size (and lifelike) figures en-
gaged in everyday tasks. *Open year-round.*
Admission charged.

71B   Tuscaloosa, AL 35402

Convention and Visitors Bureau, 2200 Uni-
versity Blvd. (205) 758-3072. From 1826 to
1846 this was the capital of Alabama. Cotton
was king, and Greek revival was the prevail-
ing architectural style. Economic conditions
declined and the capital moved to Montgomery, but reminders of ancient Greece can still
be seen in the many attractive columned
houses here. In the historic district on the
University of Alabama campus, the Gorgas
House is open to the public, and the President's Mansion is a stately example of Greek
revival. Also on the campus are the Alabama
Museum of Natural History and the Children's Hands-On Museum, good architectural
examples of their kind. Open elsewhere in
town are the Battle-Friedman House, with its
elegant chandeliers and family silver, and the
Moody-Warner House, which features excellent period furnishings and a superb collection of American art.

73   Lake Lurleen State Park

16 mi./30 min. West on Rte. 82, right on Rte.
21; follow signs. Named after Lurleen Burns
Wallace (Alabama's first woman governor and
a native of the area), Lake Lurleen is a meandering body of green water in a wooded setting. Hiking trails follow the edge of the lake
and lead into the surrounding pine forests.
Fishermen try for largemouth bass, crappie,
and catfish. Boats, canoes, and paddleboats
are for rent, and swimmers enjoy the spacious
white sand beach. *Open year-round. Admis-*
sion charged.

100   Tannehill Historical State Park

3 mi./8 min. East on Tannehill Pkwy.; follow
signs. This rustic, densely wooded park pays
tribute to Alabama's iron industry and to mid-
19th-century life in the region. Tannehill, a
major source of armament for the South in the
Civil War, was the precursor of the once-
mighty steel industry that helped create the
nearby city of Birmingham; and in the Iron
and Steel Museum all aspects of production
are explained. Close by is a reconstruction of
the furnaces, where you can climb atop the
50-foot chimney for an overview of the area.
The park has a working gristmill, and more

100. *In its wooded setting, the rustic mill is*
powered by the overshot water wheel.

than 40 other restored homes and commercial
buildings moved from other parts of the state
create the ambience of a 19th-century village,
complete with a church, a blacksmith's shop,
and farm buildings. *Open year-round. Admis-*
sion charged.

106   Oak Mountain State Park
136

Exit 106: 10 mi./15 min. East on I-459,
right on I-65 to Exit 246; follow signs.
Exit 136: 10 mi./15 min. West on I-459, left on
I-65 to Exit 246; follow signs. Opportunities
for recreation here in Alabama's largest state
park—nearly 10,000 acres set in a deep,
wooded Appalachian valley—range from canoeing, fishing, swimming, and tennis to bike
racing on a track and rugged mountain hiking.
Those interested in waterside pursuits have
three lakes to choose from, and there are some
30 miles of hiking trails. For the adventurous
there's the rough, twisting mountain road to a
parking lot and the half-mile walk to scenic
Peavine Falls. *Open year-round. Admission*
charged.

112   Bessemer Hall of History

2 mi./8 min. East on 18th St., left on Carolina
Ave. Built in 1916, this light brown brick railway station, once a stop between New York
and New Orleans (circa 1917 schedules are
still posted), is now a museum. The recent
past is represented by tools and photographs
related to the town's beginnings as a producer
of iron. Other displays include Civil War
memorabilia, old telephones, an ensemble of
gowns worn by turn-of-the-century belles, and
a large quilt collection. One exhibit portrays
every American president, and another depicts all the states. Artifacts created by the
Indian residents in the area almost 1,000 years
ago are also on display. *Open Tues.–Sat. Ad-*
mission free but donations encouraged.

125B   Birmingham, AL 35203
126A

Convention & Visitors Bureau, 2027
1st Ave. N. (205) 252-9825. The character of the city as viewed from the base of
Vulcan's statue on Red Mountain is vastly

different from the smokestack industry image that originally inspired the 55-foot cast-iron monument. Alabama's largest city now boasts an excellent museum of fine arts, a children's museum, the Southern Museum of Flight, and the unique Red Mountain Museum, where walkways along a deep road cut allow you to study some 150 million years of layers of sedimentation and fossils from ancient seas.

You'll find a conservatory of rare plants and a charming Japanese garden at the Birmingham Botanical Gardens; the excellent zoo is nearby. Arlington Antebellum Home, a handsome Greek revival house, has extensive gardens and interesting collections of furniture and decorative art. The early days of the iron industry are recalled in the reconstructed Sloss Furnaces, now a walk-through museum.

185 Women's Army Corps Museum, Fort McClellan

10 mi./20 min. North on Rte. 21; enter Ft. McClellan at fourth entrance, Galloway Gate. Founded during World War II, the Women's Army Corps served the nation until 1978, when women were integrated into the regular service. Ft. McClellan, on the outskirts of Anniston, was the corps's last training center, and the museum traces the WAC's proud history, showing the women's evolution from neatly uniformed army auxiliaries at Teletypes to armed soldiers in camouflage fatigues. Exhibits include photos, recruiting posters, medals, re-created rooms, and changing uniform styles. Drums and other musical instruments and photos recall the corps's widely admired band, which was stationed here. *Open Mon.–Fri. except holidays.* ⛺ ♿

1 John Tanner State Park

3 *Exit 1: 7 mi./15 min. South on Rte. 100, left on Rte. 16. Exit 3: 7 mi./15 min. South on Rte. 27, right on Rte. 16.* With its ample sandy beach—the largest in a Georgia state park—this secluded 136-acre park is a summer favorite with locals, who come not only to swim but also to fish and boat in its two lakes. Canoes, pedal boats, and bicycles can be rented, and there is a miniature golf course, a nature trail, and a well-used exercise

23. *The architecture of Georgia's state capitol makes a classic statement of pride and power.*

trail as well. Tall pines towering over the campgrounds provide welcome shade in this part of the country where summer can be torrid. *Open year-round, weather permitting.* ⛺ ⛺ 🚐 🚶 🏊 🎣

13 Six Flags Over Georgia

2 min. South on Six Flags Dr. At this attractive, well-landscaped theme park just outside Atlanta, the first thing you are likely to hear is the screams of anguished delight coming from patrons of such aptly named attractions as Mindbender (a loop-the-loop), Free Fall (a 10-story drop), and Great Gasp (a parachute drop). Water rides take visitors over rapids and falls and down log chutes, but for those who prefer tamer excitements there are plenty of gentler options, such as an 1820's-style train that circles the park. Other attractions include a cartoon characters theater for youngsters, game arcades, and performances by divers, acrobats, and musicians. *Open daily June–Aug.; weekends only mid-Mar.–May, Sept.–Oct. Admission charged.* ⛺ ♿

23 Atlanta, GA 30303

Convention & Visitors Bureau, 233 Peachtree St., Suite 2000. (404) 521-6600. As this bustling modern metropolis continues to grow, the essence of the Old South becomes more difficult to find. One place to look for it is the Tullie Smith House Restoration, an 1840's farmhouse with typical outbuildings, herb gardens, and craft demonstrations. On the same site is the Swan House, a 20th-century Palladian-style structure with a formal boxwood garden. The Civil War Battle of Atlanta, depicted in the circular painted cyclorama at Grant Park, has sound and light effects and is viewed from a revolving platform. The High Museum of Art, in its handsome modern building on Peachtree Street, has an excellent reputation for its collections of European and American art. The birthplace and tomb of Nobel Prize winner Martin Luther King, Jr., are honored in a two-block national historic site. Other famous Georgians are commemorated in the Hall of Fame in the capitol, also home to the State Museum of Science and Industry.

35B / 35 Georgia's Stone Mountain Park

25 mi./30 min. Exit 35B (headed east): north on I-285, right on Rte. 78. Exit 35 (headed west): proceed as above. Confederate heroes Jefferson Davis, Robert E. Lee, and Stonewall Jackson are the subjects of the world's largest bas-relief sculpture, carved on the face of Stone Mountain, a large mass of exposed granite. In spring and summer a nightly show of laser fireworks and music dramatizes the carving. Rides can be taken by cable-car, railroad, or riverboat. Other diversions include an antique car museum, a year-round ice skating rink, a golf course, miniature golf, and the 19-building Antebellum Plantation. *Open daily except Christmas. Admission charged.*

35B–35. *A memorial to Confederate heroes Davis, Lee, and Jackson is carved in stone.*

49 Hard Labor Creek State Park

6 mi./8 min. East on Newborn Rd., left on E. Dixie Hwy., right on Fairplay St. Out of the depths of the Great Depression in the 1930's came this lovely 5,805-acre park created on marginal cropland by the Civilian Conservation Corps. The young men employed in this public works program planted forests, reshaped the land, built roads and picnic and camping facilities. This is the largest state park in Georgia, with two lakes that offer boating, swimming, and fishing. Many varieties of wildlife abound in the mixed pine and hardwood forest. There are hiking and riding trails, and the public golf course is one of the finest in the Southeast. *Park open year-round; golf course and beach open Tues.–Sun. Admission charged.*

51 Madison-Morgan Cultural Center

4 min. North on Rte. 129/441. This cultural center in Madison is housed in an impressive brick structure, a former schoolhouse built in the Romanesque revival style in 1895. The past is recalled by the building itself, a history museum, and a restored classroom; the present is celebrated in changing exhibitions in four art galleries, as well as the musical and theatrical programs in the restored auditorium, which is noted for its excellent acoustics.

The museum features antique furnishings, tools, Civil War memorabilia, and a reconstructed log house. The classroom is frequently used as a learning laboratory where modern teaching methods are practiced in a setting with turn-of-the-century desks, blackboards, and accoutrements. At the center you can also get directions for seeing more of Madison, the town that Gen. William T. Sherman decreed was too beautiful to destroy on his devastating march to the sea in 1864. *Open daily except holidays. Admission charged.*

51 Uncle Remus Museum, Eatonton

20 mi./25 min. South on Rte. 129/441. Joel Chandler Harris, creator and author of the Uncle Remus stories, was born in Eatonton in 1848. As a boy he was apprenticed to Joseph Addison Turner, who published a newspaper, *The Countryman*, on his Turnwold plantation. There Harris got a solid writer's education and, through stories told by plantation slaves, the inspiration for his later literary success. Shadow boxes containing wood carvings of Br'er Rabbit, Br'er Bear, Br'er Fox, and other "critters" from Harris's writings, first editions of his works, and memorabilia are displayed in a slave cabin, authentically restored and furnished to look just as young Harris might have known it. *Open Wed.– Mon. Sept.–May. Admission charged.*

55 A. H. Stephens State Park

3 mi./6 min. North on Rte. 22, right on Rte. 278; follow signs. Although dependent on crutches and a wheelchair, farmer and lawyer Alexander H. Stephens served the South as a member of the state legislature, U.S. congressman, governor of Georgia, and vice president of the Confederacy. His home, Liberty Hall, preserved in the park, includes original furnishings; the adjacent Confederate Museum recalls the Civil War era with weapons, objects from the home front, and several of Stephens's personal belongings. The park also has a swimming pool, a bathhouse, and two lakes. There's a beaver trail and an informative pamphlet describing the life cycle of this busy rodent. *Park open year-round; historic site open Tues.–Sun. except Thanksgiving Day and Christmas. Admission charged for historic site.*

65 Augusta, GA 30913

Convention & Visitors Bureau, 1301 Greene St. (404) 826-4722. Known to golfers primarily as the home of the Masters Tournament (held during the first full week in April), Augusta also has a rich historic and architectural heritage. Perhaps the best way to appreciate the many old homes, churches, and civic buildings in Augusta is to take a walking or trolley tour of the downtown area, using the easy-to-follow map provided by the Convention & Visitors Bureau. The tour includes such notable sites as St. Paul's Episcopal Church, the Old Government House, the Victorian houses of Olde Town, the Augusta–Richmond County Museum, and Meadow Garden (home of a signer of the Declaration of Independence). The Gertrude Herbert Memorial Art Institute, built as a residence in 1818, has a striking spiral staircase as well as art exhibits.

18 Hopeland Gardens, Aiken

7 mi./14 min. South on Rte. 19, right on Dupree Pl. Live oaks tower over a carpet of English ivy, accented by wax myrtle and camellias, at the entrance to this quiet city park in Aiken. Willows and obelia grace the banks of the duck pond. Elsewhere in this charming setting, seldom disturbed by street noises, evergreens provide the shade for a pleasant landscape of water-lily ponds, brick walks, and plank terraces. A tiny rose garden grows beside a small frame house called the Dollhouse, which serves as the local garden club's headquarters and also as a library. A touch-and-scent trail for the blind (which has plaques written in braille and connected by ropes) is provided. Every Monday evening from May through August visitors can enjoy free concerts here. *Open year-round.*

55 Lexington County Museum

5 min. North on Rte. 6. This 18-building complex is rightly called a gateway to yesterday. History comes alive here—in the Oak Grove Schoolhouse; in the 1772 Corley Log House, with its single open hearth used for cooking, light, and heat; and in the eight-room Hazelius House, where an 1891 revival meeting inspired evangelist Charlie Tillman to write the spiritual, "Give Me That Old-Time Religion." Antique lovers will savor the federal-style Fox House, with furniture locally made in the style of Sheraton and Hepplewhite and a large collection of quilts. On the grounds are dairy sheds, smokehouses, ovens, beehives, rabbit hutches, herb gardens, and a cotton gin. *Open Tues.–Sun. except July 4, Thanksgiving Day, Christmas, and New Year's Day. Admission charged.*

74 Sesquicentennial State Park

5 min. North on Rte. 1. The trails here—a 3½-mile exercise course, an easy 2-mile hiking loop, and an informative quarter-mile nature trail—and the pedal boats on the 30-acre lake make this a good place to stretch your legs. This area, the Carolina Sandhills, once covered by a primeval sea, now supports a cedar bog, hardwoods, and a forest of scrub oak and pine. Evidence of an early-day turpentine plantation can be seen in the slash marks on several of the old longleaf pines. A restored two-story log cabin, built in 1756, was moved to the park and is now an artist's studio. The name of the park is derived from the 150th anniversary of the city of Columbia, when souvenir coins were sold and the proceeds used to purchase the 1,455 acres here. *Open year-round.*

98 Historic Camden

2 min. North on Rte. 521. Built in 1733–34 by royal decree, Camden, the first inland community in South Carolina, was named for Lord Camden, a member of Parliament who opposed taxation of the colonies in America. During the Revolutionary War, British troops under General Cornwallis captured the powder magazine here and occupied the town. The restored historic district is keyed primarily to the 1780–81 occupation and two battles between American and British forces. You can visit a replica of the Kershaw house, where Cornwallis had his headquarters (the original burned in 1865). Other historic buildings have been moved here, re-creating the flavor of an 18th-century village. An audiovisual presentation recounts the history of the area, and dioramas and exhibits further help to bring the past to life. *Open Tues.–Sun. and holidays. Admission charged.*

131 / 141A NMPA Stock Car Hall of Fame, Darlington

Exit 131: 11 mi./20 min. North on Rte. 401, left on Rte. 34/151. Exit 141A: 12 mi./15 min. North on I-95 to Exit 164, left on Rte. 52, left on Rte. 34/151. Located at the Darlington Raceway, this collection of stock cars and trophies won by the men who drove them provides an overview of life on the racetrack and glory at the finish line. In the museum—the dream of a famous driver, Little Joe Weatherly—you'll see record-breaking engines as well as a display of illegal parts that were found to be not "stock." Of all the displays, the most thrilling is a race simulator, where you sit in the driver's seat of a stock car and screech through two filmed laps of an actual race flashing on a screen just beyond your hood. *Open daily except Thanksgiving Day and Christmas. Admission charged.*

141A Florence Museum of Art, Science, History

8 mi./15 min. North on I-95 to Exit 164, right on Rte. 52, right on Rte. 76 (W. Palmetto St.), left on Graham St. to Spruce St. A 26-room former residence in the international style houses an unusual collection of artifacts started in the 1920's with 78 pieces of Hopi Indian pottery. Over the years the museum has added ceramic, textile, and bronze items from Chinese dynasties, Greek and Roman antiquities, African folk art, and American works of art. The South Carolina Hall of History and the museum grounds feature items related to local history, including the old town bell and a Confederate cruiser's propellers. *Open Tues.– Sat. and P.M. Sun. except Aug. and holidays.*

I-20. *Creations once on the cutting edge of science are now forever grounded.*

I-20 Florence Air and Missile Museum

4 mi./6 min. Continue on I-20 spur, left on Rte. 76; follow signs. A World War II V-2 rocket, a B-26 flown by U.S. airmen in three wars, and an F-11F retired from service with the Blue Angels (the navy's top precision flying team) are among the more than three dozen combat aircraft and missiles to be seen here. Exhibits trace aviation and space developments from the beginning of U.S. air warfare in France in 1918 to the space voyages of the Apollo project and the *Challenger* tragedy. *Open year-round. Admission charged.*

ROUTE 1 — Will Rogers State Beach, Los Angeles

5 mi./10 min. North on Rte. 1 (Pacific Coast Hwy.). This is a classic southern California beach, with glistening white sand, rolling breakers, and sailboats dotting the horizon. Mansions line the white cliffs above. The beach offers all the pleasures of the Pacific: sunbathing, swimming, volleyball, picnicking, jogging, sailboarding, surfboarding, and bodysurfing (3- to 4-foot waves are common). The water is usually tolerable from April through September. Just south of here you'll find Santa Monica State Beach and its famous pier, and south of that the equally famous Muscle Beach and Venice Beach. *Open year-round. Fee for parking.*

HAR — Los Angeles, CA 90071

Harbor Frwy. exit. Visitor Information Center, 505 S. Flower St., Level B. (213) 689-8822. The maze of freeways in and around L.A. can frustrate even the most unflappable driver, but a little aggravation is a small price to pay for this vast city's many charms. Mulholland Drive in the Hollywood Hills or the 27-story City Hall Tower downtown provides spectacular views of the city. Hollywood Boulevard has changed since the old days, but Mann's Chinese Theater is a plush reminder of the glamour that was. To see moviemaking today, take the Universal Studios tour. Those who prefer still pictures can sample the outstanding collections at the Los Angeles County Museum of Art. Griffith Park, the largest city park in the country, has over 4,000 hilly acres to explore, and the Los Angeles Zoo boasts some 2,500 animals. Among L.A.'s innumerable other attractions is an astonishing variety of plants at the 165-acre Descanso Gardens.

HAR — Norton Simon Museum of Art, Pasadena

Harbor Frwy. exit. 9 mi./15 min. North on Harbor Frwy. (becomes Pasadena Frwy.), left on N. Orange Grove Blvd., right on W. Colorado Blvd. One of the lesser-known treasures of southern California, this first-rate art collection ranges from ancient Indian and Asian religious sculpture to contemporary American works. Rodin's heroic bronze, "The Burghers of Calais," graces the entrance, and galleries are devoted to Dutch and Flemish masters, including a number of Rembrandt portraits. European paintings from the 15th to the 19th centuries are represented by Botticelli, Raphael, and others. Among the impressionists

HAR. *This masterpiece by Auguste Rodin sets the stage for treasures within.*

are Bonnard, Monet, Renoir, Cézanne, and Van Gogh. Degas's dancers fill one entire gallery, and modernists Klee, Braque, and Picasso, as well as Americans Frank Stella and Richard Diebenkorn, are also featured. *Open Thurs.–Sun. Admission charged.*

HAR — Pasadena Historical Society

Harbor Frwy. exit. 10 mi./20 min. North on Harbor Frwy. (becomes Pasadena Frwy.), left on N. Orange Grove Blvd., right on W. Walnut St. A stately beaux arts–style mansion, built in 1905 and used for many Hollywood films, houses antiques, paintings, Oriental rugs, and memorabilia that reflect the lifestyle of Pasadena's affluent families at the turn of the century. The lush Finlandia Gardens are a vivid reminder that you are in the City of Roses. On the grounds is the Finnish Folk Art Museum, featuring a quaint reproduction of a 19th-century rural Finnish home complete with an open hearth, a spinning wheel, chests, a hand-carved rocking chair, and a tall clock by the famous Könni family of clock makers. *Open P.M. Tues. and Thurs. and first, second, and the last Sun. of the month except Aug. Admission charged.*

GAR / TWN — Adobe de Palomares, Pomona

Garey Ave. exit: 3 min. North on Garey Ave., right on E. Arrow Hwy.; follow signs. Towne Ave. exit: 3 min. North on Towne Ave., left on E. Arrow Hwy.; follow signs. When Don Ygnacio Palomares built the *casa* of his dreams in 1854, the wealthy rancher established a lasting architectural style. This is unmistakably a ranch-style house. Its 13 rooms are all on one level, and the shingled roof overhangs a long porch around most of the outside. In its time it was known as the house of hospitality, for both its welcoming aspect and the fiestas, barbecues, and dances given by Don Ygnacio and his wife. Stagecoaches stopped here, as did the 20-mule-team freight wagons bringing supplies from the East. The current restoration, which includes authentic farm implements, clothing, furniture, tools, and kitchen utensils, vividly evokes southern California life in the golden days of its early Mexican rancho period. *Open P.M. Tues.–Sun. except Thanksgiving Day, Christmas, and New Year's Day.*

I-215 — Glen Helen Regional Park

15 mi./20 min. North on I-215, left on Devore Rd. With its sparkling blue lakes framed by mountain peaks and its grassy banks shaded by lovely sycamore and ash trees, this sheltered alpine glen looks like a picture postcard that has come to life. Follow the log-and-plank ecology trail through the natural marsh area. You'll find wild grapes growing free, a clear stream edged with watercress, and descriptive signs that are both informative and amusing. Two famous ski areas, Mt. Baldy and Big Bear Lake, are only a short drive away from this park. *Open daily except Christmas. Admission charged.*

I-215 — Riverside, CA 92501

7 mi./12 min. Visitors & Convention Bureau, 3443 Orange St. (714) 787-7950. Once a center of California's orange industry, Riverside is now the home of a number of museums, parks, and historical landmarks. Mission Inn, an architectural gem in the Spanish style, contains artifacts, bells, and a wedding chapel with a 300-year-old altar. The Sherman Indian Museum has dioramas on Indian culture, and in the Riverside Municipal Museum you can see exhibits on regional and natural history. Heritage House, built in 1891, is a lavishly furnished late-Victorian mansion. An excellent photography museum is located in the downtown area. At the University of California at Riverside, there's a botanic garden with 2,000 species of plants from all over the world.

ROUTE 243 | Idyllwild County Park

26 mi./45 min. South on Rte. 243. Although this site is farther from the interstate than most others, it's worth a visit if you have time. As the road climbs 5,400 feet from the Colorado Desert to the forested San Jacinto Mountains, each turn unveils a different view of the same breathtaking sight: deep green valleys and bald granite peaks set against a cobalt blue sky. At the visitor center pick up a map of the self-guiding nature trail, meandering through fragrant ponderosa pines and graceful cedars. Hikers can take Deer Spring Trail up 10,805-foot Mt. San Jacinto. In a forested valley a short walk from the park lies Idyllwild Village, with its charming shops and restaurants. *Open year-round.*

ROUTE 111 | Palm Springs Aerial Tramway

IND *Rte. 111 exit: 12 mi./20 min. Southeast on Rte. 111, right on Tramway Rd. Indian Ave. exit: 8 mi./15 min. South on Indian Ave., right on San Rafael Rd. (becomes Tramway Rd.).* Take a good deep breath before you start this 5,873-foot ascent from desert to alpine forest, because you may not take another one until this thrilling ride is over. The unforgettable 14-minute adventure in a glass-sided tram provides a bird's-eye view that encompasses 75 miles and a glimpse of vegetation from five different life zones. At the top you'll find 14,000-acre Mt. San Jacinto State Park, with 54 miles of hiking trails, mule-train rides, and campsites. The seasonal events are as varied as dogsled races in January to a spring Easter-egg hunt. *Open daily except Aug. Admission charged.*

YV PALM | Desert Hot Springs

Yucca Valley exit: 9 mi./16 min. North on Rte. 62, right on Pierson Blvd. Palm Dr. exit: 5 mi./9 min. North on Palm Dr., right on Pierson Blvd. The remains of adobe buildings testify to a simpler time before the discovery of subterranean hot springs brought rapid development to this area. Some 65 motels and resorts, ranging from simple to luxurious, attract the health-conscious with pools and spas that are nourished by natural 95° F–170° F mineral water—warm enough to counter the chill of the coolest desert air. Nonresidents can often use these facilities for a small fee. *Open year-round.*

YV PALM | Cabot's Old Indian Pueblo, Desert Hot Springs

Yucca Valley exit: 11 mi./20 min. North on Rte. 62, right on Pierson Blvd., right on Miracle Hill Rd. Palm Dr. exit: 7 mi./15 min. North on Palm Dr., right on Pierson Blvd., right on Miracle Hill Rd. In 1913 Cabot Yerxa, a confirmed eccentric, staked a claim in this then-uninhabited desert and, working with his faithful burro, Merry Xmas, built his first cabin. By 1941 he had

111–IND. *From inside the aerial tram, the unimpeded view is a thrilling spectacle.*

nestled a Hopi-style pueblo into the mountainside, using hand-mixed adobe, old railroad ties, and rusty nails. After some 20 years of painstaking labor he completed the present structure—a four-story warren with 35 rooms, 150 windows, 65 doors, and an entrance for mice-eating snakes. The building contains rough wooden furniture, an astronomical observation tower, and a long gallery of Indian artifacts, featuring Navajo blankets, a full Sioux warrior costume, and a tomahawk from the Battle of the Little Bighorn. *Open Wed.–Sun. Admission charged.*

WASH | Jensen's and Shields' Date Gardens

Washington St. exit: 5 mi./10 min. South on Washington St., left on Rte. 111. Located in the heart of the Coachella Valley, which produces over 90 percent of the dates grown in America, these family-owned farms are two of the oldest establishments in the area. Jensen's has 60-foot-tall date trees and exotic citrus trees, including one that bears nine varieties of fruit. A series of plaques details the history of the date and citrus industries. The Shields farm has a long soda fountain that features black date ice cream and date shakes. Dates of many kinds are sold at both farms. *Jensen's open daily except Thanksgiving Day, Christmas, and Easter; Shields' open daily except Christmas.*

JTM | Cottonwood Visitor Center, Joshua Tree National Monument

Joshua Tree Monument exit: 10 mi./15 min. North on Monument Rd.; follow signs. Parched golden valleys with stands of creosote bush, cholla cactus, and ocotillo delineate the Colorado Desert section of this monument. Here, too, is a man-made fan-palm oasis that supports a variety of plants and attracts a large number of birds. The odd-looking trees for which the monument is named grow in the western section of the park. Massive rock formations and dense vegetation make this the most scenic portion. If you have time, consider a drive through that area and back to I-10 via Route 62. Maps available at the visitor center show the roads, hiking trails, and other highlights. *Open year-round.*

17 Hi Jolly Camel Driver's Tomb, Quartzsite

1 min. North on Quartzsite business loop; follow signs. In the old cemetery at Quartzsite a pyramid-shaped monument of native stone topped with a metal camel marks the grave of Hadji Ali, an Arab camel driver dubbed Hi Jolly by his American companions. He came to this country from the Near East in 1856, with camels imported by the U. S. Army for its short-lived Camel Corps, and served as one of the camel drivers for the expedition that laid out the western portion of U. S. Route 66. A plaque next to the monument pays tribute to the pioneering accomplishments of Hi Jolly, who is said to have died near Quartzsite. *Open year-round.*

124 Wildlife World Zoo, Glendale

7.5 mi./15 min. North on Cotton Lane Rd., right on Northern Ave. This unusual 45-acre zoo is largely devoted to breeding and raising rare and endangered species for other institutions. The excellent bird collection includes pheasants, ostriches and other flightless birds, black curassows from South America, and a rainbow flock of lories (Australasian parrots) that eat apples from visitors' hands. Kangaroos may be seen carrying their young in their pouches. A black jaguar graces a bare branch, and there are tigers, apes, monkeys, porcupines, giraffes, and families of dromedaries and rare oryxes. Goats, llamas, baby deer, and ducklings may be found in the petting area. *Open year-round. Admission charged.*

142 Phoenix, AZ 85004

Convention & Visitors Bureau, 505 N. 2nd St. (602) 254-6500. The brilliant sunshine that accounts for the city's rapid growth also supports a surprising variety of native plants, many of which can be seen on the grounds of the state capitol. Although Phoenix is considered a mecca for retirees, many attractions here appeal to children as well. The Phoenix Art Museum has a junior gallery and some appealing miniature rooms, as well as fine collections of sculpture and Asian art. The Arizona Historical Society includes toys, an

7TH–150. *Stone shelters—built to last—frame views of the valley and distant mountains.*

early drugstore, and a children's room. The Arizona Museum of Science and Technology features a young people's discovery area. And children as well as adults will be intrigued by the extensive collection of colorful kachina dolls at the excellent Heard Museum of Anthropology and Primitive Art.

7TH / 150 South Mountain Park, Phoenix

7th Ave. exit: 6 mi./12 min. South on 7th Ave., left on Baseline Rd., then right on Central Ave. Exit 150: 7 mi./20 min. South on 24th St., right on Baseline Rd., left on Central Ave. Extensive hiking and saddle trails crisscross this 16,000-acre former Indian hunting ground, which is now a large municipal park in Phoenix. From Dobbins Lookout high in the park's jagged Salt River Mountains, the sprawling outlines of Phoenix are visible. Hieroglyphics, a natural bridge and tunnel, and views that include the Superstition, White Tank, and Estrella mountains can also be enjoyed. Horses are available for rent. *Open year-round.*

153A McCormick Railroad Park, Scottsdale

8 mi./25 min. North on 48th St., right on Camelback Rd., left on Scottsdale Rd. A good introduction to this 30-acre park devoted to

trains is to board a diesel train. The train takes passengers through the McCormick Railroad Arboretum (a part of this park), where more than 100 desert plants and shrubs form a panorama of color and texture. On weekends a Paradise & Pacific $^5/_{12}$"-scale steam locomotive follows the same route. Visitors will also enjoy a ride on the 1929 antique carousel. Near the brick railroad station several refurbished full-size cars from the Santa Fe line are displayed. And a model train runs through a Disneyland-like setting, with gnomes, cartoon characters, piles of candy, and alpine scenery. *Open year-round. Fee charged for rides.*

153A Papago Park, Phoenix

5 mi./18 min. North on 48th St., right on Van Buren St., left on Galvin Pkwy. In one of the busiest parts of the city, among an outcropping of red sculpted boulders, are the Desert Botanical Garden, Phoenix Zoo, riding stables, and a golf course. The Desert Botanical Garden boasts an in-depth collection of plants from deserts worldwide, including organ-pipe cactus, teddy bear cholla, living rocks, and the exotic upside-down boojum tree. The zoo specializes in birds and animals from the warmer regions of the world, many of them endangered species. *Open year-round. Admission charged for zoo and garden.*

153B Big Surf, Tempe

6 mi./25 min. East on Broadway Rd., left on McClintock Rd. (becomes Hayden Rd.). This surprising attraction brings the ocean to the Arizona desert. Palm trees sway over a wide, sandy beach while a huge man-made lagoon resounds with 3- to 5-foot breakers that are generated by a wave machine. There are scheduled times for swimming and rafting, and shallow areas for children. A long winding water slide passes through the belly of a whale, and for the more adventurous there's a steep slide from a 3½-story tower into a 100-foot-long pool. Boogie boards to ride the waves can be rented. *Open daily Mar.–Sept. Admission charged.*

154 Mesa Southwest Museum

8 mi./30 min. East on Rte. 360, left on Country Club Dr., right on 1st St. Displays of Pima and Apache artifacts, Spanish armor, and a reconstructed Hohokam pit house are imaginatively presented to portray the early history of this area. Sparkling geodes and minerals set the stage for the story of the Lost Dutchman's Mine. A re-creation of a Mesa street scene evokes the 1920's, and visitors can pan for gold in a small stream. Murals and a life-size automated model of a triceratops dramatize prehistoric times, while models and illustrations of space explorations suggest what the future may hold in store. *Open year-round. Admission charged.*

154 Champlin Fighter Museum, Mesa

7 mi./23 min. East on Superstition Frwy. (Rte. 360), left on Greenfield Rd., right on McKellips Rd.; follow signs to Falcon Field Airport. Two large hangars house a collection of more than 30 fighter aircraft dating from World War I to the Korean War. All are beautifully refurbished or reproduced and in flying condition. The visitor can get a close-up view of such famous planes as the French Nieuport, the German Fokker and Messerschmitt, the English Sopwith Camel and Spitfire, and the American P-47 Thunderbolt and P-40 Warhawk. Separate exhibits feature a large collection of machine guns and other weapons, and numerous autographed photos of flying aces from various countries, the aviators dashingly attired in goggles and silk scarves. *Open year-round. Admission charged.*

194 Casa Grande Valley Historical Society Museum

6 mi./10 min. West on Rte. 287. A former church, this unusual rough stone building recalls the colorful history of the Casa Grande area from the time of the Hohokam Indians, through the silver and copper booms, to the rich farming economy of today. Displays include three "pioneer rooms" furnished in turn-of-the-century style, collections of Indian artifacts, early mining tools, dolls and tin toys, a 1900's storefront, a 1929 fire engine, and an elaborate map system detailing the flow of precious water here. Clippings and photographs recall the con man James Reavis, "Baron of Arizona," who used fake royal Spanish deeds to lay claim to more than 1 million acres of the state and live lavishly off rents he demanded from ranchers. *Open Tues.–Sun. mid-Sept.–mid-June. Admission free but donations encouraged.*

219 Picacho Peak State Park

5 min. South on Picacho Peak Rd. Picacho Peak's distinctive horn-shaped summit has long been a landmark for travelers, and the pass it guards was the site of Arizona's only Civil War battle. Tucked against the steep slope of the mountain, the park offers lovely vistas of the desert valley below, where forests of saguaro cactus grow amid dark red rock. A 2-mile trail climbs some 1,500 feet to the top, and it's so steep in one part that cables are provided. Going up and back takes 4 to 5 hours. You can also drive along the base of the mountain on a scenic route where there are cliffside picnic shelters and short hiking trails. *Open year-round. Admission charged.*

219. *The harsh, forbidding landscape is lightened by a bright drift of Mexican gold poppies.*

260. *The fired adobe facade of the mission fairly glows in the warm light of late afternoon.*

---

258 | Tucson, AZ 85701

Convention & Visitors Bureau, 130 S. Scott Ave. (602) 624-1817. The life and architecture of this sunshine-filled city reflect the four cultures that built it: Indian, Spanish, Mexican, and frontier American. Among the desert-style buildings that still exist is La Casa Cordova, dating from the 1850's. Nearby is the John C. Frémont House, a restored mid-19th-century dwelling where walking tours begin. One of the sites on the tour is the Wishing Shrine, where according to local lore your wish will come true if a candle placed at the shrine's base continues to burn until daylight.

One of the highlights of Tucson is the University of Arizona, founded in 1885 on 300 acres that are now part of the city center. Attractions to be seen on the university's campus include the Arizona State Museum, which has an unusual archeological collection, and the University Art Gallery, where the Kress Collection of Renaissance Art is housed.

260 | Old Tucson

12 mi./18 min. South on I-19 to Exit 99, right on Rte. 86, right on Kinney Rd. The small whitewashed church, a yellow clapboard depot, a ramshackle post office, and dusty Front Street in this sprawling Old West town may well look familiar. Since it was built in 1939 for the movie *Arizona*, the remarkably authentic-looking town has served as a setting for more than a hundred films, as well as innumerable television shows and commercials; an 8-minute movie has clips from several. Attractions include action-packed gunfights and stunt shows, country music performances, and costumed dancing girls in the saloons. For rides, there's a stagecoach, a carousel, a narrow-gauge railroad, and miniature cars. *Open year-round. Admission charged.*

260 | The Arizona–Sonora Desert Museum

14 mi./22 min. South on I-19 to Exit 99, right on Rte. 86, right on Kinney Rd. Celebrating the desert and the surprising number of plants and animals that survive in it, this renowned and innovative complex is a combination of zoo, botanical garden, natural history museum, and mountain park. An extensive series of exhibits presents more than 500 species of desert animals and plants in settings that are extraordinarily realistic and very instructive. Among the exhibits are a huge walk-through aviary, an earth sciences center, a grotto for small cats, through-the-glass views of underwater and burrowing creatures, a grove of towering saguaro cacti, and a man-made "cavern" so real that it fools a flock of bats. *Open year-round. Admission charged.*

260 | Saguaro National Monument, Tucson Mountain Unit

16 mi./26 min. South on I-19 to Exit 99, right on Rte. 86, right on Kinney Rd. The gentle slopes covered with tall cacti and the ever-changing magenta and orange light on the desert horizon make this one of the most beautiful spots in Arizona. A 6-mile drive loops through the luxuriant stands of ironwood trees and a saguaro forest that is one of the densest in the country. For those who want to experience the beauty of the desert more closely, there are about 8 miles of trails, ranging from an easy, well-marked half-mile nature walk near the visitor center to one that follows a mountain ridge and passes the ruins of several copper mines. Water as well as maps of the monument are available at the visitor center. *Open year-round.*

260 | Mission San Xavier del Bac

7 mi./10 min. South on I-19 to Exit 92; follow signs. The pristine beauty of this Franciscan church, on the Papago Indian Reservation near the Santa Cruz River, stands out against the desert landscape. Built between 1783 and 1797 near the site of a mission founded a century earlier, it is an intriguing blend of Spanish, Moorish, Byzantine, and Mexican styles of architecture. The church is adorned with many statues, paintings, wood carvings, and plaster moldings. The intricately carved wooden altar is watched over by several brightly colored religious figures. According to legend, when the cat perched on one side of the altarpiece behind the altar catches the mouse on the other side, the end of the world will have arrived. *Open year-round.*

275 | Saguaro National Monument, Rincon Mountain Unit

13 mi./25 min. North on Houghton Rd., right on Escalante Rd.; follow signs. In this 57,000-acre preserve, where saguaro cacti flourish, is a forest of 150- to 200-year-old specimens, some more than 30 feet tall. This vast grove can be seen from the 8-mile Cactus Forest Drive. The monument includes more than 75 miles of hiking and horseback trails, crossing the desert scrubland and going up into the pine and fir forests of the higher elevations. A hike along the quarter-mile Desert Ecology Trail takes about 40 minutes. The saguaros, which provide nesting places for many species of birds, bloom in spring and summer, along with other desert plants. Camping is by permit only. *Open year-round.*

279 | Colossal Cave

7 mi./16 min. North on Vail–Colossal Cave Rd. The water that formed the stalactites, stalagmites, and smooth, folded stone draperies has long since stopped dripping, making this one of the largest dry caverns in the world. Going through the spacious chambers that yawn into darkness overhead may seem more like touring an ancient castle than a cave. Bones, artifacts, and soot marks indicate that from ancient times Indians used the site—as did fleeing train robbers in the 1880's. Spelunkers still explore the cave's unmapped reaches and dream of stumbling onto aban-

275. *It took a very large cactus to produce this bouquet of a dozen saguaro flowers.*

doned loot. The cave entrance is on a high mountain slope, and the park there offers a memorable view of the desert highlands. The road to the cave is narrow and winding. *Open year-round. Admission charged.*

318 | Amerind Foundation

3 min. East on Triangle T Rd.; follow signs. Amerind is a scholar's contraction of American Indian, and this foundation, started in 1937 by amateur archeologist William S. Fulton, is devoted to the study of Native American history and culture. Exhibits in the Spanish-style museum run by the foundation include artifacts from archeological digs in the Southwest and Mexico, as well as fine examples of Indian clothing, beadwork, pottery, basketry, and other handiwork. The Hopi ceremonial dance costumes are of special interest. A separate art gallery displays works with western themes. Unusual massive rock formations in the surrounding canyon are another attraction. *Open daily Sept.–May; Wed.–Sun. June–Aug. except holidays. Admission charged.*

331 | Pearce Ghost Town

23 mi./35 min. South on Rte. 666; follow signs. Pearce is one of many Arizona ghost towns—such as Goldfield, Goldroad, Paradise, and Tombstone—that are forlorn reminders of the boom days when gold and silver fever gripped the West and the railroads came pushing through. The town was named for Johnny Pearce, whose 1894 gold strike became the Commonwealth Mine, the richest in southern Arizona. The deserted buildings here include a post office, a mill, and adobe houses. A window in an adobe general store still carries a faded sign: "This store is protected by a loaded shotgun three days a week. You guess which days." *Open year-round.*

340 | Museum of the Southwest, Wilcox

3 min. Exit west, right on Circle I Rd. Brightly painted tepees frame the entrance of the tourist information center and set the tone for the museum it houses. The extensive exhibits concentrate on the history of Cochise County,

especially on the Chiricahuas, a formidable Apache tribe that used this rugged terrain to outmaneuver the Spaniards, Mexicans, and Americans for some 300 years. There are fascinating pictures of the great chiefs Cochise and Geronimo, along with weapons used by their braves and a full-scale wickiup, a hut that these nomads used for shelter. Exhibits also display memorabilia related to other tribes, and to ranching and railroading. *Open Mon.– Sat. and P.M. Sun.*

340 | Fort Bowie National Historic Site
366

Exit 340: 22 mi./36 min. Southeast on Rte. 186, left on Apache Pass Rd.; follow signs. Exit 366: 18 mi./30 min. West into Bowie, left on Apache Pass Rd.; follow signs. Ft. Bowie is a rich source of frontier lore: Chiricahua Apache chief Cochise and his 10-year wars against white settlers; Geronimo, fighting vainly to retain Indian lands. The fort, established in 1862 to guard Apache Pass, the route of the vital Butterfield stagecoach line, was the army's headquarters for its campaigns against the Indians. Ringed by lofty mountains, the ruins of the fort and the old stagecoach station can only be reached by foot, along a 1½-mile path that starts in the parking area and winds through a valley of mesquite with eagles and hawks soaring overhead. A park ranger is on duty at this historic site most of the time. *Open year-round.*

82A | Rock Hound State Park

13 mi./25 min. South on Rte. 11, left on Rock Hound Rd. Perched at the foot of the Little Florida Mountains, this ruggedly beautiful desert park lives up to its reputation as a paradise for rock enthusiasts. A display near the entrance shows the types of rocks commonly found along the steep mountain trails, which are flanked by barrel cacti and prickly pear and studded with boulders and rough outcroppings. Likely mineral finds include blue agate, common opals, jasper, quartz crystals, and perlite. One ridge is noted for variegated jasper, geodes, and thunder eggs. Each visitor can take up 20 pounds of rocks. *Open year-round. Admission charged.*

85 Deming Luna Mimbres Museum

1.5 mi./8 min. Exit south across overpass; continue on Spruce St., left on Silver St. Housed in an imposing old brick armory building, this large, rambling museum includes a very fine collection of Indian pottery and extensive exhibits of western and local memorabilia. The delicate white Indian pottery is decorated with remarkably sophisticated black and red geometric designs, animal figures, and scenes from daily life. It was found in the burial grounds of the Mimbres Indians, who mysteriously left this region some 800 years ago.

85. *The elegance of Mimbres pottery is typified by this bowl's lightning motif.*

Other exhibits include saddles and tack, a restored chuck wagon, a jail cell, a beauty salon, and household furnishings used by local settlers. Impressive collections of dolls, quilts and lace, polished and raw minerals, and Stetson hats are on view. *Open Mon.–Sat. and P.M. Sun. except Thanksgiving Day, Christmas, and New Year's Day. Admission free but donations encouraged.*

102 Bowlin's Akela Flats Trading Post

1 min. North from exit. This trading post is modeled on the one Claude Bowlin established in northwestern New Mexico at the turn of the century. He encouraged Indians to trade with him by offering them free coffee and tobacco. Free coffee is still offered to passersby who stop here to investigate the brightly colored buildings. A store sells Western souvenirs, jewelry, Indian pottery, and fresh pecans that are grown on a 105-acre farm behind the store. The post has a museum featuring a life-size diorama of Pueblo Indians in a cliff dwelling, along with examples of Zuni prayer sticks, antique kachina dolls, and traditional pottery, including many examples of the deep black vessels made by the Santa Clara Indians. *Open daily except Thanksgiving Day and Christmas.*

140 La Mesilla Historic Village

2 mi./15 min. South on Rte. 28; follow signs. This quaint Spanish-style village was Mexican until 1854, when the Gadsden Purchase was signed and the American flag was raised in its plaza. The area's largest settlement and a natural crossroads, it thrived as a major stop on the Butterfield overland stagecoach route. The town's colorful history includes capture by Confederates for a short period, bloody political shoot-outs during the cattle wars, a trial of Billy the Kid, and harassment by the Apache war chief Geronimo. Today La Mesilla, which was bypassed by the railroad, looks much as it did in the 19th century. The mission-style church of San Albino dominates the plaza, and many restored adobe buildings house restaurants, gift shops, and galleries. The Gadsden Museum has many fascinating items related to local history, including a chapel filled with the charming religious figures known as *santos*, which are carved from wood and colorfully painted. *Museum open daily except Thanksgiving Day, Christmas, and Easter. Admission charged for museum.*

I-25 Fort Selden State Monument

19 mi./28 min. North on I-25 to Exit 19, west on access road. Set on the banks of the Rio Grande, this fort was established in 1865 to protect settlers in the Las Cruces area from Apaches. The troops were also responsible for escorting travelers along the dangerously dry Jornada del Muerto ("Journey of Death") desert trail

140. *The stone gate's arch echoes the rounded form of the prickly pear cactus.*

to the north. To re-create life in the remote outpost in the 19th century, exhibits in the visitor center make use of models, photographs, weapons, and uniforms, including the Prussian-style coats and plumed hats of the Buffalo soldiers, a famed black cavalry unit. The remains of the extensive fort's adobe walls are well marked with signs explaining how the rooms were used. *Open daily except holidays. Admission charged.*

I-25 Leasburg Dam State Park

20 mi./30 min. North on I-25 to Exit 19, left on access road. This rugged park extends from a bluff overlooking the Rio Grande down to the river shore. From the hiking trail there are extensive views of the river as it makes its way through the surrounding desert and backs up against the dam here. A sandy area for swimmers near the dam, fishing below the dam, and a shaded trail along the grassy shoreline offer pleasant diversions. *Open year-round. Admission charged.*

DNTN El Paso, TX 79901 and Ciudad Juárez, Mexico

Downtown exit: Tourist Information Center, 5 Civic Center Plaza. (915) 534-0686. Shopping seems to be in order on both sides of the border: at flea markets, farmers' markets, and factory outlets in El Paso and in nearby Juárez at the government-sponsored ProNaF Center, where prices are fixed, and the Central Market, where bargaining is expected. To cross the border and return, you need two proofs of

U.S. citizenship or residence (a birth certificate and a driver's license, for example). El Paso has the skyline of a modern city, but it dates back to the late 16th century, and its long and colorful history is recalled at the Fort Bliss Museum and the Magoffin Home State Historical Site. The El Paso Museum of Art is noted for its fine collection of European old masters. On the Mexican side of the border you can visit the excellent Museum of History and Art and the Museum of Archeology.

32 | Tigua Indian Reservation, El Paso

5 min. South on Zaragosa Rd., left on Alameda St., right on Old Pueblo Rd. The Tiguas settled here in 1681 after being forced to move south with retreating Spaniards during the great Pueblo uprising. A museum building made of adobe is devoted to Pueblo Indian culture. In the adjacent courtyard, restored pueblo buildings have displays and shops devoted to weaving, pottery making, and other crafts. There is a round ceremonial kiva and an open-air clay stage where young Tiguas perform traditional dances every weekend and on weekdays during the summer. *Open daily except Thanksgiving Day, Christmas, and New Year's Day. Admission charged for dance performances.*   ♿

206 / 209 | Balmorhea State Recreation Area

Exit 206: 5 min. South on Rte. 2903, right on Rte. 290. Exit 209: 7 mi./12 min. West on Rte. 290. With wide lawns, white stucco buildings, and an enormous spring-fed swimming pool edged with cottonwoods and willows, this park provides a welcome relief from the surrounding desert plains. The 1¾-acre pool, with stone grottoes and ledges along its sides, looks more like a lake than a pool. Fish and other aquatic creatures live in the clear, fresh waters around the mouth of the spring, and scuba divers love to explore its depths. In canals meandering through the park, two rare and endangered species, the Comanche Springs pupfish and the Pecos gambusia, can be seen. *Park open year-round; pool open late May–Labor Day. Admission charged.*   ⛺ △ 🚐 🏊

261 | Old Fort Stockton

2 mi./10 min. West on Rte. 290 to Main St.; follow signs. With its abundant water, Comanche Springs became a stopping place for the stagecoaches and wagon trains that brought immigrants to the West in frontier days. In 1858 the U.S. Army established a fort to provide protection from hostile Indians. It was abandoned to the Confederates during the Civil War, but the army returned in 1867 and stayed on until 1886. Today the remains of the fort are surrounded by the town that bears its name. The old compound can be traced by following an interpretive trail that goes past the parade ground. The stone guardhouse, with barred windows and shackles on the floor, still stands, as do three houses on officers' row. *Open year-round.*

392 | Caverns of Sonora

8 mi./11 min. South on Caverns of Sonora Rd.; follow signs. Discovered about 1900 when a rancher's dog chased a raccoon down a hole,

392. *A close look will reveal a great variety of calcite shapes in just one place.*

these remarkably varied and beautiful caverns have become a major attraction. The 1½-mile subterranean tour reveals a long passage with calcite formations resembling popcorn or miniature mushrooms. There are clusters of crystals that resemble chandeliers, translucent columns of stone, and colorful crystal shapes as varied as ocean waves, burning candles, firecrackers, and cauliflower. The evolution of this amazing netherworld of stalagmites, stalactites, flowstone, and helictites is described by well-informed guides. *Open daily except Christmas. Admission charged.*   ⛺ △ 🚐

508 | Cowboy Artists of America Museum

5 mi./10 min. South on Rte. 16, left on Bandera Hwy. This museum, opened in 1983, features the work of more than 30 artists, many of whom were part-time cowpunchers with a passion for realistic paintings of western scenes. To present the Old West as it really was, the museum acquires only historically authentic art works. The building has mesquite hardwood floors and an area with 23 brick domes, constructed by a method derived from the Moors and now practiced by only a few Mexican craftsmen. There's a shop that sells reproductions. *Open Mon.–Sat. and P.M. Sun. Memorial Day–Labor Day; Tues.–Sat. and P.M. Sun. rest of year except Thanksgiving Day, Christmas, New Year's Day, and Easter. Admission charged.*   ♿

508 | Kerrville State Recreation Area

7 mi./13 min. South on Rte. 16, left on Rte. 173. This 500-acre park on the shores of Flatrock Lake and the Guadalupe River is divided into two areas. The Lake Unit has a walk along the river, with picnic tables shaded by oaks and willows. Swimming and tubing are allowed in the lake area; and there's fishing for crappie, catfish, and bass. The Hill Country Unit offers miles of trails through terrain ranging from wooded hills to rocky arroyos. Mesquite, sumac, buckeye, and bluebonnets are abundant, as are birds, jackrabbits, and white-tailed deer. It's the kind of country seen in cowboy movies. *Open year-round. Admission charged.*   ⛺ △ 🚐 🚶 🏊 🎣 ♿

574 *Visitor Information Center, 317 Alamo Plaza. (512) 299-8155.* The Alamo, of course, is the major historical treasure here. The second best-known attraction is the Paseo del Rio, a below-street-level string of sidewalk cafés, clubs, hotels, and artisans' shops that line the banks of the meandering San Antonio River. A good spot for an overview is the top of the 750-foot-high Tower of the Americas. Be sure to visit the San Antonio Museum of Art and the Witte Museum's displays of anthropology, history, and natural science. The 1749 Spanish Governor's Palace and the Alamo's four sister missions further reveal the city's heritage.

609 Max Starckey Park, Seguin

3 mi./6 min. South on Rte. 123 (business). The open green fields and flowering trees of this well-equipped municipal park offer a welcome respite from the surrounding plains. An 18-hole golf course, a swimming pool, a baseball field, volleyball courts, and secluded picnic spots overlooking the Guadalupe River are among the park's amenities. The spacious stone picnic shelters with long pits for Texas-style barbecues and the stone terraces with tables are all set on the steep riverbank. A scenic drive shaded by pecan trees runs along the river, with views of the Victorian houses and gardens on the opposite shore. *Open year-round.*

ROUTE 183 Palmetto State Park

4 mi./6 min. South on Rte. 183, right on Park Rd. 11. Spread along the winding shores of the San Marcos River, these 263 acres of swampy woodlands offer a remarkable contrast to the open terrain surrounding them. Lush hedgerows of dwarf palmettos and other subtropical plants grow along the main road, and willow forests line the river's edge. All told, more than 500 eastern and western plant species grow in the area. Many are marked along 1½ miles of trails. Chameleons, armadillos, and rabbits are among the animals commonly seen, and some 240 bird species have

183. *Reflections in Ottine Swamp double the impact of its mysterious beauty.*

been spotted. Swimming, tubing, and fishing are popular. After a rainstorm, watch your step as you walk along the river. The banks turn into a slippery, impassable slime that locals like to call gumbo mud. *Open year-round. Admission charged.*

ROUTE 183 Gonzales County Jail

13 mi./15 min. South on Rte. 183, left on St. Lawrence St. The Old West comes to life (and death) in this three-story yellow limestone jailhouse built in 1887 and used as the county's lockup until 1975. Six-shooters, gun belts, ten-gallon hats, and saddles used by 19th-century lawmen are displayed in the lobby along with vintage photographs, handcuffs, and weapons ingeniously crafted by inmates. Here, too, is the story of the notorious gunman John Wesley Hardin, who opened a law office in town after studying for the bar while in prison. In the cells crisscrossed bars cover windows and doors, and inmates' names are scratched on the black steel walls. There's also a grim, lightless dungeon and, on the second floor, cagelike cells surrounding a worn gallows with a hangman's noose. *Open daily except holidays.*

ROUTE 183 Gonzales Memorial Museum

13 mi./15 min. South on Rte. 183, left on St. Lawrence St. Texas's war for independence began in 1835 when the American settlers in Gonzales refused to surrender a small cannon to Mexican troops. Instead, they unfurled a crude banner with the motto "Come and Take It" stitched on it and used the cannon to help rout the Mexicans. The cannon, the flag, and other items from the revolution can be seen in this impressive structure with art deco touches built in 1937 to commemorate Texas's centennial. In another wing, books, clothing, and household items recall the lives of early settlers. A pleasant park surrounds the building, and a memorial by a reflecting pool pays tribute to 32 Gonzales men who fought their way into the Alamo and died there. *Open Tues.–Sun. except holidays. Admission charged.*

674 Monument Hill State Historic Site

16 mi./18 min. North on Rte. 77, left on Spur 92. Hostilities with Mexico continued for years after Texas won independence. In 1842 36 Texans died at the Battle of Salado Creek. The next year, in the Black Bean Episode, their Mexican captors shot 17 others, forced to draw beans from a pot to see who would be executed. Here on a high bluff overlooking the Colorado River, their remains are entombed, and the site is marked with a 48-foot tower of shellstone on which brightly colored friezes illustrate some of the events. The design, ironically, has a Mexican influence. Also here you'll find the ruins of a three-story stone brewery built in the early 1870's and, still standing, the home of the Kriesche family, who ran it. The visitor center has memorabilia related to the brewery. *Open year-round. Admission charged.*

674 N. W. Faison Home, La Grange

17 mi./19 min. North on Rte. 77. N. W. Faison is a Texas hero who spent 2 hard years in a Mexican prison after being captured at the Battle of Salado Creek, in September 1842, during the struggle to keep the republic's hard-won independence. Faison, who was a surveyor and county clerk, worked tirelessly after his release to have the remains of the men who fought by his side removed from their shallow battlefield graves and reburied at nearby Monument Hill. Faison's home, a modest one-story clapboard house with gingerbread trim, stands shaded by old oaks on one of La Grange's main streets. Iron hitching posts on the front lawn recall earlier days, and flowering plants form a Texas star on the back terrace. Inside, the furnishings reveal the lifestyle of Texans during the formative years of the Lone Star State. *Open P.M. Sun. Apr.–May and Sept.–Oct. Admission charged.*

723 | Stephen F. Austin State Historical Museum

5 min. North on Rte. FM 1458. It's no wonder that Stephen Austin selected this site for Texas's first American colony in 1824. These woodlands and fields where cattle now graze at roadside are some of the most pleasant in Texas. The 664-acre park is devoted entirely to recreation, with an 18-hole golf course and a large swimming pool among the facilities. Some artifacts from the original town of Austin and an imposing bronze statue of the Father of Texas are at the J. J. Josey General Store Museum on Route FM 1458 just north of the park entrance. *Open year-round. Admission charged.*

763 | Astroworld, Houston

775A | *Exit 763: 10 mi./20 min. South on I-610 Loop. Exit 775A: 15 mi./25 min. South on I-610 Loop.* A bright high-tech atmosphere prevails at this enormous theme park across from the Houston Astrodome. The state-of-the-art rides include a sleek roller coaster that plunges downward at 50 feet per second. The park has Japanese, Mexican, German, and Italian sections as well as Gay Nineties and Wild West areas. Each has activities, restaurants, and shops related to the theme. The entertainment includes performances by magicians, dolphins, and divers. For children the Enchanted Kingdom offers elaborate play equipment and a cartoon theater. The admission price is relatively high but includes all rides and shows. Waterworld, with a body

slide, surfing, and rapids to shoot, has a separate admission. *Open Tues.–Sun. Memorial Day–Labor Day; weekends Apr.–May and Sept.–Oct. Admission charged.*

769A. *The Pillot House in Sam Houston Park is a refreshing evocation of times gone by.*

769A | Houston, TX 77002

Convention and Visitors Bureau, 3300 Main St. (713) 523-5050. Houston's dramatic modern skyline suggests that the present and the future are of primary interest in this city. The past, however, is recalled right in the heart of downtown in Sam Houston Park, where you can tour seven historic buildings dating from the early 19th century to the early 20th century. And the Museum of Texas History displays artifacts going back to the early 16th century. The Museum of Fine Arts presents an extensive collection, from pre-Columbian pieces to contemporary sculpture. The 15 halls of the Museum of Natural Science in Hermann Park house exhibits ranging from gems and minerals to the petroleum sciences and space exploration. A zoo, a garden center, and a miniature train ride complete this park's attractions.

787 | San Jacinto Battleground State Historical Park, La Porte

4 mi./10 min. South on Rte. 134; take free ferry leaving every 10 min. It took only 18 minutes for Sam Houston and his men to avenge the Alamo and win Texas independence in the bloody battle fought here in 1836. A sleek 570-foot limestone tower topped by a lone star marks the site. Displays in the museum relate not only to the battle but to the history of Texas from the days of Indians and

conquistadors until it achieved statehood. The tower's observation deck, accessible by elevator, offers a sweeping view of Houston's skyline. Visitors can board the 573-foot U.S.S. *Texas,* the only surviving battleship that saw duty in both world wars. *Park open daily except Christmas; museum and tower open daily except Christmas Eve and Christmas. Admission charged for tower.*

787. *A proud and elegant symbol of independence dominates the battleground and park.*

851 | Art Museum of Southeast Texas, Beaumont

5 min. South on Pearl St., left on Bowie St., right on Main St. Capped with an imposing glass pyramid, this striking postmodern–art deco structure stands out in the center of downtown Beaumont. The interior, too, is Texas-scale, with 20-foot ceilings, polished stone floors, glass walls, and gleaming metal trim. The permanant collection is not large, and some of the extensive space will be used for concerts, lectures, multimedia shows, and changing exhibits. The emphasis is usually on local, ethnic, and folk art. *Open Tues.–Sun. Admission charged.*

| 29 | **Imperial Calcasieu Museum, Lake Charles** |
| 30 | |

Exit 29: 5 mi./10 min. South on N. Lakeshore Dr., left on Watkins St.; follow signs. Exit 30: 4 mi./9 min. South on Ryan St., right on Mill St., left on Lakeshore Dr.; proceed as above. The museum is on the site of a homestead established in the late 1700's by Charles Sallier, for whom the city of Lake Charles was named. The facade, in Louisiana colonial style, incorporates bricks, columns, and balustrades salvaged from historic buildings in the area. The past is also recalled in the interior, with a richly decorated turn-of-the-century parlor, a country kitchen, and a bedroom with a massive rosewood bedstead. There's a pharmacy display, with colorful bottles in glass cases, and a barbershop with antique fixtures and personalized shaving mugs. The Gibson Library houses a fine collection of Audubon prints and excerpts from the diary the artist kept while he lived in Louisiana. A fine arts gallery, opened in 1984, features changing exhibits. On the grounds is the magnificent 300-year-old Sallier live oak. *Open year-round.* ⛲ ♿

33 Sam Houston Jones State Park

7 mi./12 min. North on Rte. 171, left on Rte. 378, right on Rte. 378 spur; follow signs. This is a refreshing watery domain between the Calcasieu River and a cypress lagoon. Picnic tables are set on raised decks and shelters are located near the river, with adjacent lawns for impromptu games. The park features a pen of white-tailed deer and a pond where beavers and nutrias can be seen. Ducks, geese, and other waterfowl enliven the surface of the deep-green cypress swamp. There are canoes for rent and a boat launch area. *Open year-round. Admission charged.* ⛲ ⛺ 🚐 🚶 🐟

64 Zigler Museum, Jennings

5 min. South on Rte. 26, left on Clara St.; follow signs. This former home of a prominent local family now houses an impressive collection of art from medieval times to the 20th century, including works by Rembrandt, Van Dyck, and Whistler, and landscape paintings by artists of the Hudson River school. Events in the history of painting that affected each work are described, providing an interesting walking tour of art history. In the gallery of wildlife art, recorded birdcalls follow your tour through a gallery of prints by Audubon and other wildlife painters, as well as a selection of lifelike waterfowl wood carvings. *Open Tues.–Sun. except holidays. Admission free but donations encouraged.* ♿

100. *As the church was central to the Acadian way of life, so it is in this village.*

100 Acadian Village, Lafayette

8 mi./18 min. South on Ambassador Caffery Rd., right on Ridge Rd., left on W. Broussard Rd. Original cabins with whitewashed fronts and steeply sloping roofs evoke the way of life of the 19th-century Acadians, popularly called Cajuns. Their French Catholic ancestors settled in southern Louisiana after they were exiled from Nova Scotia and New Brunswick by the British in 1755. The village, with its schoolhouse, chapel, and general store, sits on a bayou amid 10 acres of gardens and woodlands. The cabins contain the simple wooden furniture, moss-filled mattresses, and homespun coverlets of the period. Songbooks, records, and photographs of musicians document the importance of music and dance in the Cajun culture. *Open daily except holidays; open evenings only, first 2 weeks in Dec. Admission charged.* ⛲ 🚐 🚶

| 101 | **Lafayette Natural History Museum and Planetarium** |

5 mi./15 min. South on University Ave., right on Taft St. (becomes Girard Park Dr.). A glittering room with distorted mirrors and unusual lenses illustrates the imaginative approach of this museum. Butterflies, minerals, skulls, an alligator skin, a turtle shell, tree branches, and fossils make up the permanent collection. The museum also features changing exhibits pertaining to natural history and Louisiana culture. At the planetarium you might see special programs devoted to astronomy and space. *Museum open year-round; planetarium open P.M. Sun.–Tues. Admission free but donations encouraged.* ⛲

| 103 | **Acadiana Park Nature Station, Lafayette** |

3 mi./8 min. South on Rte. 167, left on Willow St., left on Louisiana Ave., right on E. Alexander St. The Acadiana Nature Trail leads through dense oak woods along a small creek, passing an environment typical of these southern prairies and floodplain forests. From observation decks up among the treetops at the three-story Nature Station, you can view the park with the help of enthusiastic naturalists and available binoculars. There are exhibits of the animals and plants that inhabit the park today, and tool fragments and spearpoints from the Indians whose land this was before the 18th century. *Open year-round.*

⛲ ⛺ 🚐 🚶

| 155B | **Baton Rouge, LA 70801** |

Convention and Visitors Bureau, New State Capitol, State Capitol Dr. (504) 342-7317. The 34-story state capitol building dominates the skyline, and from the observation tower there's a panoramic view of the surrounding countryside and the mighty Mississippi River. In contrast, the Old State Capitol has the eccentric charm of the 19th century, when architects reached deep into the past for symbols to express the power of government.

The Louisiana Arts and Science Center offers a more intimate view of the river and port, along with paintings, sculpture, a country store, a 1918 steam engine, and an Egyptian mummy. One can also wander the riverfront in Catfish Town, where old warehouses have been converted into shops and restaurants.

179 Houmas House Plantation

4 mi./10 min. South on Rte. 44, right on Rte. 942; follow signs. This classic plantation home, with its 14 stately columns and its formal gardens enhanced by classical Greek sculpture, was built in 1840 in the Greek revival style. The mansion was restored a century later and has been the backdrop for many Hollywood epics. Here the atmosphere and elegance of the Old South live on within view of the Mississippi, the lifeline of the plantation system. Guides in period dress conduct tours of the house. *Open daily except Thanksgiving Day, Christmas, and New Year's Day. Admission charged.*

182 Oak Alley Plantation, Vacherie

18 mi./24 min. West on Rte. 70 over Sunshine Bridge, left at bottom of bridge onto service road, right on Rte. 18. Twenty-eight magnificent live oaks spread their branches to form a spectacular quarter-mile *allée* leading to a Greek revival-style mansion with two-story pillars and wide verandas, built in 1837–39 for a French sugar planter. The 250-year-old trees and the opulence of the mansion have made this the setting for movies and television shows. House tours are conducted by former servants of the last family to live here, and a bygone era comes to life with their anecdotes. *Open daily except Thanksgiving Day, Christmas, and New Year's Day. Admission charged.*

234A/234C New Orleans, LA 70112

235A
Tourist & Convention Commission, 1520 Sugar Bowl Dr. (504) 566-5011. The music, food, architecture, history, and ambience make this one of America's most celebrated cities. Jackson Square in the heart of the French Quarter, the city's best-known area, is a good place to start a walking tour. On the square you'll see the beautiful St. Louis Cathedral and the superb wrought-iron balco-

234A/C–235A. *The stately symmetry of St. Louis Cathedral as seen from Jackson Square.*

nies of the Pontalba Apartments. The nearby French Market features outdoor cafés and eye-catching displays of produce. At night the sound of music—blues, ragtime, Cajun zydeco, country, and of course New Orleans jazz—emanates from clubs and bars that line the length of Bourbon Street. The St. Charles streetcar still clangs and rattles through the Garden District, an area of large live oaks and handsome antebellum houses that also rewards strolling. To get the feel of the Mississippi River, which loops dramatically around the city, try the free ferry or one of the cruises.

ROUTE 90B Jean Lafitte National Historical Park, Barataria Unit

235B
17 mi./30 min. Rte. 90B exit (headed east): east across Greater New Orleans Bridge, southwest on Rte. 90 (business; West Bank Expy.), left on Rte. 45 (Barataria Blvd.). Exit 235B (headed west): proceed as above. Named for the noted Louisiana resident—and sometime pirate—who helped the American forces defeat the British at the battle of New

Orleans, this park preserves the Mississippi Delta's rich blend of early American history, French culture, and magnificent wildlife. The Barataria Unit, with some 8,600 acres of coastal wetlands, was settled by the first Native Americans around 300 B.C. Three different trails wind through this dense, misty jungle of hardwood forest, cypress swamp, and freshwater marsh that is shared by white-tailed deer, alligators, giant spiderwebs, and some 200 species of birds. The visitor center offers exhibits on hunting, trapping, and fishing. *Open daily except Christmas.*

247 Jean Lafitte National Historical Park, Chalmette Unit

10 mi./20 min. South on Rte. 47, right on St. Bernard Hwy. (Rte. 46); follow signs. The battle of New Orleans, famed in song and story, erupted along this narrow Mississippi riverbank on a foggy Christmas Eve morning in 1814 and raged for 2 weeks. The 1½-mile driving tour along the battlefield follows the progress of the conflict in which Gen. Andrew Jackson's American forces fought to keep New Orleans from falling into British hands.

At the visitor center, exhibits, paintings, and a slide show depict scenes from the War of 1812, and in summer a guide in an 1812-style soldier's uniform tells about the action and demonstrates the use of a musket. A tall granite monument commemorates those who fell in battle. *Open year-round.*

247. *The lack of firepower in 1814 was compensated for in sartorial splendor.*

57. *Although they seem a world apart, the Gulf islands' fascinating vistas of sand and slash pines (and the occasional full moon) are but a short boat ride from the Mississippi mainland.*

267 1 Fontainebleau State Park

20 mi./30 min. Exit 267 (headed east): west on I-12 to Exit 74, left on Rte. 434, right on Rte. 190. Exit 1 (headed west): proceed as above. The open areas around Lake Pontchartrain combine with dense forest to give this area its unique character. In the park, once part of Bernard de Marigny de Mandeville's estate, Fontainebleau, are the crumbling brick ruins of a sugar mill, on which at least one of his many reputed fortunes was founded. The swimming pool and picnic shelters invite you to linger, and a nature trail through the oak forests introduces the area's local plant and animal life. *Open year-round.*

2 13 Buccaneer State Park

Exit 2: 15 mi./25 min. East on Rte. 607, right on Rte. 90; follow signs. Exit 13: 11 mi./20 min. South on Rte. 603, right on Beach Blvd. The park's name acknowledges the profession of Jean Lafitte and others who once terrorized this stretch of coast. Violence in another context is recalled by the Old Hickory Nature Trail, named for Andrew Jackson, who camped here and used it as a base during the battle of New Orleans. All is peace and quiet now on the wooded ridge and swampy lowlands where muskrats, rabbits, and aquatic birds play the leading roles. In another section of the park you'll find a wave pool, tennis courts, and another nature trail. Crowded on weekends in summer. *Open year-round. Admission charged.*

44 Beauvoir

8 mi./15 min. South on Rte. 15, right on Rte. 90. The gracious, magnolia-shaded home of Confederate President Jefferson Davis is one of a row of antebellum mansions on the Gulf Coast in Biloxi. It is a stately white Greek revival house flanked by two square pavilions. Davis moved into the house at the age of 69, and it was here that he wrote his famous treatise, *The Rise and Fall of the Confederate Government.* You will see his writing desk and pen in the library pavilion. The airy rooms are filled with rich tapestries, lace, and fine Mallard furniture from New Orleans; many pieces belonged to the Davis family. A museum of the family's personal effects is on the ground floor, and there's a Confederate Museum on the grounds. *Open year-round. Admission charged.*

57 Gulf Islands National Seashore, Mississippi District

5 mi./10 min. South on Rte. 57, right on Rte. 90. At the headquarters in Ocean Springs on Davis Bayou on the mainland, you'll get an informative introduction to the barrier islands that lie offshore here. Exhibits trace the region's history and display its flora and fauna. A 28-minute film provides a colorful view of the islands in a whirlwind tour, and the satellite and aerial photographs provide added perspective. The bayou winds through pinewood flats, which can be investigated on two short nature trails. Boat trips to West Ship Island are available in both Gulfport and Biloxi. *Open year-round.*

15A Bellingrath Gardens and Home, Theodore

12 mi./15 min. West on Rte. 90, left on Bellingrath Rd. Floral exuberance and abundance characterize these 65 acres of gardens, created in the midst of a semitropical riverfront jungle. One of the first delights along the walking tour is the Oriental-American garden. Here a wooden teahouse sits between a carp stream and a placid lake, where swans glide against a backdrop of weeping Yoshima cherry trees. Near the imposing brick house are brilliant beds of perennials. The wheel-shaped rose garden is an inviting source of color and fragrance for 9 months of the year. In the fall the landscape here is brightened by one of the world's largest outdoor displays of chrysanthemums—some 80,000 plants. A conservatory houses orchids and other exotics.

Antique furnishings and objets d'art are displayed in the Walter D. Bellingrath home, and the nearby Boehm Gallery houses more than 230 of the famed Edward Marshall Boehm porcelain sculptures. *Open year-round. Admission charged for garden and home.*

26A Mobile, AL 36602

Chamber of Commerce, 451 Government St. (205) 433-6951. In this charming city one feels the essence of the Old South: the magnolias, live oaks, crape myrtles, camellias, and azaleas in abundance and scores of gracious antebellum houses. The five historic districts and adjacent neighborhoods constitute a veritable museum of architectural styles, from federal to late Victorian, including the Richards-D.A.R. House, embellished with ornate lace ironwork, and Oakleigh, a classic of southern Greek revival design. Other highlights are the City Museum and a reconstructed French fort. In Battleship U.S.S. *Alabama* Memorial Park, you can board the World War II battleship as well as a submarine and see a B-52 bomber and other aircraft of the era.

35   Historic Blakeley State Park

6 mi./12 min. North on Rte. 98, right on Rte. 31, left on Rte. 225. Set on the Tensaw River, this wooded 3,800-acre park memorializes the last great battle of the Civil War, where fighting continued for hours on April 9, 1865, after General Lee had surrendered in Virginia. Self-guiding maps of the Blakeley park and battleground are available from the park ranger. One trail traverses woodlands atop well-preserved Confederate breastworks; near the beaver pond, a bucolic picnic and cane pole fishing spot, you can see the incongruously peaceful remains of a gun emplacement. In early April the park sponsors an annual reenactment of the South's bold last stand.

Another trail leads to the 1,000-year-old Jury Oak, which early 19th-century settlers from the now vanished town of Blakeley reportedly used as a courthouse. The judge sat in a fork among the lower branches, the defendant stood below, and if the verdict was guilty, the Hanging Tree was just a few steps away. Be warned: the dirt roads into and through the park can be quite rough. *Open daily except Christmas. Admission charged.*

53   Styx River Water World

2 min. North on Wilcox Rd. It would be difficult for any child —and most adults—to resist the charms of this delightful aquatic playground. The park features a swinging rope bridge that leads to the Tarzan ride, where would-be ape-men can swing from a rope and drop into the pool below. There are high-speed water slides, an inner-tube rapids ride,

and a small lake with separate areas for bumper boats, paddleboats, and miniature speedboats. For quieter enjoyment, try a 2-hour trip down the sandy Styx River on an inner tube; a bus takes tubers upstream to float back to the park. Tots will enjoy the kiddies' pool, a dinosaur trampoline, climbing equipment, and every hour two animated shows: one of a rock band and the other of a western band. A frog and a pelican wander through the park and greet visitors. *Open daily June–Labor Day; weekends Apr.–May. Admission charged.*

4   Gulf Islands National Seashore, Florida Section

22 mi./30 min. South on Rte. 110, left on Rte. 98, right on Rte. 399; follow signs. The two most popular areas, both on Santa Rosa Island, are Ft. Pickens, built between 1829 and 1834 to protect the Gulf Coast from invaders, and

4. *A great blue heron strides confidently into the surf in search of a meal of fresh fish.*

the Santa Rosa Area, where the warm, clear waters of the Gulf are bordered by an idyllic sandy beach that stretches for miles.

During the Civil War Ft. Pickens was occupied by Union forces, and from 1886 to 1888 a group of Chiricahua Apaches, including the famous Geronimo, was imprisoned here.

Visitors can enjoy swimming and picnicking at both areas. Lifeguards are on duty in the summer. Scuba diving is popular in the mild waters, and schools of brightly colored fish are visible even to the cautious wader. *Open year-round.*

10   Blackwater River State Park
11

Exit 10: 7 mi./10 min. North on Rte. 87, left on Rte. 90; follow signs. Exit 11: 12 mi./15 min. North on Rte. 189, right on Rte. 90; follow signs. This rustic park has the ambience of a Huck Finn adventure, with schoolboys practicing daredevil dives from an old bridge, fishermen dropping lines from another, and troops of raccoons, sheltered by the sandy woodlands, cautiously creeping to the edge of the river to catch fish.

The slow-moving waters and wide sandy banks, with picnic tables nearby, entice both sunbathers and swimmers. A nature trail rambles along the swamps to a chain of small lakes. One of several bridges in the park leads to the campground. *Open year-round. Admission charged.*

12   Sasquatch Canoe Rentals

7 mi./10 min. North on Rte. 85, left on Rte. 90. Canoeing here on the Shoal River, a shallow stream with many wide sandbars that invite swimmers and picnickers, offers a quiet, relaxing outing past chalky cliffs and dense stands of oaks and cypresses. Trips vary from 4 hours to a full day or even overnight. In addition to canoes, other related equipment is available.

Although named for the elusive manlike creature whose wanderings have been reported in this area, Sasquatch Canoe Rentals has heard of no such sightings by any of their customers. *Open Apr.–Nov., river level permitting. For reservations call (904) 682-3949.*

13 Fred Gannon Rocky Bayou State Recreation Area

20 mi./30 min. South on Rte. 285, left on Rte. 20; follow signs. Tall pines shelter the sandy shore along the southern edge of Rocky Bayou, a narrow finger of salt water stretching up from the Choctawhatchee Bay of the Gulf of Mexico. Boating is especially popular here, and there are several nature trails, including one through the sand pine forest, a wooded area for which the park is noted. At man-made Puddin Head Lake you may be able to see alligators seeking their prey in the brackish water. The campsites are set along the bayou, where the sunsets are truly spectacular. *Open year-round.*

15 Ponce de Leon Springs State Recreation Area

3 mi./10 min. North on Rte. 81, right on Rte. 90, right on Rte. 181A; follow signs. Although they are not the Fountain of Youth, legend suggests the springs' name stems from the refreshing quality of their clear, cool waters. These springs have two boils whose flow keeps the water at 68° F year-round. First enjoyed by the Smithgall family, who bought the property in 1925 and created a parklike setting here, the springs today have Spanish-style bathhouses and sunning platforms. Their waters flow into Sandy Creek, where fishermen cast for chain pickerel and largemouth bass. *Open year-round.*

18 Falling Waters State Recreation Area

10 mi./15 min. South on Rte. 77; follow signs. Sheltered by a forest of white oaks, American beeches, and southern magnolias, the park contains several geological sinks. Over the years acids in rainwater slowly dissolve the underlying limestone and create these interesting depressions on the surface. Falling Waters Sink, the most unusual of those found here, is named for the gentle, sparkling waterfall that drops for 100 feet down straight, smooth, fern-fringed walls. Timbers from a gristmill that once stood here can be seen at the bottom. Campsites and a man-made lake round out the attractions. *Open year-round.*

20–21. *An unpredictable flow of mineral-laden waters produced these amazing shapes.*

20 Florida Caverns State Park

21

Exit 20: 10.5 mi./12 min. North on Rte. 167 through Marianna; follow signs. Exit 21: 7.5 mi./10 min. North on Rte. 71, left on Rte. 90 to Marianna, right on Rte. 167; follow signs. A long stairway here leads you to an extraordinary underground world where stalactites, stalagmites, sodastraws, rimstone, columns, flowstone, and draperies are commonplace. The last-named, stone stretched as thin as fabric and beautifully translucent, are the most amazing. The mineral-laden water that over the ages formed the limestone caves is still oozing and dripping, slowly and imperceptibly changing the intricate structure. Water that collects in pools clearly reflects the surroundings. At 65 feet underground, you will feel the impact of total darkness when the guide turns off the light. Aboveground you can enjoy the nature trails and a spring-fed swimming hole. *Open year-round. Admission charged.*

24 Torreya State Park

16 mi./20 min. North on Rte. 270 toward Chattahoochee, left on Rte. 269; follow signs. Taking its name from the rare and endangered torreya tree, which originally grew only along the Apalachicola River, the park combines the charm of a southern plantation house with a wooded setting laced with inviting hiking trails through the steep and wooded ravines.

Gregory House, a typical planter's home in the Greek revival style, sits on the high bluffs overlooking the Apalachicola. In the 1930's it was moved to this site from an old cotton plantation across the river. *Open year-round. Admission charged.*

29 Tallahassee, FL 32302

Chamber of Commerce, 100 N. Duval St. (904) 224-8116. The historic Old Capitol, built in the 1840's, is now a museum furnished in late 19th-century style. It houses an extensive collection of Florida artifacts. The new capitol, dedicated in 1978, stands nearby. The Museum of Florida History contains wide-ranging exhibits related to the era when mastodons roamed through this area, the days of the Spanish explorers, the Civil War, and the 20th century. Of particular interest to children is the Tallahassee Junior Museum, a 52-acre attraction featuring historic buildings, several trails, and native wildlife in natural habitats.

30 Alfred B. Maclay State Gardens, Tallahassee

5 min. North on Rte. 319. Wide brick pathways flanked by magnolias, dogwoods, crape myrtles, and torreya trees lead through a stunning world of dazzling color and richly textured foliage. Formal flower beds, reflecting pools, and sparkling fountains enhance the lavishly furnished former residence of the Alfred B. Maclay family. Few flowers bloom here year-round, but the colorful azaleas in February and March and the lovely camellias from November through April are the real glory of the gardens. *Open year-round. Admission charged.*

30 Pebble Hill Plantation

24 mi./30 min. North on Rte. 319. The elegant mansion—with its spacious lawns, gardens, tennis court, swimming pool, stables, carriage house, cow barn, and dairy—bespeaks a way of life enjoyed by a privileged few. It was the winter home of a wealthy Cleveland family and was bequeathed to a private trust.

The owner's interest in the hunt is apparent in paintings, carvings, and sculptures of horses and hounds. Collections of silver, crystal, shells, and Indian relics, along with antiques, reflect the family's discerning taste. *Open Tues.–Sun. Oct.–Aug. Admission charged. Children under 12 not admitted.* 🪑

38 39 Suwannee River State Park

Exit 38: 10 mi./13 min. North on Rte. 255 to Lee, right on Rte. 90. Exit 39: 5 min. West on Rte. 90. The haunting echoes of steamboat whistles resounding from the banks of the Suwannee and the Withlacoochee have long since faded. But the rivers, as seen from the rustic overlook in this park, can still stir the imagination. Here, too, are some Civil War earthworks, grim reminders of that tragic conflict. Interesting plants and landforms can be seen on two trails, one going through the hardwood hammock and the other traversing a sparse pine forest. *Open year-round. Admission charged.* 🪑 ⛺ 🚐 🚶 🎣 ♿

43 Stephen Foster State Folk Culture Center

12 mi./15 min. North on Rte. 41 through White Springs; follow signs. The familiar strains of "Old Folks at Home," "Oh, Susanna," and other Stephen Foster melodies ring out from the carillon tower. While listening, the visitor can peruse the composer's handwritten manuscripts and scores, see a piano he composed on, and admire the instruments and costumes of the minstrel bands that played such an important role in popularizing his music—all on display on the mezzanine of the carillon tower.

In the visitor center elaborately ingenious mechanized dioramas depict the themes of his most famous songs: horses run in the "Camptown Races," steamboats ply the Suwannee River, and cowboys gather around to hear "Oh, Susanna." Traditional crafts are represented by Seminole Indian baskets, Cuban cigars, and artifacts from local turpentine camps. Headphones bring you the music of the region, played on banjos and by steel bands and a Latin dance band. *Open year-round. Admission charged.* 🪑 ♿

45 Olustee Battlefield State Historic Site

8 mi./10 min. West on Rte. 90. In these flat pinewoods Confederate and Union soldiers met on February 20, 1864, in one of the bloodiest battles of the the Civil War. The fierce struggle for an important communications link and supply route raged relentlessly for some 5 hours. When the Union soldiers finally retreated into the woods, they left behind 1,861 dead; the Confederates lost 946 men in the battle. At the interpretive center you can observe a fascinating exposition of this historic and deadly confrontation, and from an observation platform you can look out over the battlefield as you listen to a poignant taped account read by an "eyewitness." *Open year-round. Admission charged.* 🪑

I-95 Jacksonville, FL 32202

Convention & Visitors Bureau, 33 S. Hogan St. (904) 353-9736. The bend in the St. John's River here has been a crossing place and focal point since prehistoric times. Today you can enjoy the river from either side: Jacksonville Landing, on the north side, offers stores, markets, and restaurants, Riverwalk, on the opposite side, features restaurants, entertainment, and a boardwalk more than a mile long. Elephant rides and a Safari train are attractions at the Jacksonville Zoological Park. The Cummer Gallery of Art, the Jacksonville Museum of Arts and Sciences, the Jacksonville Art Museum, the Jacksonville Fire Museum, and the Lightner Museum provide an abundance of artistic, scientific, and historical riches.

38–39. *Lush growth along the banks, the mysterious play of light and shadow, and the sound of its name all contribute to the charm of the Suwannee River, famed in song and story.*

I-95. *The waterscape here at Riverwalk is as attractive by day as it is by night.*

ROUTE 209 — Cabrillo National Monument

10 mi./20 min. South on Rte. 209; follow signs. Juan Rodríguez Cabrillo was the first European to explore this section of the Pacific Coast, and it was this windswept finger of land that greeted him when he sailed into the harbor here. Today, at this park named in his honor, he wouldn't recognize the view to the east: a panorama of ocean freighters against a backdrop of San Diego's white skyscrapers. But to the west is the vast unchanged Pacific, where whale watching is now popular from late December to mid-March. Exhibits in the visitor center concentrate on the peninsula's history and natural features, local Indian artifacts, and Spanish explorers. There is also a restored lighthouse; and a 2-mile round-trip nature trail, edged by chaparral, runs alongside the harbor. *Open year-round.*

ROUTE 163 — San Diego Zoo

5 mi./10 min. South on Rte. 163 to Park Blvd. exit; follow signs. With a population of 3,200, representing some 800 species from around the world, this outstanding 100-acre zoo is a veritable United Nations of the animal kingdom. If you have enough time, take the 40-minute guided bus tour for orientation, then return to your favorite exhibits on foot or via outdoor escalators and moving walkways. You will see Australian koalas, highland gorillas, miniature deer, giant anteaters, Mongolian wild horses, and the world's largest collection of parrots and parrotlike birds. The children's zoo is scaled to four-year-olds and features a nursery where baby mammals are bottle-fed, bathed, and diapered. There are elephant and camel rides, animal shows, an overhead Skyfari, "behind the scenes" group tours, and special facilities for the disabled. *Open year-round. Admission charged.*

MG — Mission Basilica San Diego de Alcala

Mission Gorge Rd. exit: 4 mi./12 min. North on Mission Gorge Rd., left on Twain Ave. Known as the Mother of Missions, this was the first of the early California missions and was built by Father Junípero Serra in 1769. The mission's tall white walls enclose an inner sanctuary of gardens and candle-lit shrines. A *campanario* with bells in its arches stands guard at the church's main entrance. Inside, the decor is surprisingly simple: a red tile floor, a flat ceiling, and a rough-hewn wooden altar. The cavelike rooms where the friars lived are equally stark, but the religious vestments and vessels on display are richly ornate. Other exhibits detail the mission's history, and hibiscus and other tropical plants give color to the main courtyard. In the mission garden there is a wishing well reputed to bring answers to prayers. *Open year-round. Admission charged.*

MG. *These were the humble quarters of the Franciscan friar Father Junípero Serra.*

ROUTE 79 — Cuyamaca Rancho State Park

8 mi./15 min. North on Rte. 79. With its rugged oak and evergreen forests, boulder-strewn streams, and stretches of grassy meadows, this spacious mountain park offers a surprising change of pace from the surrounding desert. More than half of the 25,000 acres are a wilderness area that can be explored on trails following the cascading Sweetwater River or leading to the top of Cuyamaca Peak and to other summits. The area's unusual beauty can also be enjoyed from numerous lookouts and roadside picnic areas and two campgrounds. A museum displays artifacts left by Indians and gold miners. Adjacent to the park's north end, Cuyamaca Lake, set in an inviting green basin, has a wooded island, a long white fishing pier, and shoreside trails. *Open year-round. Admission charged.*

ROUTE S2 — Anza-Borrego Desert State Park

18 mi./28 min. North on Rte. S2. In this setting of arid beauty, striking rock formations and hidden canyons punctuate spacious stretches of open desert land, and the forbidding brown peaks of the Superstition Mountains darken the horizon. Five hundred miles of primitive dirt roads crisscross the 600,000-acre park, and primitive camping is permitted in most areas. At Bow Willow campground there are wooden shelters at campsites and well-marked trails leading into the nearby rocky arroyos. Farther north along Highway S2, Agua Caliente County Park, with its hot springs, is an oasis of trees and flowers. The campground offers an enclosed mineral-water pool as well as an outdoor swimming pool. There are equestrian trails throughout the park. *Open year-round.*

IKP — Desert View Tower

In-Ko-Pah exit. Headed east: 5 mi./7 min. Left on Old Hwy. 80. Headed west: 5 mi./7 min. Right on Old Hwy. 80. This tall round tower of fitted stone, built in 1922 by a local businessman to honor the pioneers, is now a registered historic landmark that houses a museum of desert Americana. Exhibits in the four-story structure include Indian masks, Navajo blankets, and paintings of cowboys. Antique china and beaded dresses are among the items for sale in the first-floor shop. From the observation tower, where you can see for 110 miles on a clear day, there's a spectacular view of the Coyote Mountains. Outside is a garden of rocks from around the world. Don't miss the animal caves, with a bulbous frog, an alligator family, a raven's head, and a buffalo carved from the stone in the caverns. *Open year-round. Admission charged.*

CA | AZ

See E—W book,
sec. 49.

100

76

10

GIS

102

178 End I-8

ROUTE 111   Mexicali, Mexico

10 mi./21 min. South on Rte. 111 and cross border by car. Or south on Rte. 111, left on 1st St. to parking lot in Calexico and cross border on foot. The Mexican border towns offer the most immediate contrast between one culture and another, and this one is no exception. Avoid a long wait at customs by parking in Calexico and crossing the border on foot. The arcades are lined with shops selling sombreros, woven wool blankets and rugs, huaraches, embroidered clothing, pottery, and all manner of souvenirs and trinkets. In the open-air produce market 7 blocks south on Calle Mexico, you can get a step closer to the real Mexico and see colorful mounds of fresh fruit, peppers, and other vegetables invitingly displayed for the local populace.

GIS   Quechan Indian Reservation, Yuma

Giss Pkwy. exit: 5 min. West on Giss Pkwy., right on Gila St., right on 1st St., right on Indian Hill Rd. This cluster of tile-roofed buildings overlooking an ancient Colorado River crossing is one of the area's oldest settlements. And it is a study in contrasts. A white Spanish mission church with a single-scalloped bell tower has a flower-filled garden with palm-shaded benches and tile birdbaths. Next door is an Indian cultural center made of rough-hewn logs and painted with bright animal designs. A former frontier military post, Ft. Yuma, houses an Indian museum, with exhibits of Quechan baskets and pottery as well as displays on the fort and the missionary era. A reconstructed Quechan adobe house is in the yard. *Open Mon.–Fri. except holidays. Admission charged.*

GIS   Yuma Territorial Prison State Historic Park

Giss Pkwy. exit: 5 min. Headed east: east on Giss Pkwy., left on Prison Hill Rd. Headed west: west on Giss Pkwy., right on Prison Hill Rd. Photographs and case histories of 15-year-old thieves, female murderers, Indians victimized by the white man's whiskey, and others imprisoned here between 1876 and 1909 reveal the scope of crime in the Arizona Territory. Despite its thick caliche walls, iron bars, and 6- by 10-foot cells, the prison was not a hellhole. It was a model institution for its time, where prisoners learned to read and write (one of the area's first public libraries was built here) and produced crafts, such as the delicate lacework, leather goods, and horsehair ropes on display. *Open daily except Christmas. Admission charged.*

GIS   Yuma, AZ 85364

Giss Pkwy. exit. Chamber of Commerce, 377 S. Main St. (602) 782-2567. Chances are you won't be caught in a rainstorm in Yuma, one of the sunniest and least humid places in the country. When you have had all the sun you need, there are a number of inviting indoor places to visit. The Century House Museum, the former home of a pioneer businessman, has exhibits on the early Arizona Territory as well as gardens and exotic birds. Both traditional and present-day art can be seen at the Yuma Art Center, located in a restored railroad depot. You can enjoy the historic Colorado River by taking a boat tour (2 hours) or a train ride (2½ hours) along the river.

102   Painted Rock State Historical Park

15 mi./30 min. North on Painted Rock Rd. Arid stretches of white sand desert surround a mound of black basalt boulders carved with 1,000-year-old petroglyphs of animals, birds, people, and geometric designs. You can climb to the top, where the workings can be seen close up. In pioneer times the rocks were important as a landmark for travelers through the desert, including those who followed the Mormon Battalion Trail, which went by here around 1846. *Open year-round. Admission charged.*

178   Casa Grande Ruins National Monument

24 mi./30 min. West on I-10 to Exit 185, east on Rte. 387, right on Rte. 87. The purpose of this towering, symmetrical, ocher-colored building is as mysterious as the fate of pre-Columbian Hohokam Indians who built it some 650 years ago. Named by a Spanish explorer in the 17th century, it is distinguished by inwardly sloping earth walls. They dominate the remains of a 2-acre compound that once contained more than 60 rooms, a ball court, and segments of a 600-mile network of irrigation canals. Fragments of pottery, cloth, and copper bells in the visitor center provide tantalizing glimpses into the lives of the vanished Hohokams. *Open year-round. Admission charged.*

S2. *Surrealistic scene of cholla and rocks beautifully backlit on a morning in May.*

Credits and acknowledgments

The editors gratefully acknowledge the assistance of the many individuals, chambers of commerce, tourist bureaus, and state and local park, highway, and police departments that helped make this book possible.

Driver-reporters (and the routes they drove)
Gregory Archbald (I-80), Thomas Barr (I-80, I-84, I-90), Kent and Donna Dannen (I-70), Jon and Jane Farber (I-40), Cory Kilvert (I-20, I-40, I-64, I-70, I-90), Robert Lancaster (I-20), George Marsden (I-40, I-64, I-70, I-90), Richard Marshall (I-70, I-80, I-90, I-94), Barbara Roether (I-8, I-10, I-20).

Picture credits

The numbers in **bold type** below refer to the section numbers at the bottom of each page. The positions of the photos are indicated thus: (l) left, (m) middle, (r) right, (t) top, (b) bottom.

Cover B. Taylor/H. Armstrong Roberts. **Introduction** Jay Maisel. **1** Ray Atkeson. **2** (l) Larry and Jan Aiuppy; (r) Jeff Gnass. **3** (l) © David Muench Photography 1988; (r) Mark E. Gibson. **4** (l) © David Muench Photography 1988; (m) Jeff Gnass; (r) Positive Reflections. **5** (l) © David Muench Photography 1988; (r) Ken Dequaine. **6** (l) James P. Rowan: Click/Chicago; (r) Joseph Jacobson /Journalism Services. **7** (l) Indiana State Parks Department of Natural Resources; (tr) Wolfgang Weber; (br) Jim Schafer/View Finder. **8** (l) Zefa/H. Armstrong Roberts; (bl, r) Doris Gehrig Barker. **9** (l) Naoki Okamoto; (r) Mark E. Gibson. **10** (l) Montana Travel Promotion; (r) © David Muench Photography 1988. **11** (l) Clayton Wolt; (r) Wilford L. Miller. **12** Positive Reflections. **13** (l) R. Krubner/H. Armstrong Roberts; (r) William Meyer/Third Coast. **14** (l) Dave Gustafson/Kalamazoo Aviation History Museum; (r) Lee Foster. **15** (l, bl) © David Muench Photography 1988; (tr) D. C. Lowe; (br) Lynda Hatch/Ric Ergenbright Photography. **16** (l) © David Muench Photography 1988; (r) Kent and Donna Dannen. **17** (l) D. C. Lowe/Shostal Associates; (r) Joseph Beckner/Amwest. **18** D. Muench/H. Armstrong Roberts; (tr) Ravell Call/Hillstrom Stock Photo; (br) G. Ahrens/H. Armstrong Roberts. **19** (l) Jeff Gnass; (r) Kent and Donna Dannen. **20** (l) Kent and Donna Dannen; (r) Nebraska Game and Parks Commission. **21** (l) Mike Whye; (r) Tom Bean. **22** Positive Reflections. **23** (l) Ray F. Hillstrom/Hillstrom Stock Photo; (m) Bill Thomas; (r) Ruth Chin. **24** (l) Mark E. Gibson; (r) Carl Lindquist/View Finder. **25** E. R. Degginger. **26** (tl) Kent and Donna Dannen; (bl) © David Muench Photography 1988; (r) Larry Burton. **27** (l) Todd Powell; (r) Kent and Donna Dannen. **28** (l, tr) Dick Herpich; (br) Daniel Dancer. **29** (l) Jack Zehrt; (r) Bets Anderson Bailly/Unicorn Stock Photos. **30** (l) Ken Dequaine/Third Coast; (r) Audrey Gibson. **31** (l) Larry Hamill; (r) Arnout Hyde, Jr. **32** (l) Steve Solum/West Stock; (r) Shostal Associates. **33** (l) Thomas Peters Lake; (r) Patrick L. Pfister. **34** (l) Charles Westerfield; (r) Arnout Hyde, Jr. **35** © David Muench Photography 1988. **36** (l) © David Muench Photography 1988; (r) Eduardo Fuss. **37** (l) Willard Clay; (r) M. Schneiders/H. Armstrong Roberts. **38** Positive Reflections. **39** (l) Positive Reflections; (tr) Mark E. Gibson; (br) E. Cooper/H. Armstrong Roberts. **40** (l) Matt Bradley; (r) R. Krubner/H. Armstrong Roberts. **41** (l) John Netherton; (r) Chip Henderson. **42** (l) James P. Valentine; (br) Don C. Olive; (tr) Jack Dermid. **43** (l) © David Muench Photography 1988; (br) Scott Berner/The Stockhouse, Inc.; (tr) Laurence E. Parent. **44** (l) Kent and Donna Dannen; (r) Mark E. Gibson. **45** (l) Louisiana Purchase Gardens and Zoo; (r) © David Muench Photography 1988. **46** (l) Ed Malles/Photo Options; (r) Aerial Photography Services. **47** (l) Ken Dequaine; (r) Danny C. Booker. **48** (l) Richard B. Spencer/Shostal Associates; (r) Mark E. Gibson. **49** (l) Tom Bean; (r) © David Muench Photography 1988. **50** (l) Willard Clay; (r) © David Muench Photography 1988. **51** (l) Todd Powell; (m) Eduardo Fuss; (r) John Ward/Unicorn Stock Photos. **52** (l) © David Muench Photography 1988; (m) Mark E. Gibson; (r) © David Muench Photography 1988. **53** (l) Thomas Peters Lake; (tr) Philip Gould; (br) Jackson Hill. **54** Connie Toops. **55** (l) Florida Caverns State Park; (m) Don C. Olive; (r) W. Bertsch/H. Armstrong Roberts. **56** (l) Mark E. Gibson; (r) Jeff Gnass. **Back cover** (tl) Clayton Wolt; (bl) Kent and Donna Dannen; (r) © David Muench Photography 1988.

Library of Congress Cataloging in Publication Data

Reader's Digest Association.
    On the road, U.S.A.

    Includes index.
    Contents: v. 1. North–South routes—v. 2. East–West routes.
    1. United States—Maps, Tourist. 2. United States—Description and travel—Guide-books. I. Title.
G1201.E635R4 1989   912'.73   88-675238
ISBN 0-89577-318-X (set)
ISBN 0-89577-316-3 (v. 1)
ISBN 0-89577-317-1 (v. 2)

Index

The letter **N** in **bold type** preceding a section number indicates the North–South book; **E** indicates this book, the East–West volume.